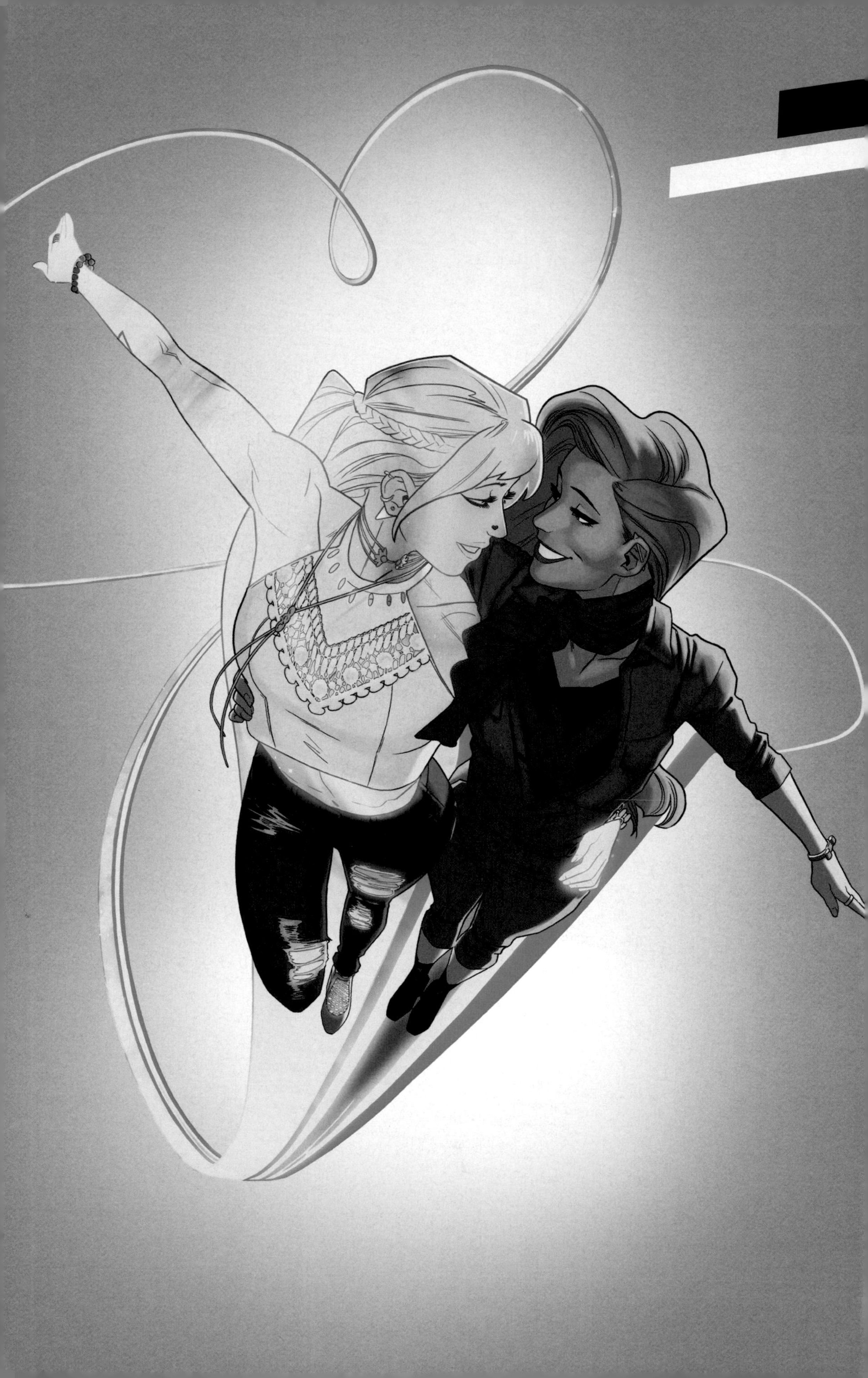

RUNAWAYS

Best Friends Forever

WRITER **RAINBOW ROWELL**

PENCILER **KRIS ANKA**

INKERS **KRIS ANKA** WITH **CRAIG YEUNG** (#9)

COLOR ARTISTS **MATTHEW WILSON** (#7, #10-12)
& **TRÍONA FARRELL** (#8-9)

LETTERER **VC'S JOE CARAMAGNA**

COVER ART **KRIS ANKA**

ASSISTANT EDITOR **KATHLEEN WISNESKI**
EDITOR **NICK LOWE**

RUNAWAYS CREATED BY **BRIAN K. VAUGHAN** & **ADRIAN ALPHONA**

COLLECTION EDITOR **JENNIFER GRÜNWALD** | ASSISTANT EDITOR **CAITLIN O'CONNELL** | ASSOCIATE MANAGING EDITOR **KATERI WOODY**
EDITOR, SPECIAL PROJECTS **MARK D. BEAZLEY** | VP PRODUCTION & SPECIAL PROJECTS **JEFF YOUNGQUIST**
SVP PRINT, SALES & MARKETING **DAVID GABRIEL** | BOOK DESIGNER **JAY BOWEN**
EDITOR IN CHIEF **C.B. CEBULSKI** | CHIEF CREATIVE OFFICER **JOE QUESADA**
PRESIDENT **DAN BUCKLEY** | EXECUTIVE PRODUCER **ALAN FINE**

RUNAWAYS BY RAINBOW ROWELL & KRIS ANKA VOL. 2: BEST FRIENDS FOREVER. Contains material originally published in magazine form as RUNAWAYS #7-12. First printing 2018. ISBN 978-1-302-91197-3. Published by MARVEL WORLDWIDE, INC., a subsidiary of MARVEL ENTERTAINMENT, LLC. OFFICE OF PUBLICATION: 135 West 50th Street, New York, NY 10020. **Printed in Canada.** DAN BUCKLEY, President, Marvel Entertainment; JOHN NEE, Publisher; JOE QUESADA, Chief Creative Officer; TOM BREVOORT, SVP of Publishing; DAVID BOGART, SVP of Business Affairs & Operations, Publishing & Partnership; DAVID GABRIEL, SVP of Sales & Marketing, Publishing; JEFF YOUNGQUIST, VP of Production & Special Projects; DAN CARR, Executive Director of Publishing Technology; ALEX MORALES, Director of Publishing Operations; DAN EDINGTON, Managing Editor; SUSAN CRESPI, Production Manager; STAN LEE, Chairman Emeritus. For information regarding advertising in Marvel Comics or on Marvel.com, please contact Vit DeBellis, Custom Solutions & Integrated Advertising Manager, at vdebellis@marvel.com. For Marvel subscription inquiries, please call 888-511-5480. **Manufactured between 8/24/2018 and 9/25/2018 by SOLISCO PRINTERS, SCOTT, QC, CANADA.**

10 9 8 7 6 5 4 3 2 1

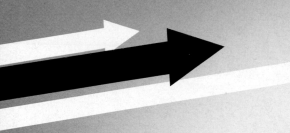

PREVIOUSLY

WHEN THEY WERE YOUNGER, NICO MINORU, CHASE STEIN, GERTRUDE YORKES, KAROLINA DEAN, MOLLY HAYES AND ALEX WILDER BECAME FRIENDS THROUGH CIRCUMSTANCE: HANGING OUT ONCE A YEAR WHILE THEIR PARENTS HAD WHAT THEY CLAIMED WAS A DINNER PARTY. AFTER DISCOVERING THEIR PARENTS WERE ACTUALLY THE SUPER VILLAIN TEAM KNOWN AS THE PRIDE, THE KIDS RAN. THE RUNAWAYS LEARNED TO USE POWERS AND RESOURCES INHERITED FROM THEIR PARENTS, AND RETURNED TO DEFEAT THEM. THE EXPERIENCE MADE THEM A FAMILY, BUT THAT WASN'T ENOUGH TO KEEP THEM SAFE.

THE RUNAWAYS, AND ALL THEIR PROBLEMS, ARE TOGETHER UNDER ONE (UNDERGROUND) ROOF! NOW THAT THE EASY STUFF — LIKE BRINGING VICTOR'S HEAD AND GERT BACK FROM THE DEAD, CONVINCING KAROLINA TO SIDELINE COLLEGE LIFE AND RESCUING MOLLY FROM HER MAD SCIENTIST GRANDMOTHER — IS DONE, THEY CAN GET BACK TO THE BUSINESS OF GROWING UP.

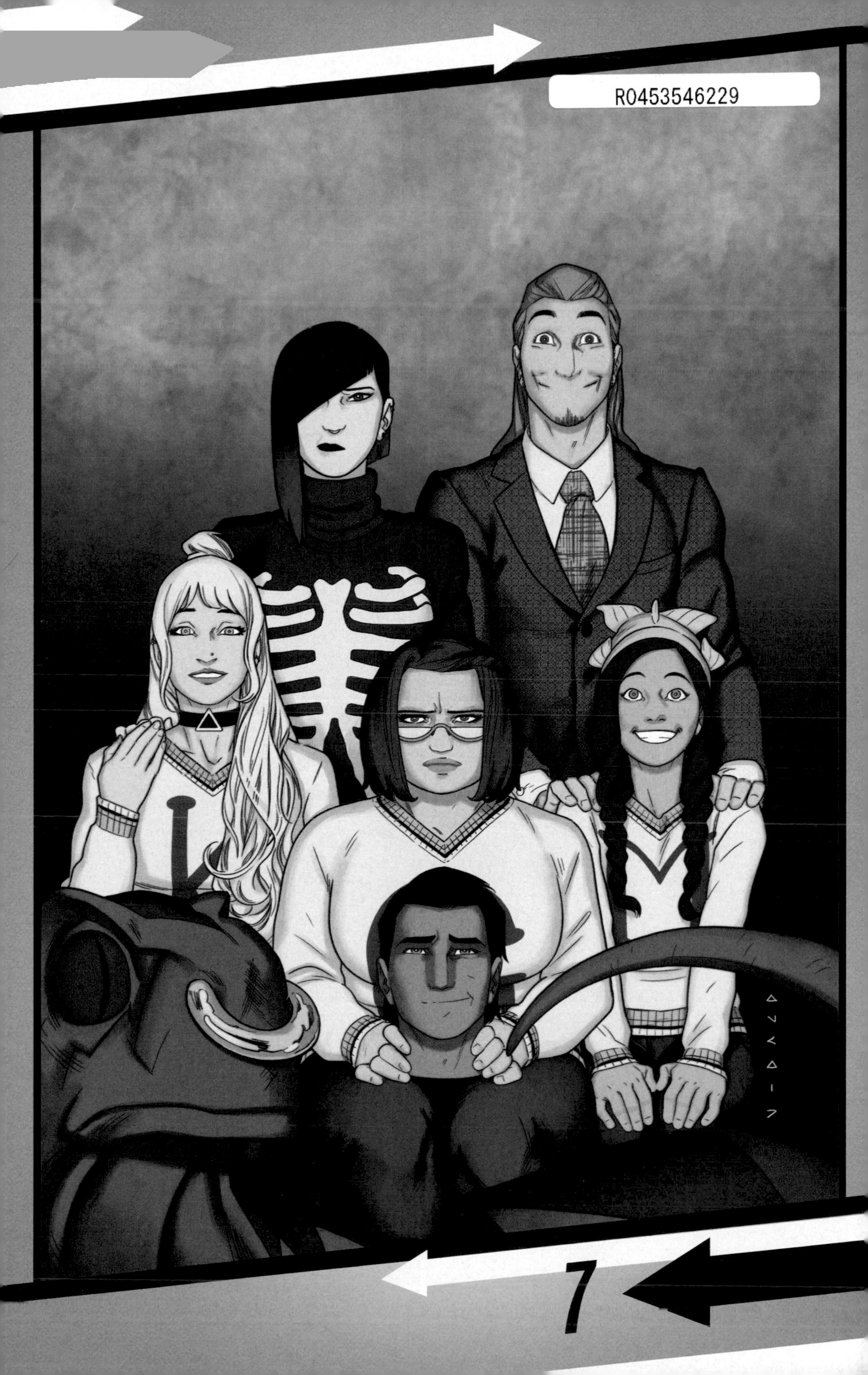

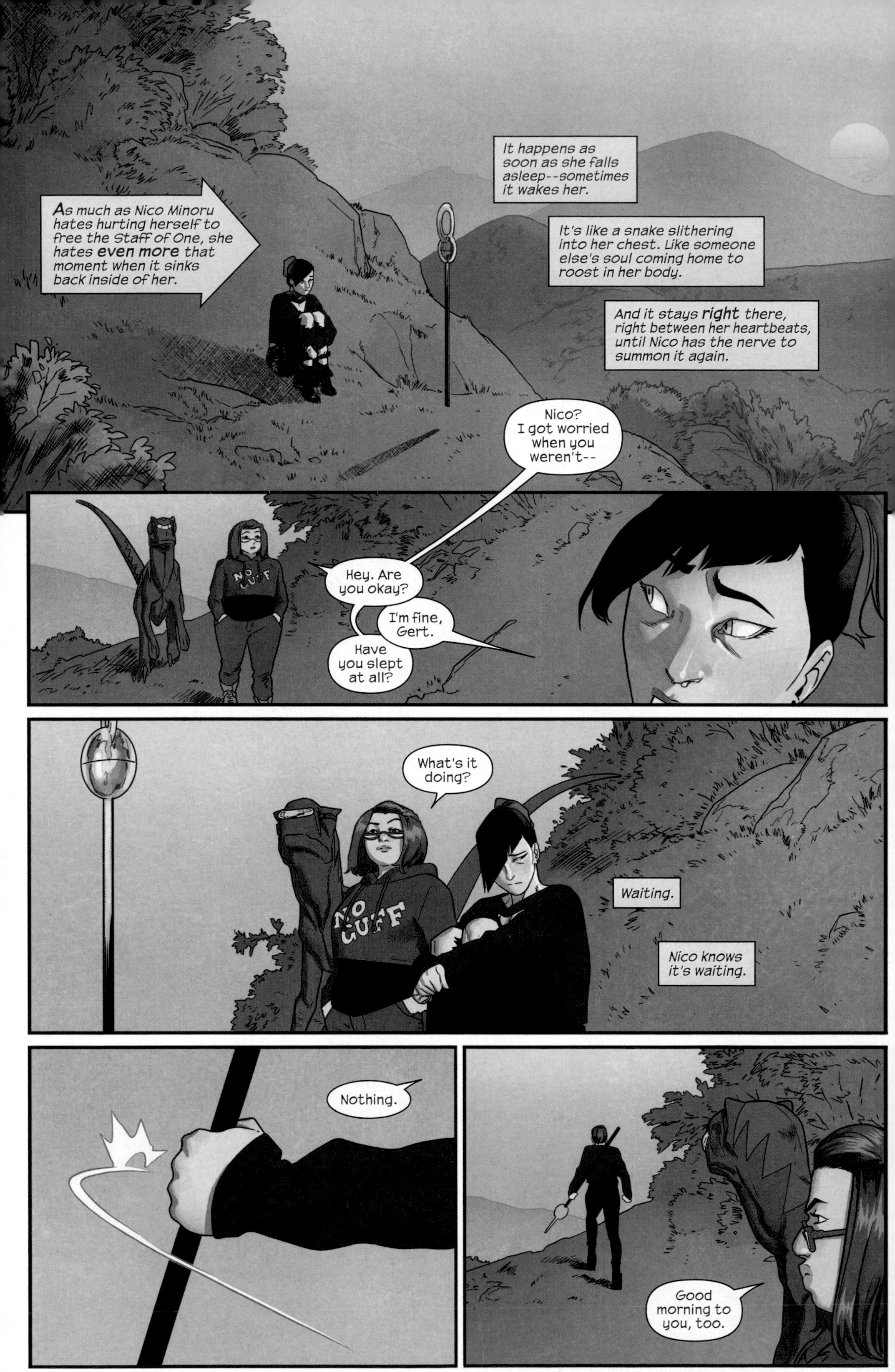
As much as Nico Minoru hates hurting herself to free the Staff of One, she hates **even more** that moment when it sinks back inside of her.
It happens as soon as she falls asleep--sometimes it wakes her.
It's like a snake slithering into her chest. Like someone else's soul coming home to roost in her body.
And it stays **right** there, right between her heartbeats, until Nico has the nerve to summon it again.
Nico? I got worried when you weren't--
Hey. Are you okay?
I'm fine, Gert.
Have you slept at all?
What's it doing?
Waiting.
Nico knows it's waiting.
Nothing.
Good morning to you, too.

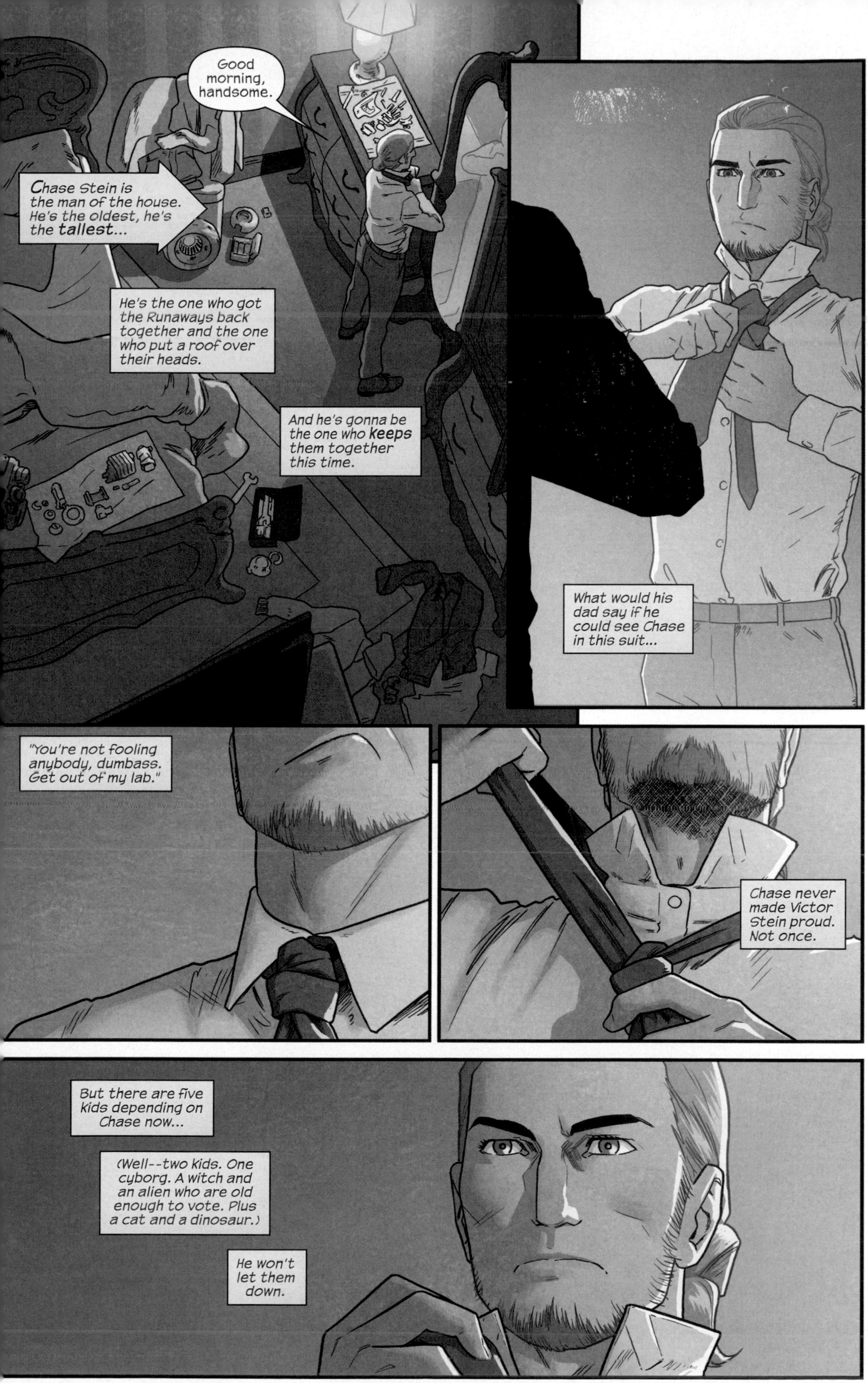

Good morning, handsome.
Chase Stein is the man of the house. He's the oldest, he's the tallest...
He's the one who got the Runaways back together and the one who put a roof over their heads.
And he's gonna be the one who keeps them together this time.
What would his dad say if he could see Chase in this suit...
"You're not fooling anybody, dumbass. Get out of my lab."
Chase never made Victor Stein proud. Not once.
But there are five kids depending on Chase now...
(Well--two kids. One cyborg. A witch and an alien who are old enough to vote. Plus a cat and a dinosaur.)
He won't let them down.

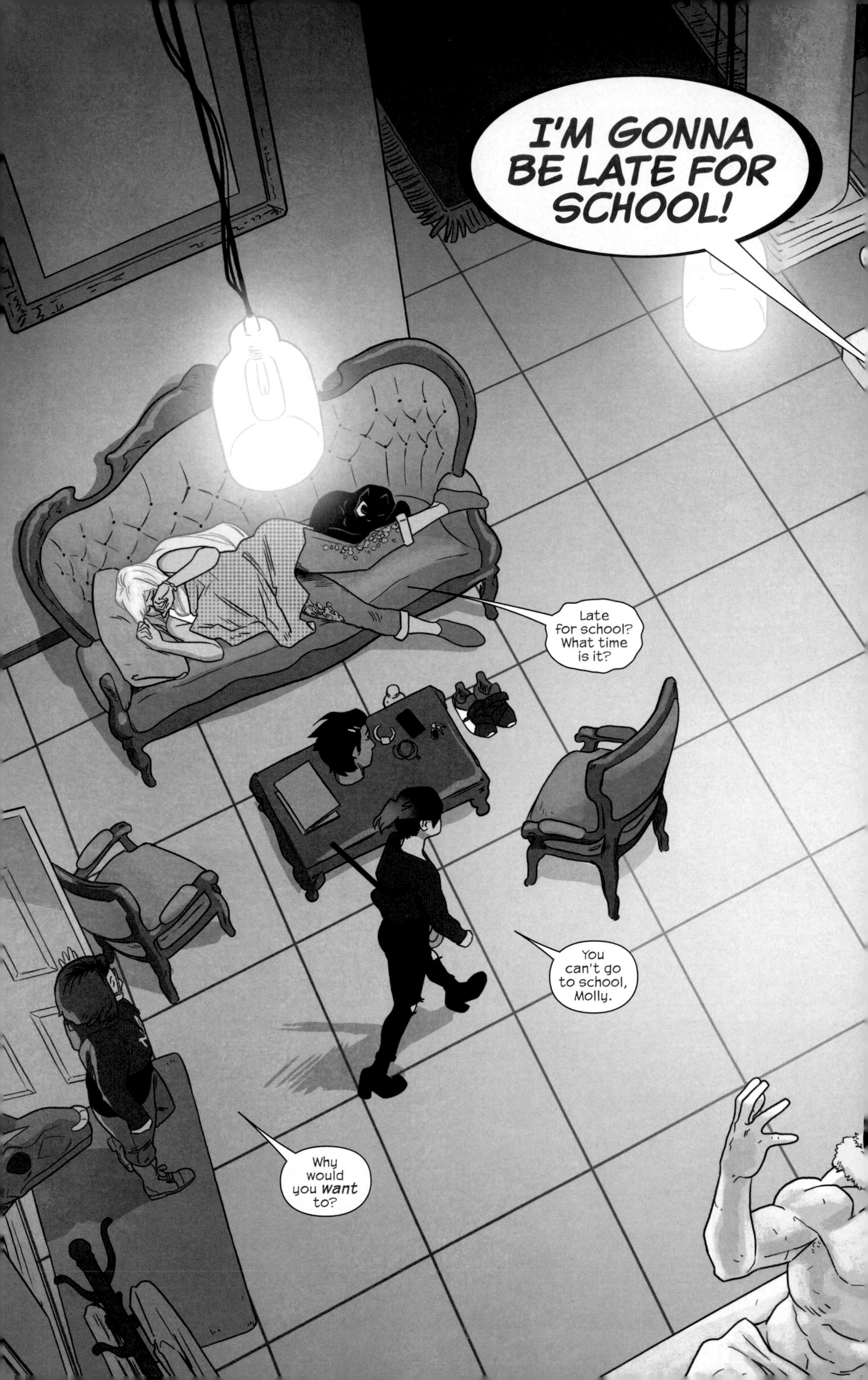
I'M GONNA BE LATE FOR SCHOOL!
Late for school? What time is it?
You can't go to school, Molly.
Why would you *want* to?

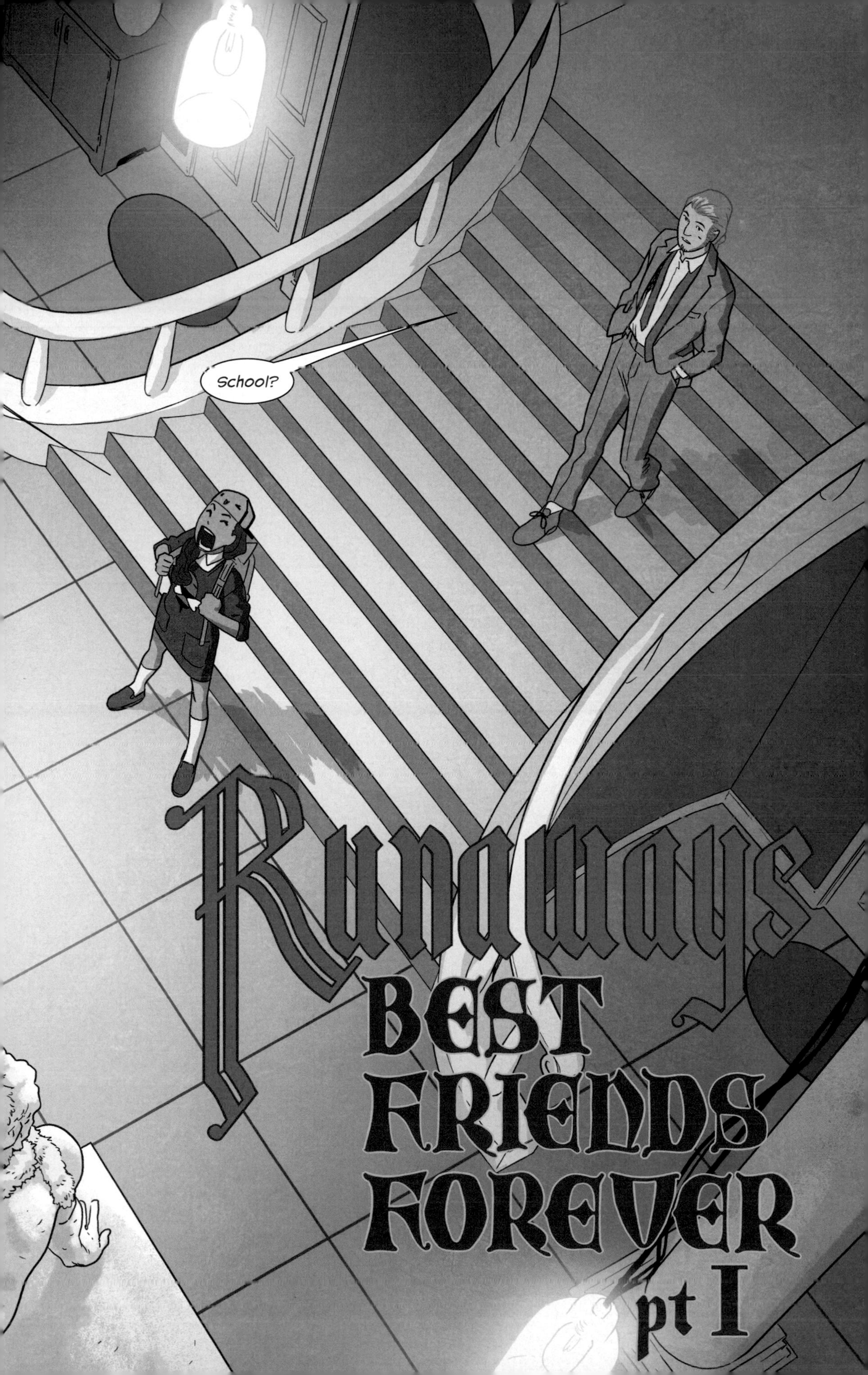
School?
Runaways
BEST FRIENDS FOREVER
pt I

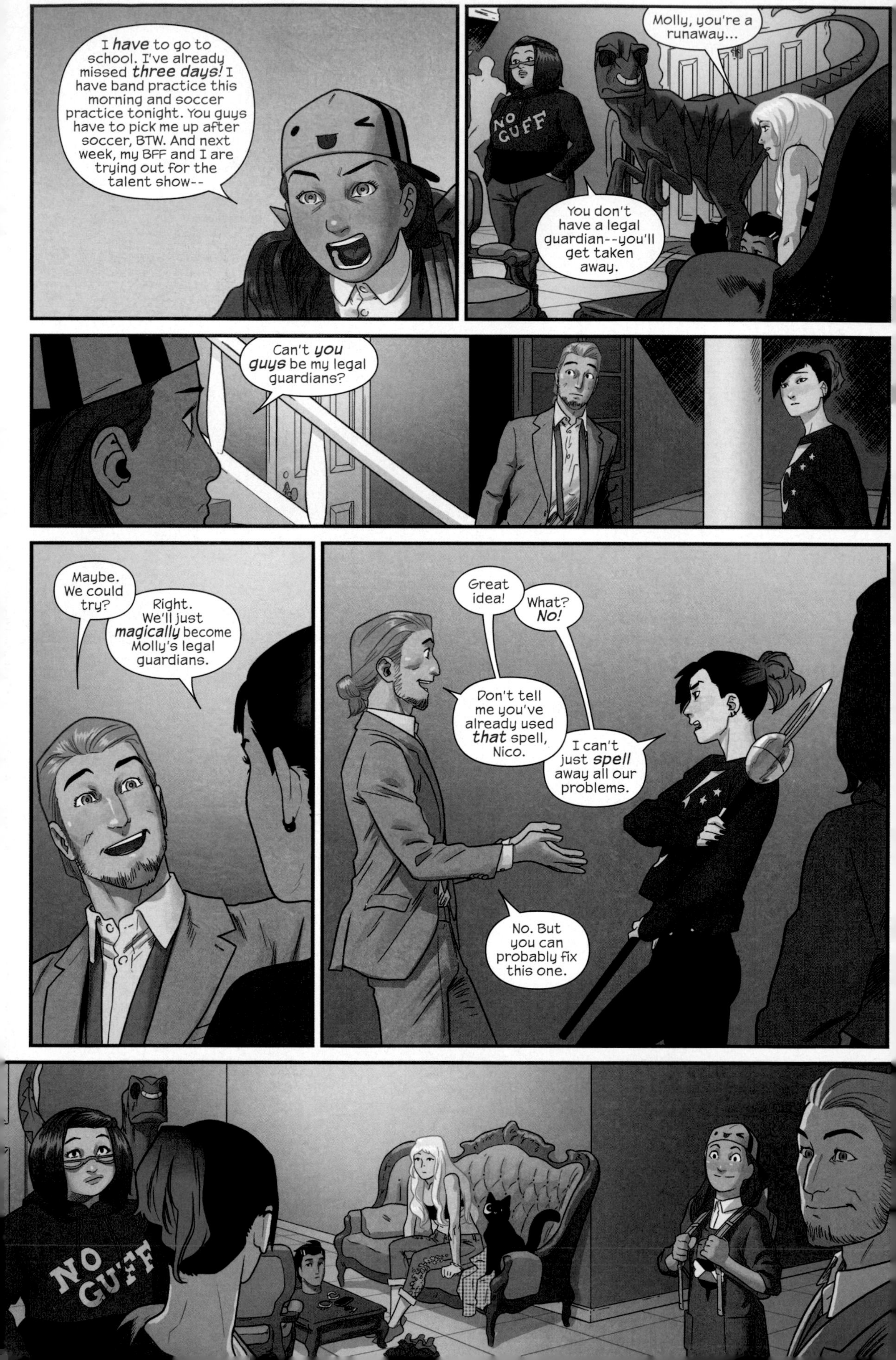
I have to go to school. I've already missed three days! I have band practice this morning and soccer practice tonight. You guys have to pick me up after soccer, BTW. And next week, my BFF and I are trying out for the talent show--
Molly, you're a runaway...
NO GUFF
You don't have a legal guardian--you'll get taken away.
Can't you guys be my legal guardians?
Maybe. We could try?
Right. We'll just magically become Molly's legal guardians.
Great idea!
What? No!
Don't tell me you've already used that spell, Nico.
I can't just spell away all our problems.
No. But you can probably fix this one.
NO GUFF

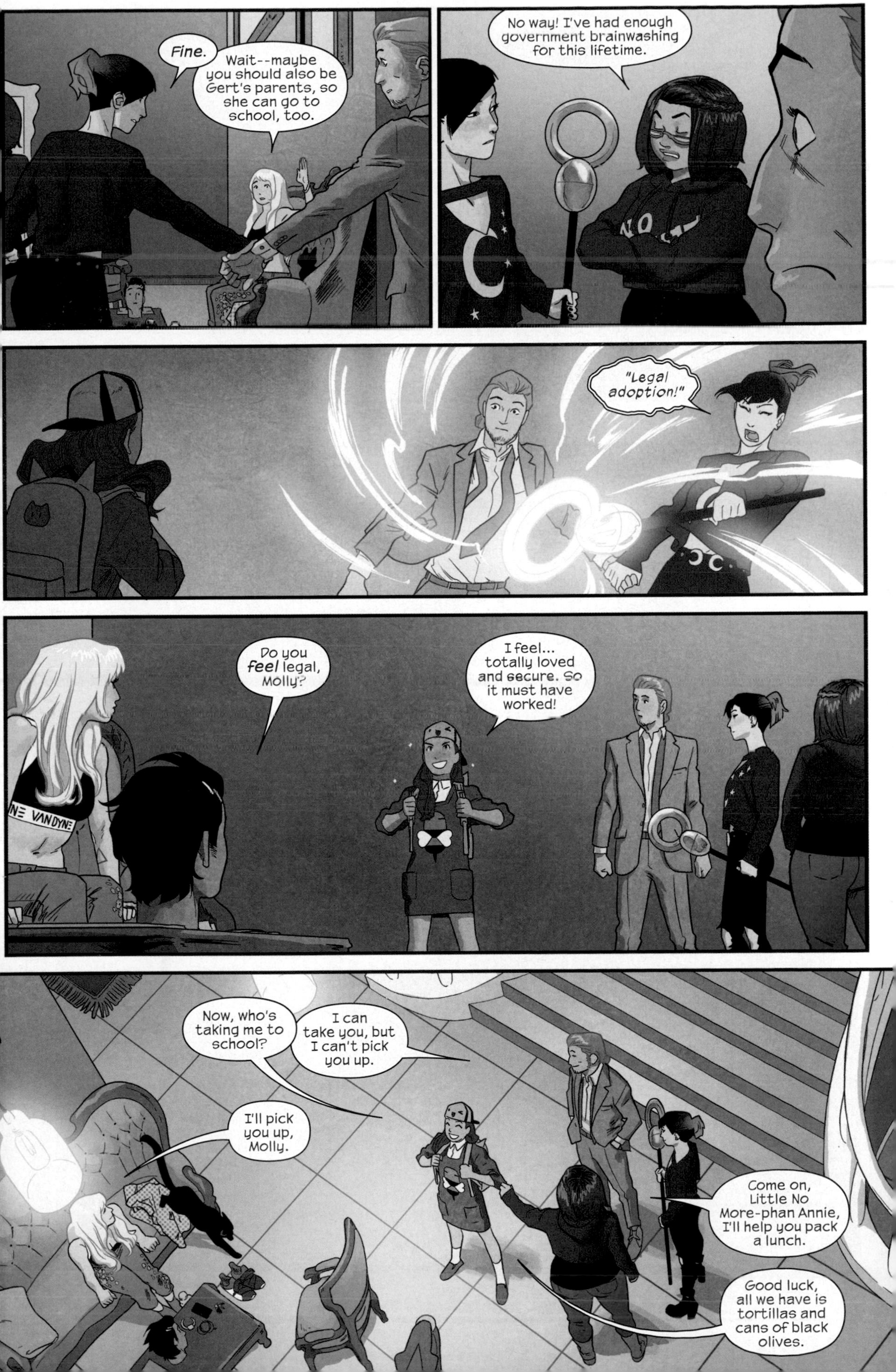
Fine.
Wait--maybe you should also be Gert's parents, so she can go to school, too.
No way! I've had enough government brainwashing for this lifetime.
"Legal adoption!"
Do you feel legal, Molly?
I feel... totally loved and secure. So it must have worked!
Now, who's taking me to school?
I can take you, but I can't pick you up.
I'll pick you up, Molly.
Come on, Little No More-phan Annie, I'll help you pack a lunch.
Good luck, all we have is tortillas and cans of black olives.

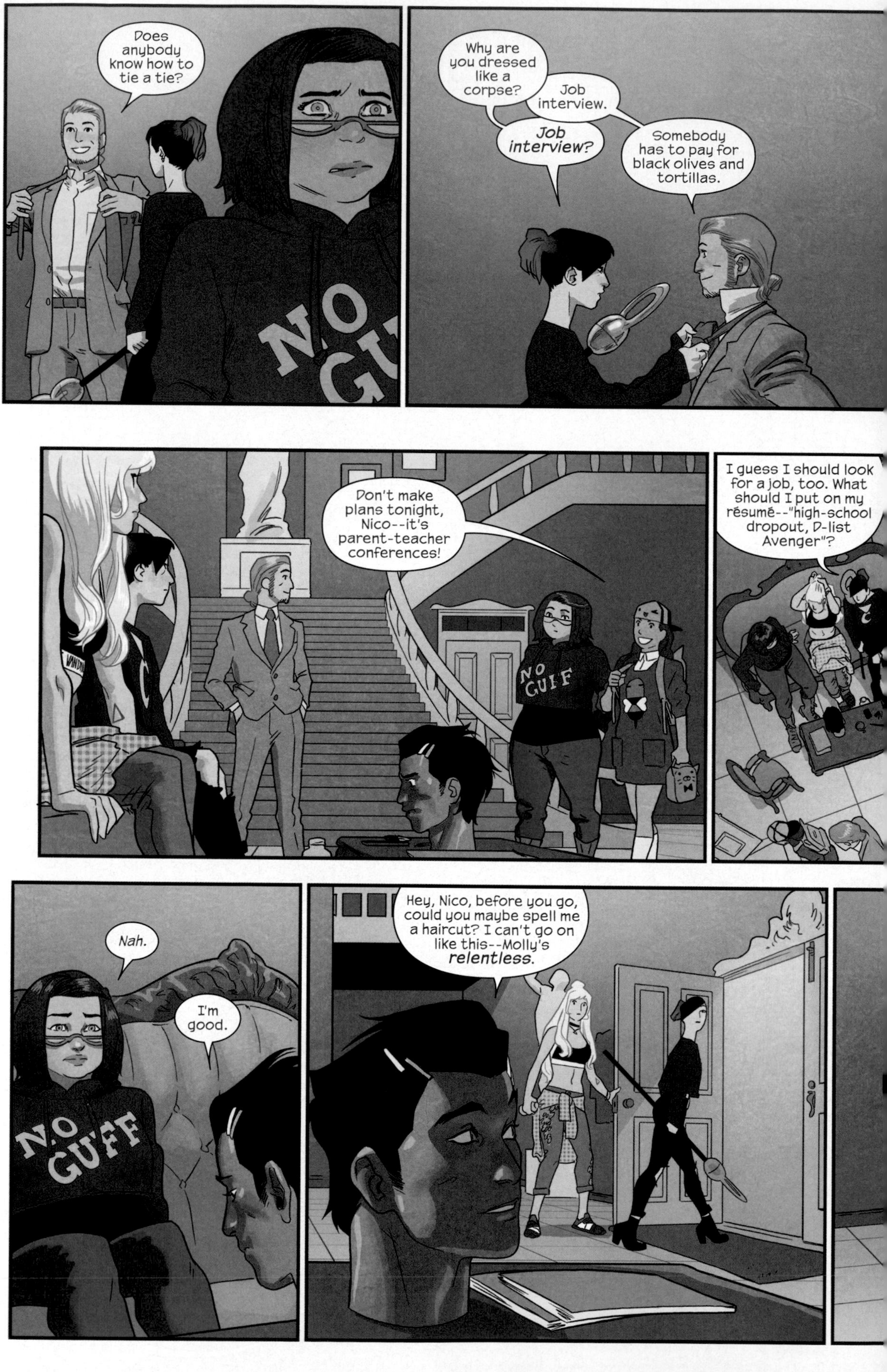
Does anybody know how to tie a tie?
Why are you dressed like a corpse?
Job interview.
Job interview?
Somebody has to pay for black olives and tortillas.
Don't make plans tonight, Nico--it's parent-teacher conferences!
I guess I should look for a job, too. What should I put on my résumé--"high-school dropout, D-list Avenger"?
Nah.
I'm good.
Hey, Nico, before you go, could you maybe spell me a haircut? I can't go on like this--Molly's relentless.

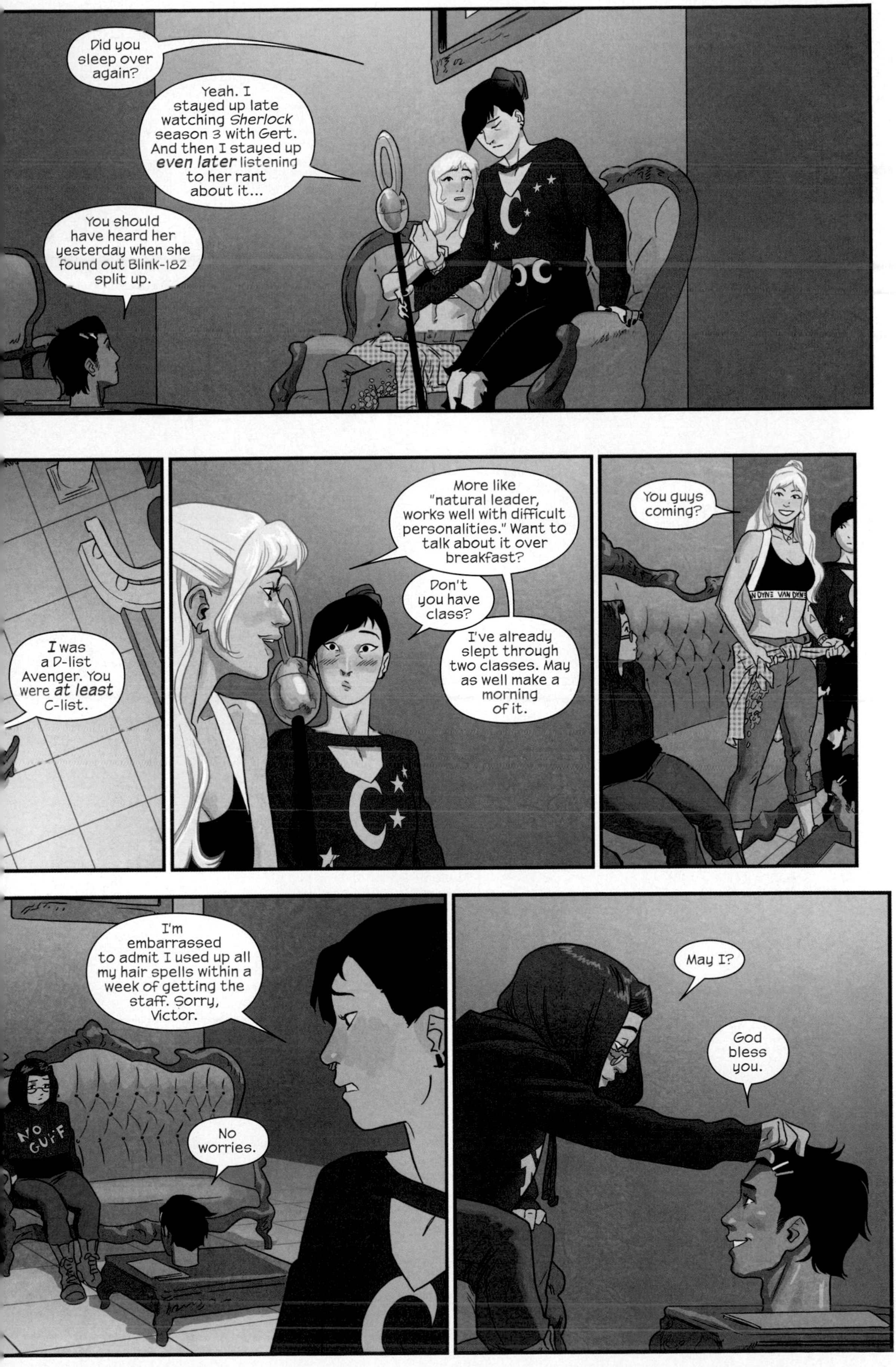

Did you sleep over again?
Yeah. I stayed up late watching Sherlock season 3 with Gert. And then I stayed up even later listening to her rant about it...
You should have heard her yesterday when she found out Blink-182 split up.
I was a D-list Avenger. You were at least C-list.
More like "natural leader, works well with difficult personalities." Want to talk about it over breakfast?
Don't you have class?
I've already slept through two classes. May as well make a morning of it.
You guys coming?
VAN DYNE VAN DYNE
I'm embarrassed to admit I used up all my hair spells within a week of getting the staff. Sorry, Victor.
No worries.
NO GUFF
May I?
God bless you.

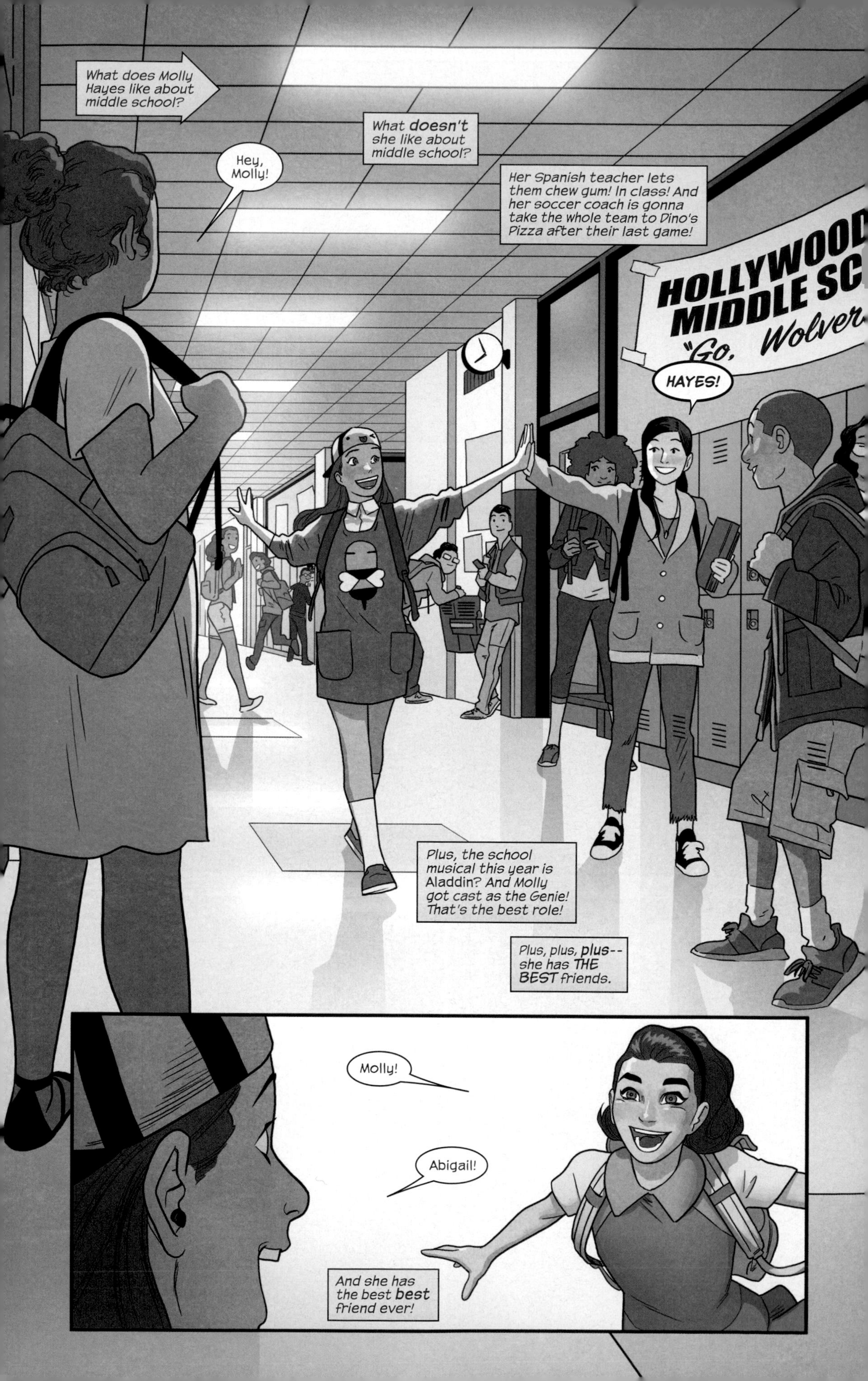
What does Molly Hayes like about middle school?
What **doesn't** she like about middle school?
Hey, Molly!
Her Spanish teacher lets them chew gum! In class! And her soccer coach is gonna take the whole team to Dino's Pizza after their last game!
HOLLYWOOD MIDDLE SC
"Go, Wolver
HAYES!
Plus, the school musical this year is Aladdin? And Molly got cast as the Genie! That's the best role!
Plus, plus, **plus**-- she has **THE BEST** friends.
Molly!
Abigail!
And she has the best **best** friend ever!

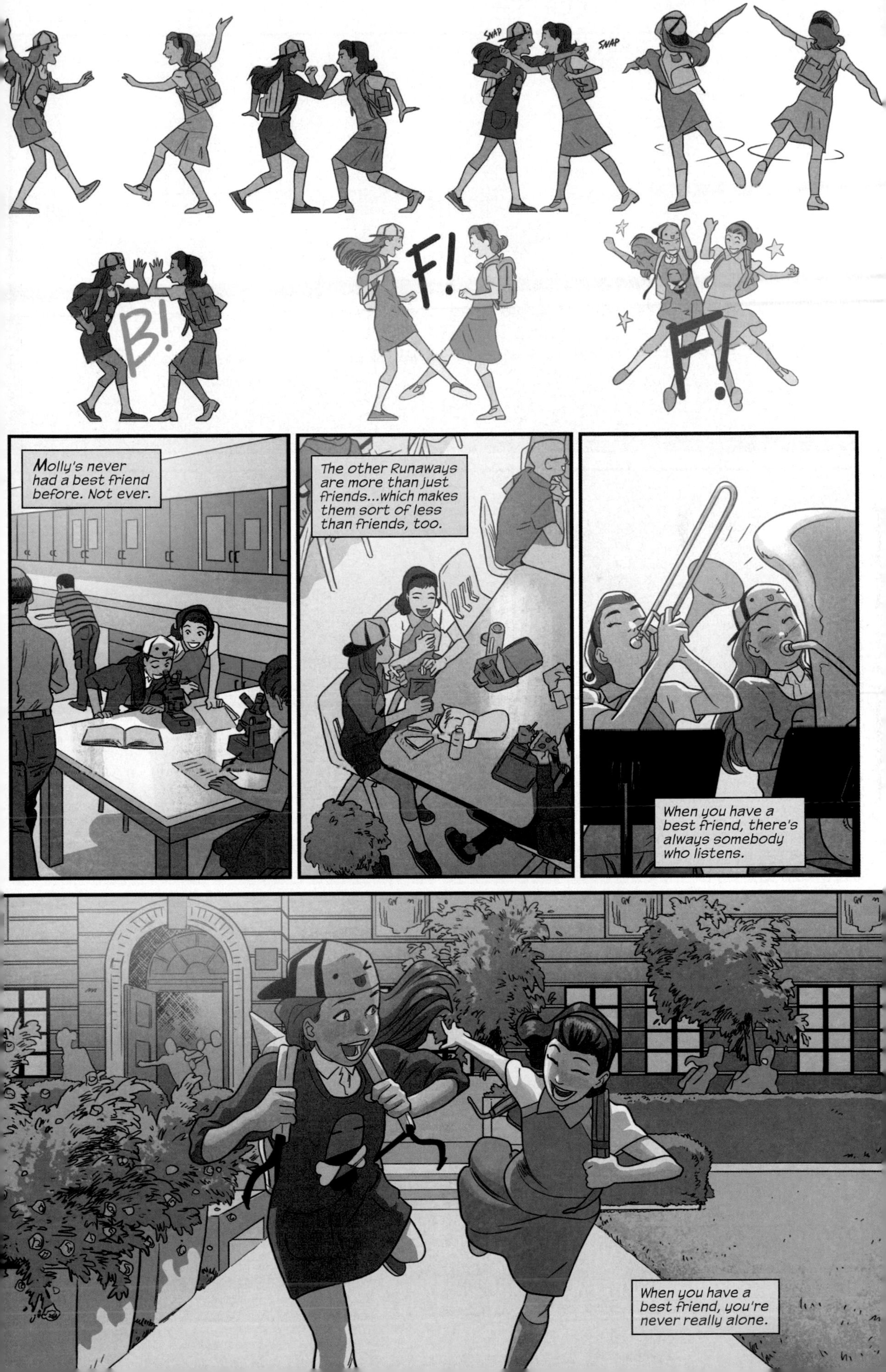
SNAP
SNAP
B!
F!
F!
Molly's never had a best friend before. Not ever.
The other Runaways are more than just friends...which makes them sort of less than friends, too.
When you have a best friend, there's always somebody who listens.
When you have a best friend, you're never really alone.

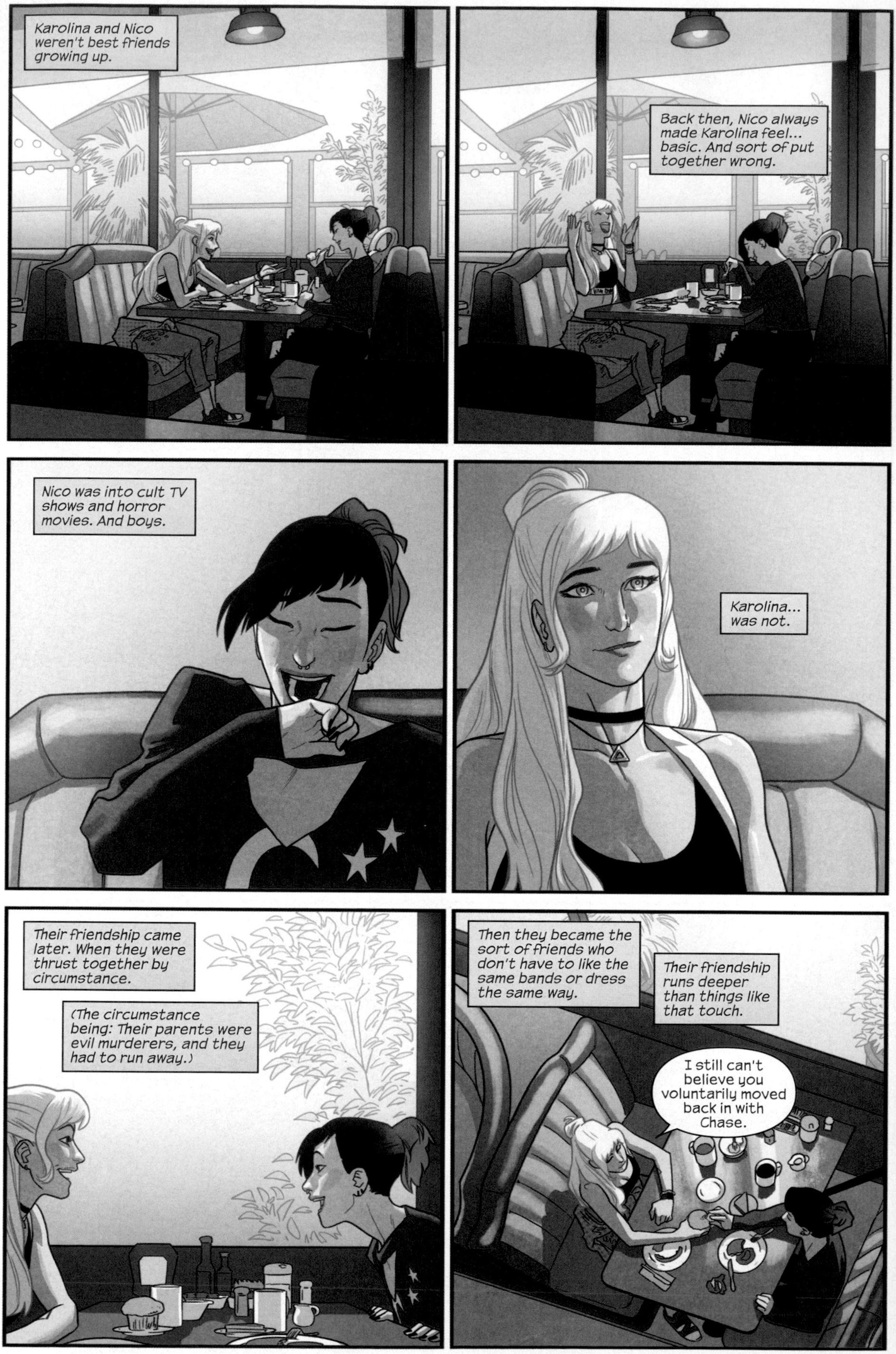
Karolina and Nico weren't best friends growing up.
Back then, Nico always made Karolina feel... basic. And sort of put together wrong.
Nico was into cult TV shows and horror movies. And boys.
Karolina... was not.
Their friendship came later. When they were thrust together by circumstance.
(The circumstance being: Their parents were evil murderers, and they had to run away.)
Then they became the sort of friends who don't have to like the same bands or dress the same way.
Their friendship runs deeper than things like that touch.
I still can't believe you voluntarily moved back in with Chase.

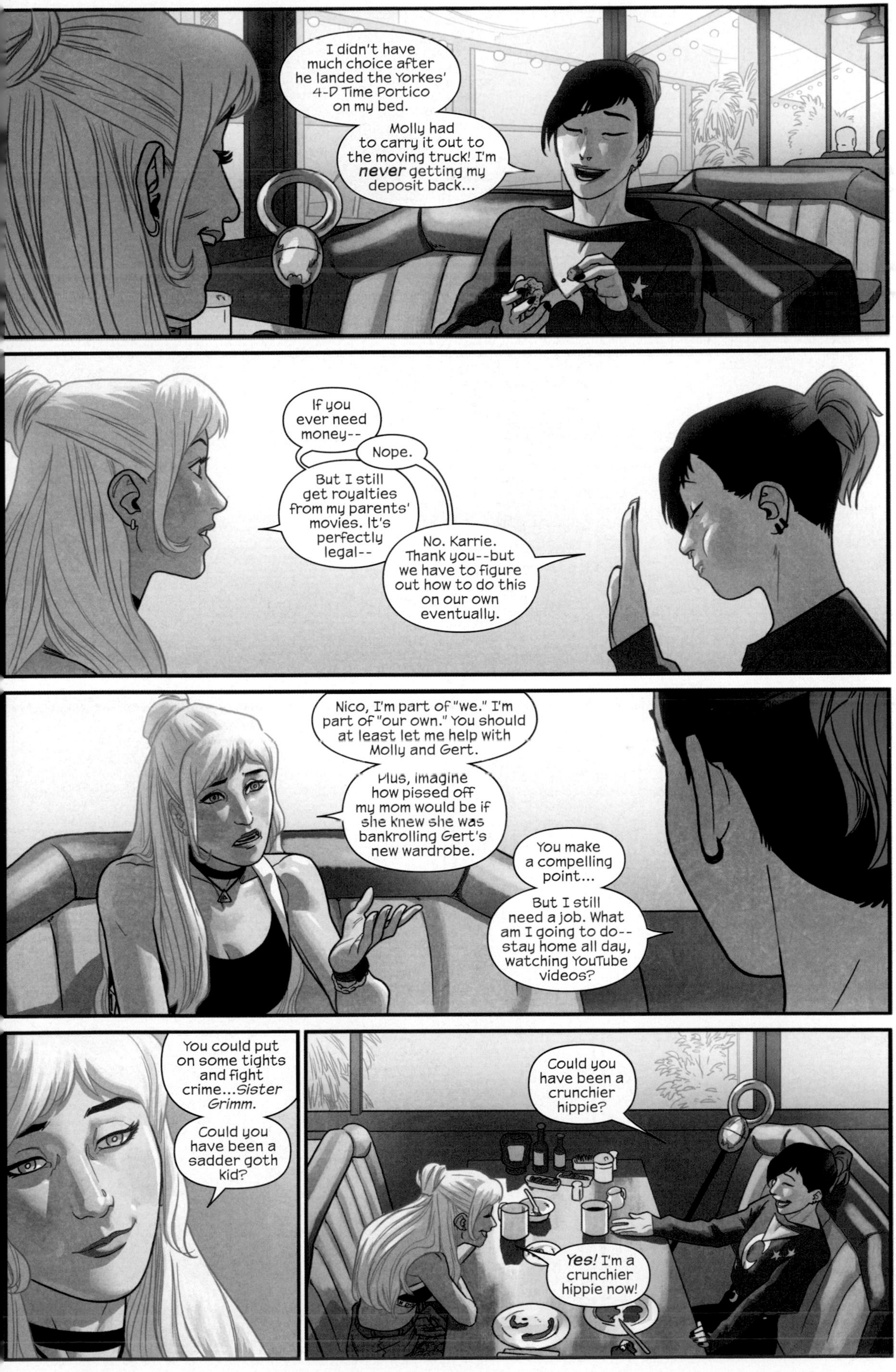

I didn't have much choice after he landed the Yorkes' 4-D Time Portico on my bed.
Molly had to carry it out to the moving truck! I'm *never* getting my deposit back...
If you ever need money--
Nope.
But I still get royalties from my parents' movies. It's perfectly legal--
No. Karrie. Thank you--but we have to figure out how to do this on our own eventually.
Nico, I'm part of "we." I'm part of "our own." You should at least let me help with Molly and Gert.
Plus, imagine how pissed off my mom would be if she knew she was bankrolling Gert's new wardrobe.
You make a compelling point...
But I still need a job. What am I going to do--stay home all day, watching YouTube videos?
You could put on some tights and fight crime...*Sister Grimm.*
Could you have been a sadder goth kid?
Could you have been a crunchier hippie?
Yes! I'm a crunchier hippie now!

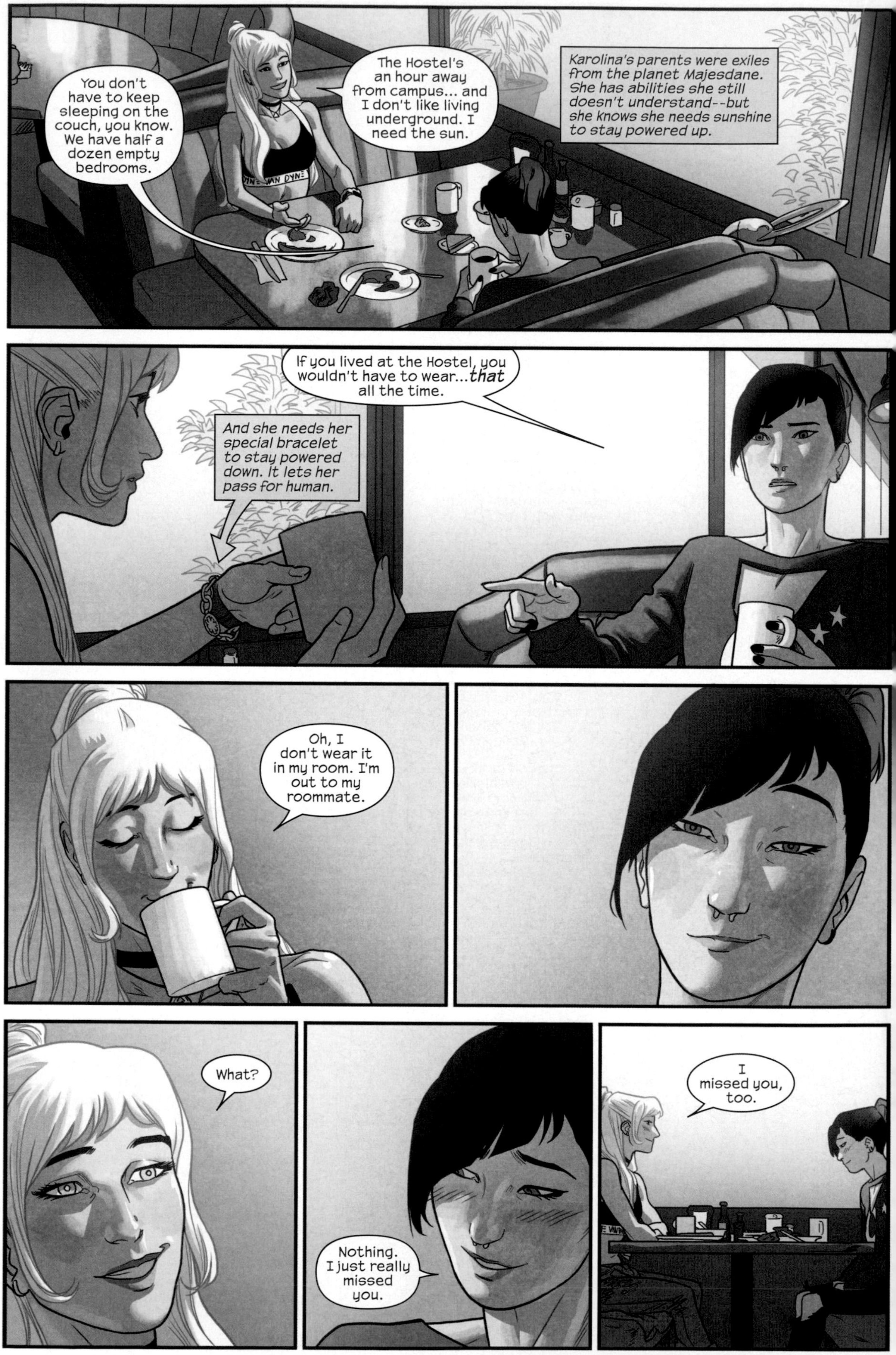

You don't have to keep sleeping on the couch, you know. We have half a dozen empty bedrooms.
The Hostel's an hour away from campus... and I don't like living underground. I need the sun.
Karolina's parents were exiles from the planet Majesdane. She has abilities she still doesn't understand--but she knows she needs sunshine to stay powered up.
If you lived at the Hostel, you wouldn't have to wear...that all the time.
And she needs her special bracelet to stay powered down. It lets her pass for human.
Oh, I don't wear it in my room. I'm out to my roommate.
What?
Nothing. I just really missed you.
I missed you, too.

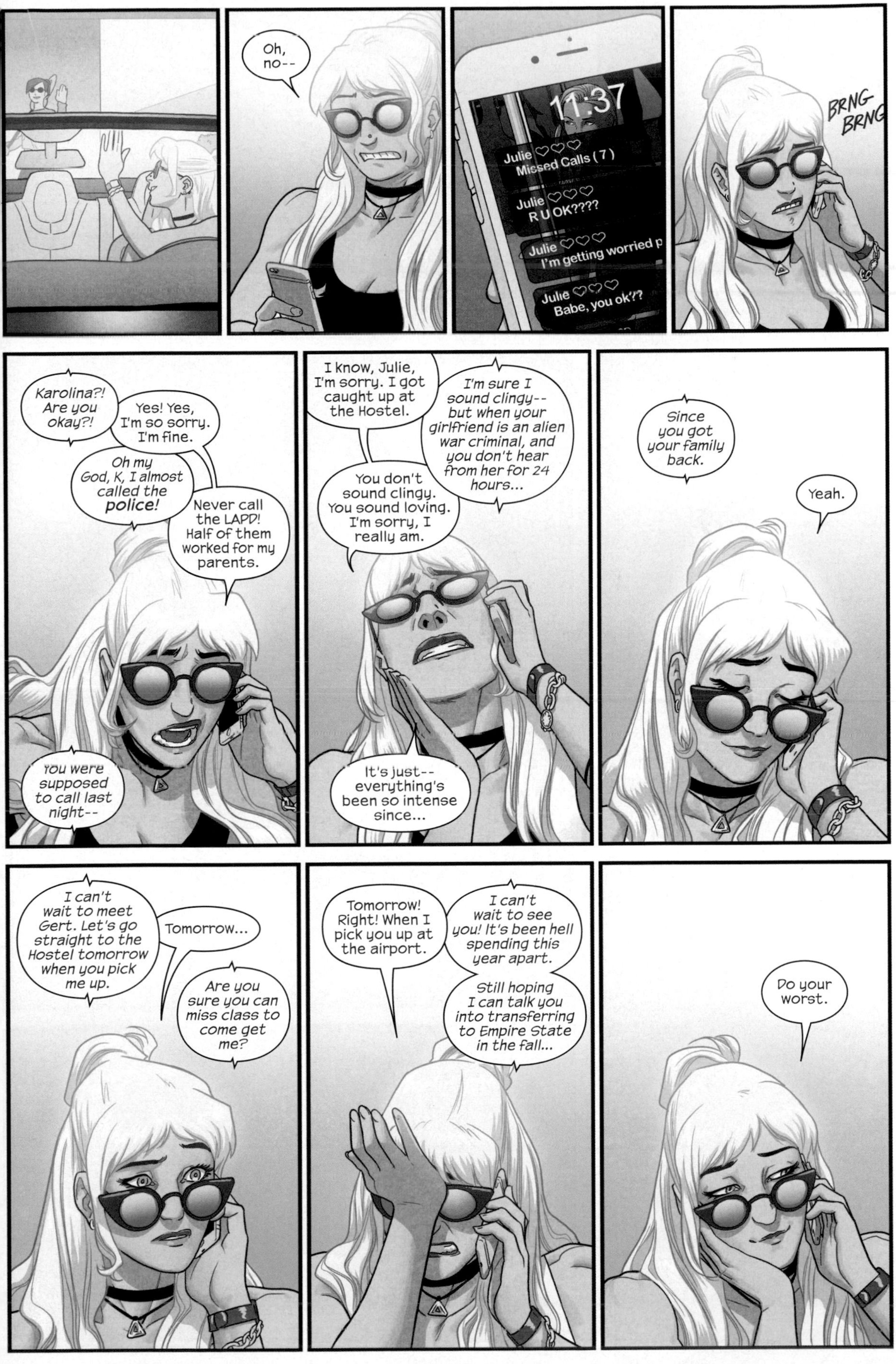
Oh, no--
11:37
Julie ♡♡♡ Missed Calls (7)
Julie ♡♡♡ R U OK????
Julie ♡♡♡ I'm getting worried
Julie ♡♡♡ Babe, you ok?
BRNG BRNG
Karolina?! Are you okay?!
Yes! Yes, I'm so sorry. I'm fine.
Oh my God, K, I almost called the police!
Never call the LAPD! Half of them worked for my parents.
You were supposed to call last night--
I know, Julie, I'm sorry. I got caught up at the Hostel.
I'm sure I sound clingy-- but when your girlfriend is an alien war criminal, and you don't hear from her for 24 hours...
You don't sound clingy. You sound loving. I'm sorry, I really am.
It's just-- everything's been so intense since...
Since you got your family back.
Yeah.
I can't wait to meet Gert. Let's go straight to the Hostel tomorrow when you pick me up.
Tomorrow...
Are you sure you can miss class to come get me?
Tomorrow! Right! When I pick you up at the airport.
I can't wait to see you! It's been hell spending this year apart.
Still hoping I can talk you into transferring to Empire State in the fall...
Do your worst.

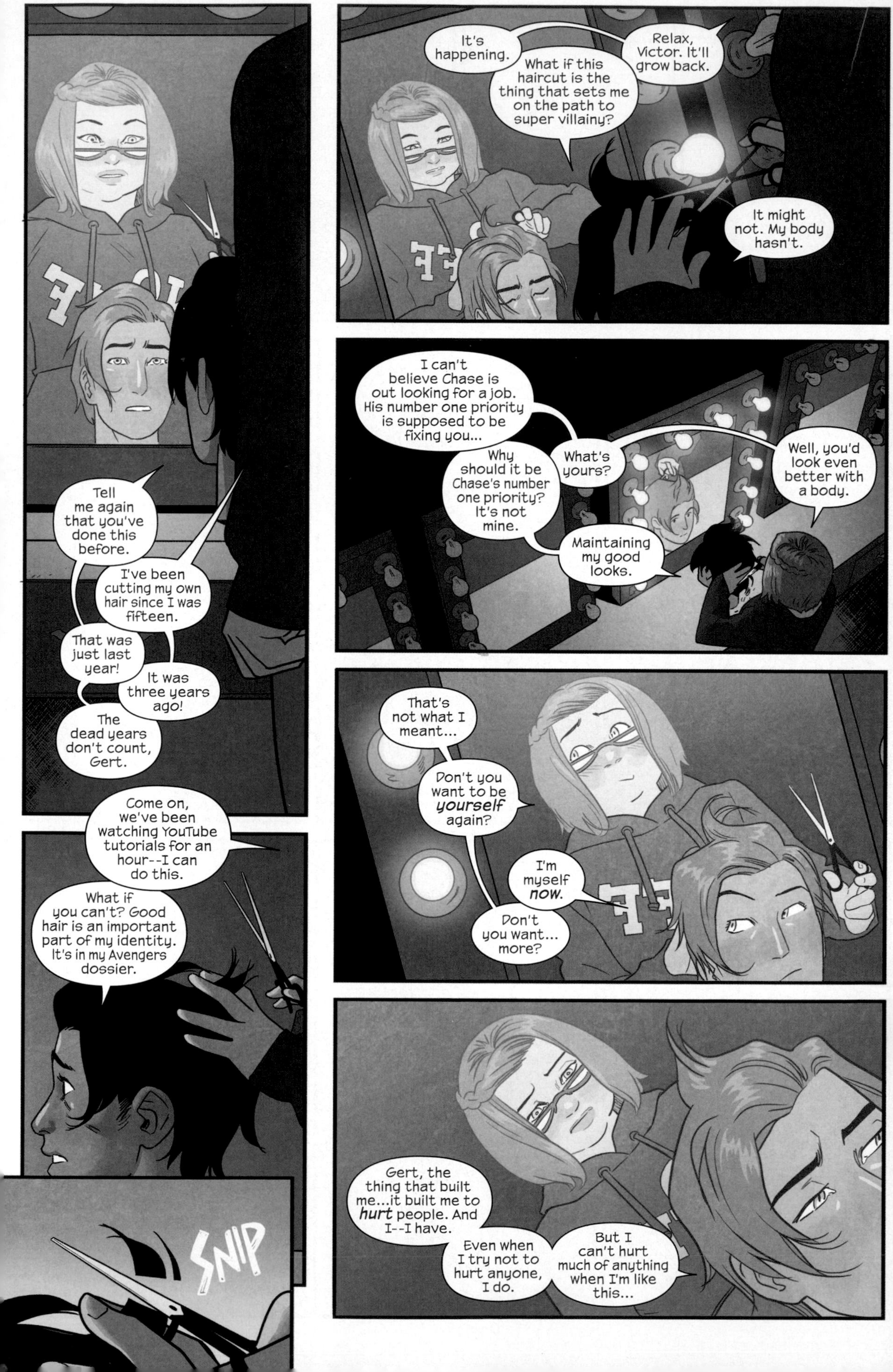
It's happening.
What if this haircut is the thing that sets me on the path to super villainy?
Relax, Victor. It'll grow back.
It might not. My body hasn't.
Tell me again that you've done this before.
I've been cutting my own hair since I was fifteen.
That was just last year!
It was three years ago!
The dead years don't count, Gert.
I can't believe Chase is out looking for a job. His number one priority is supposed to be fixing you...
Why should it be Chase's number one priority? It's not mine.
What's yours?
Maintaining my good looks.
Well, you'd look even better with a body.
Come on, we've been watching YouTube tutorials for an hour--I can do this.
What if you can't? Good hair is an important part of my identity. It's in my Avengers dossier.
SNIP
That's not what I meant...
Don't you want to be *yourself* again?
I'm myself *now*.
Don't you want... more?
Gert, the thing that built me...it built me to *hurt* people. And I--I have.
Even when I try not to hurt anyone, I do.
But I can't hurt much of anything when I'm like this...

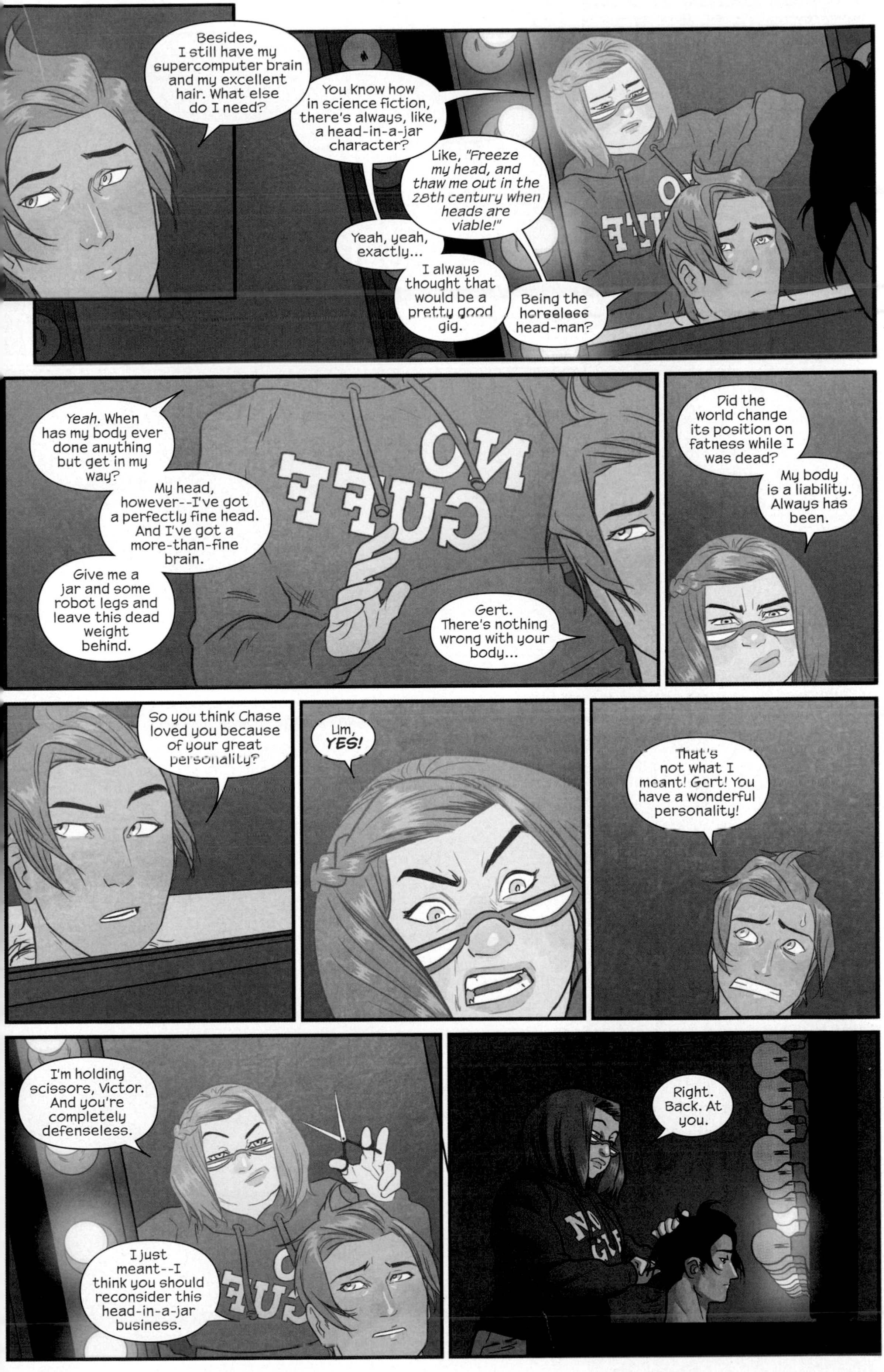
Besides, I still have my supercomputer brain and my excellent hair. What else do I need?
You know how in science fiction, there's always, like, a head-in-a-jar character?
Like, "Freeze my head, and thaw me out in the 28th century when heads are viable!"
Yeah, yeah, exactly...
I always thought that would be a pretty good gig.
Being the horseless head-man?
Yeah. When has my body ever done anything but get in my way?
My head, however--I've got a perfectly fine head. And I've got a more-than-fine brain.
Give me a jar and some robot legs and leave this dead weight behind.
Gert. There's nothing wrong with your body...
Did the world change its position on fatness while I was dead?
My body is a liability. Always has been.
So you think Chase loved you because of your great personality?
Um, YES!
That's not what I meant! Gert! You have a wonderful personality!
I'm holding scissors, Victor. And you're completely defenseless.
I just meant--I think you should reconsider this head-in-a-jar business.
Right. Back. At you.

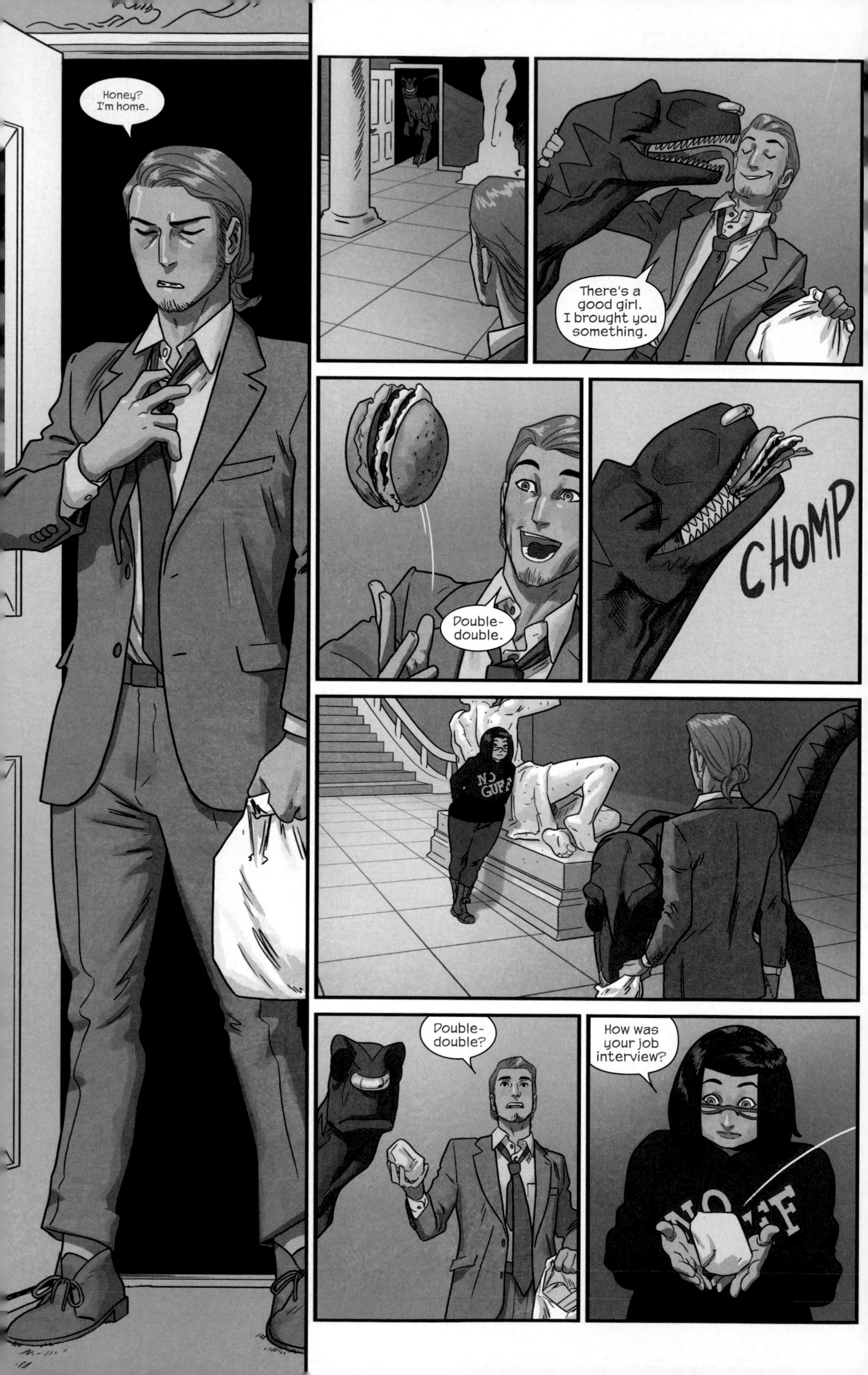
Honey?
I'm home.
There's a good girl. I brought you something.
Double-double.
CHOMP
Double-double?
How was your job interview?

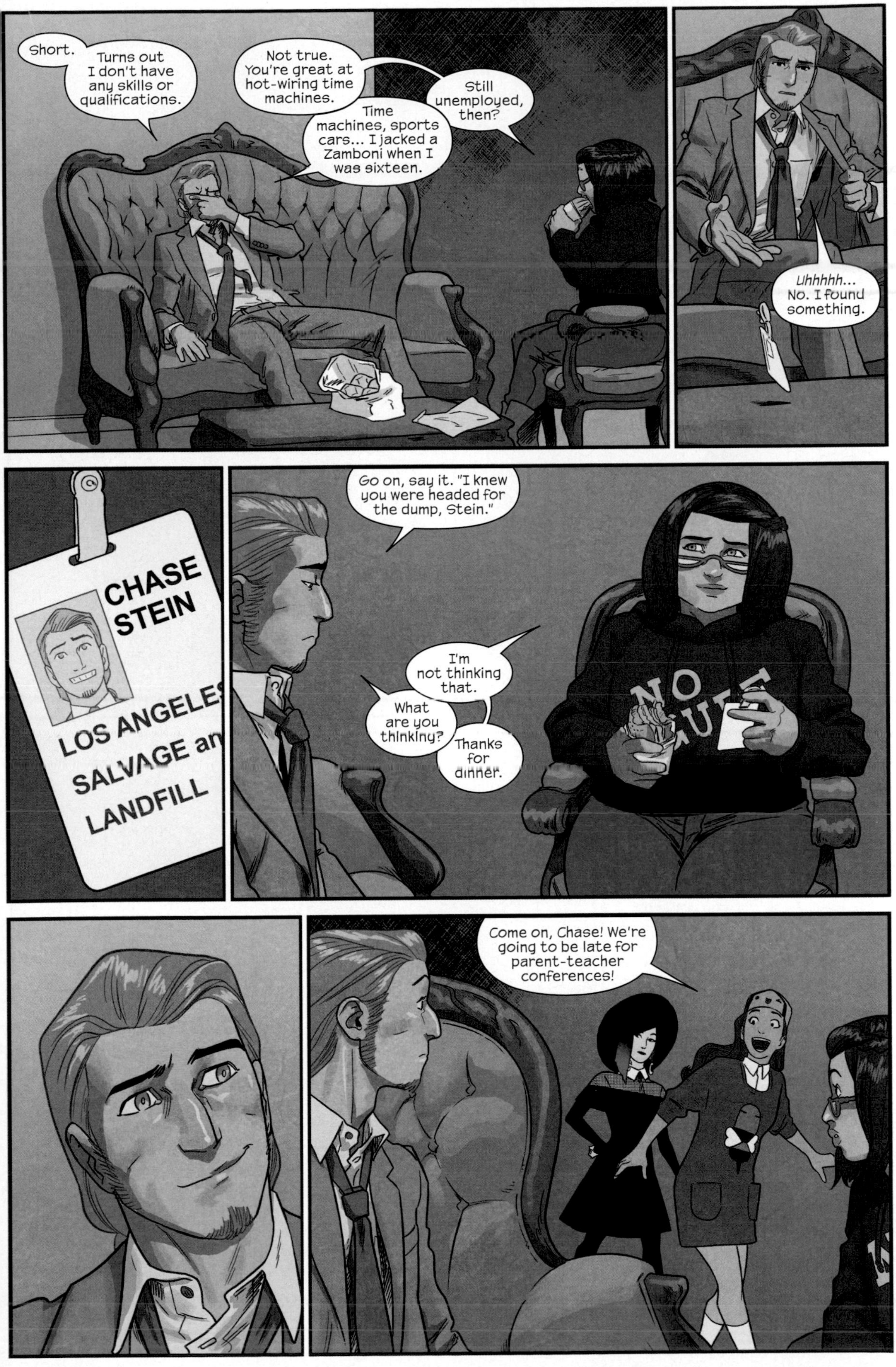
Short.
Turns out I don't have any skills or qualifications.
Not true. You're great at hot-wiring time machines.
Still unemployed, then?
Time machines, sports cars... I jacked a Zamboni when I was sixteen.
Uhhhhh... No. I found something.
CHASE STEIN
LOS ANGELES
SALVAGE an
LANDFILL
Go on, say it. "I knew you were headed for the dump, Stein."
What are you thinking?
I'm not thinking that.
Thanks for dinner.
Come on, Chase! We're going to be late for parent-teacher conferences!

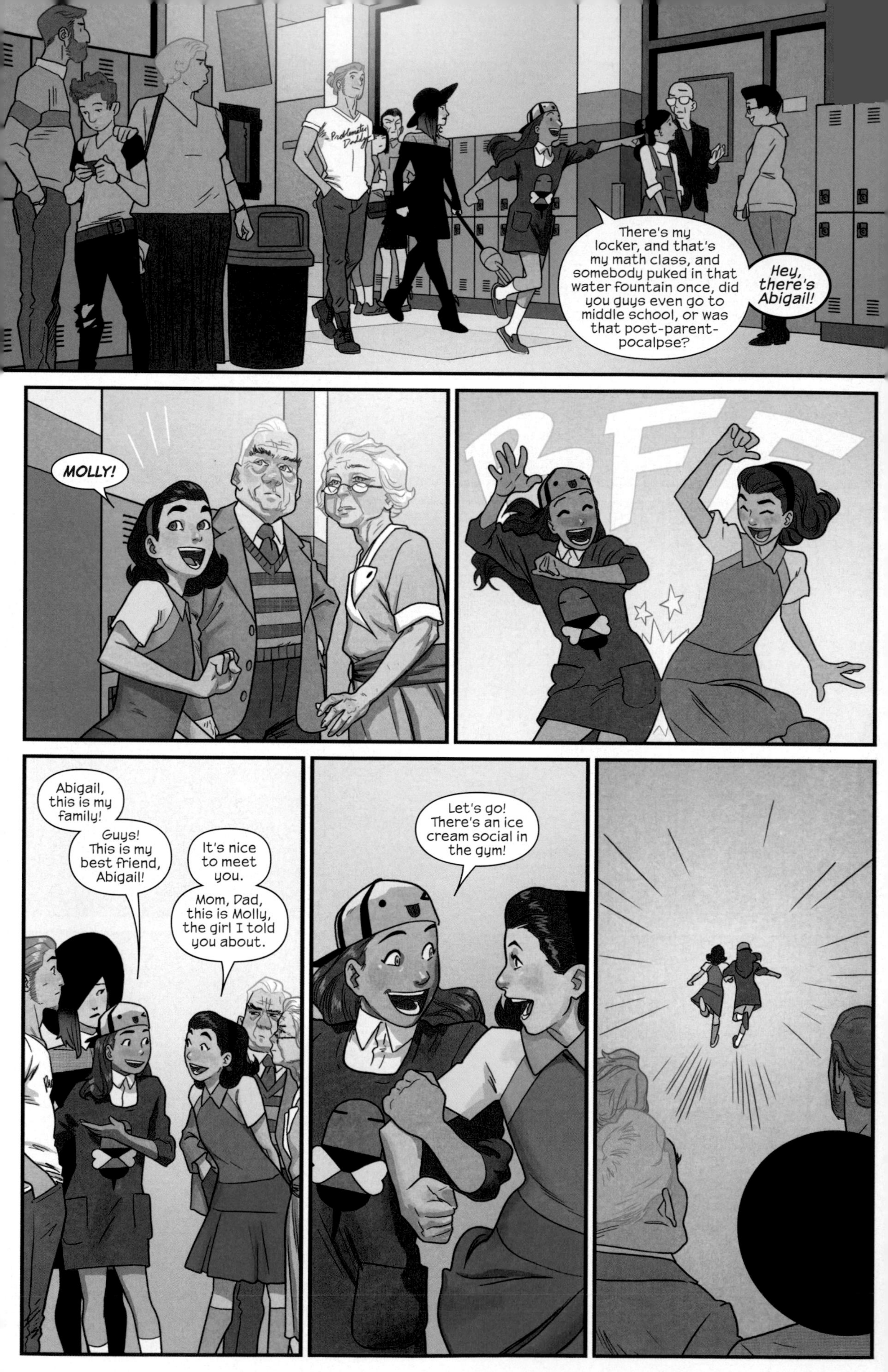
There's my locker, and that's my math class, and somebody puked in that water fountain once, did you guys even go to middle school, or was that post-parent-pocalpse?
Hey, there's Abigail!
MOLLY!
BFF
Abigail, this is my family!
Guys! This is my best friend, Abigail!
It's nice to meet you.
Mom, Dad, this is Molly, the girl I told you about.
Let's go! There's an ice cream social in the gym!

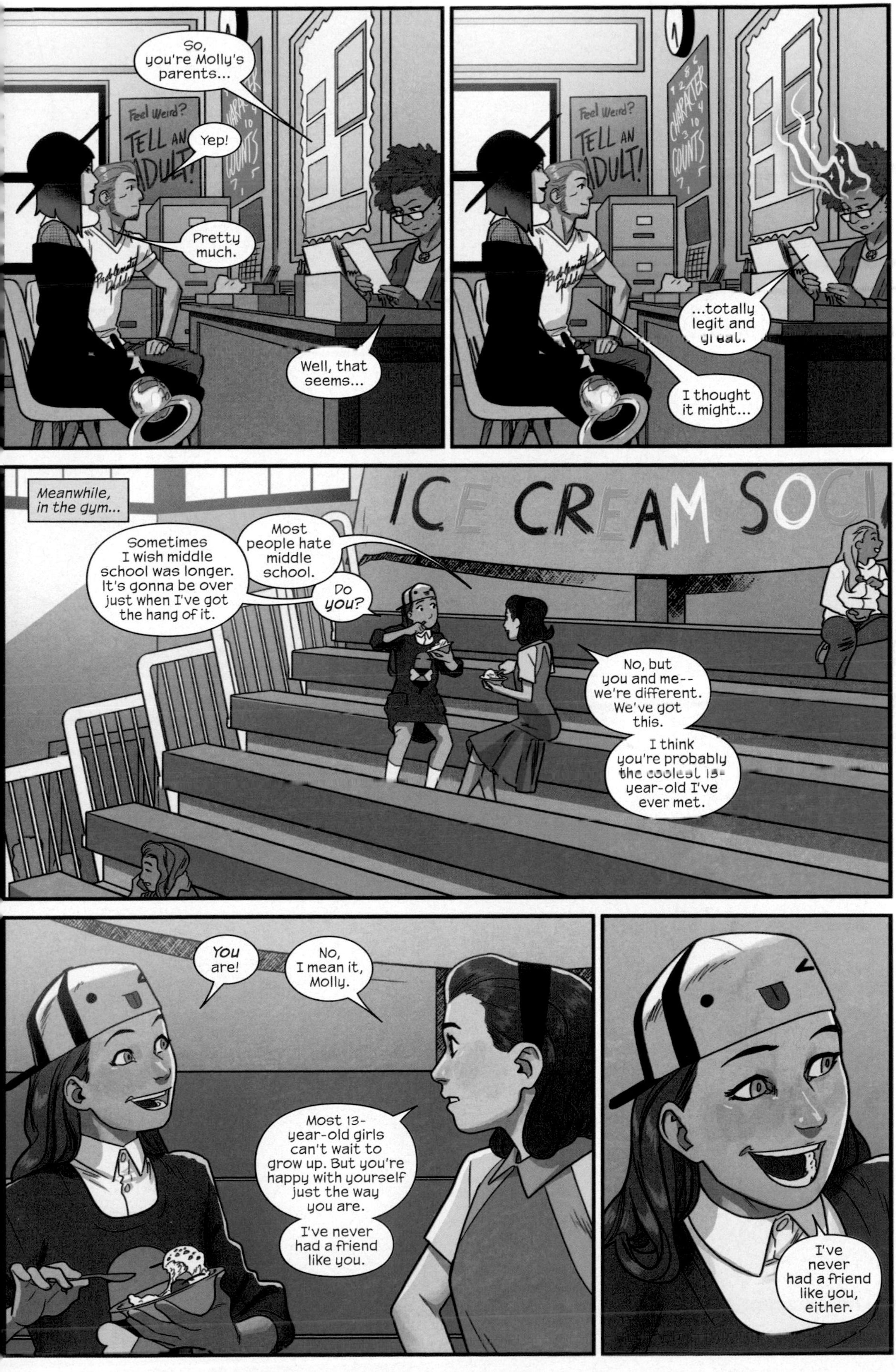
So, you're Molly's parents...
Feel Weird? TELL AN ADULT!
CHARACTER COUNTS
Yep!
Pretty much.
Well, that seems...
...totally legit and great.
I thought it might...
Meanwhile, in the gym...
ICE CREAM SOC
Sometimes I wish middle school was longer. It's gonna be over just when I've got the hang of it.
Most people hate middle school.
Do *you*?
No, but you and me-- we're different. We've got this.
I think you're probably the coolest 13-year-old I've ever met.
You are!
No, I mean it, Molly.
Most 13-year-old girls can't wait to grow up. But you're happy with yourself just the way you are.
I've never had a friend like you.
I've never had a friend like you, either.

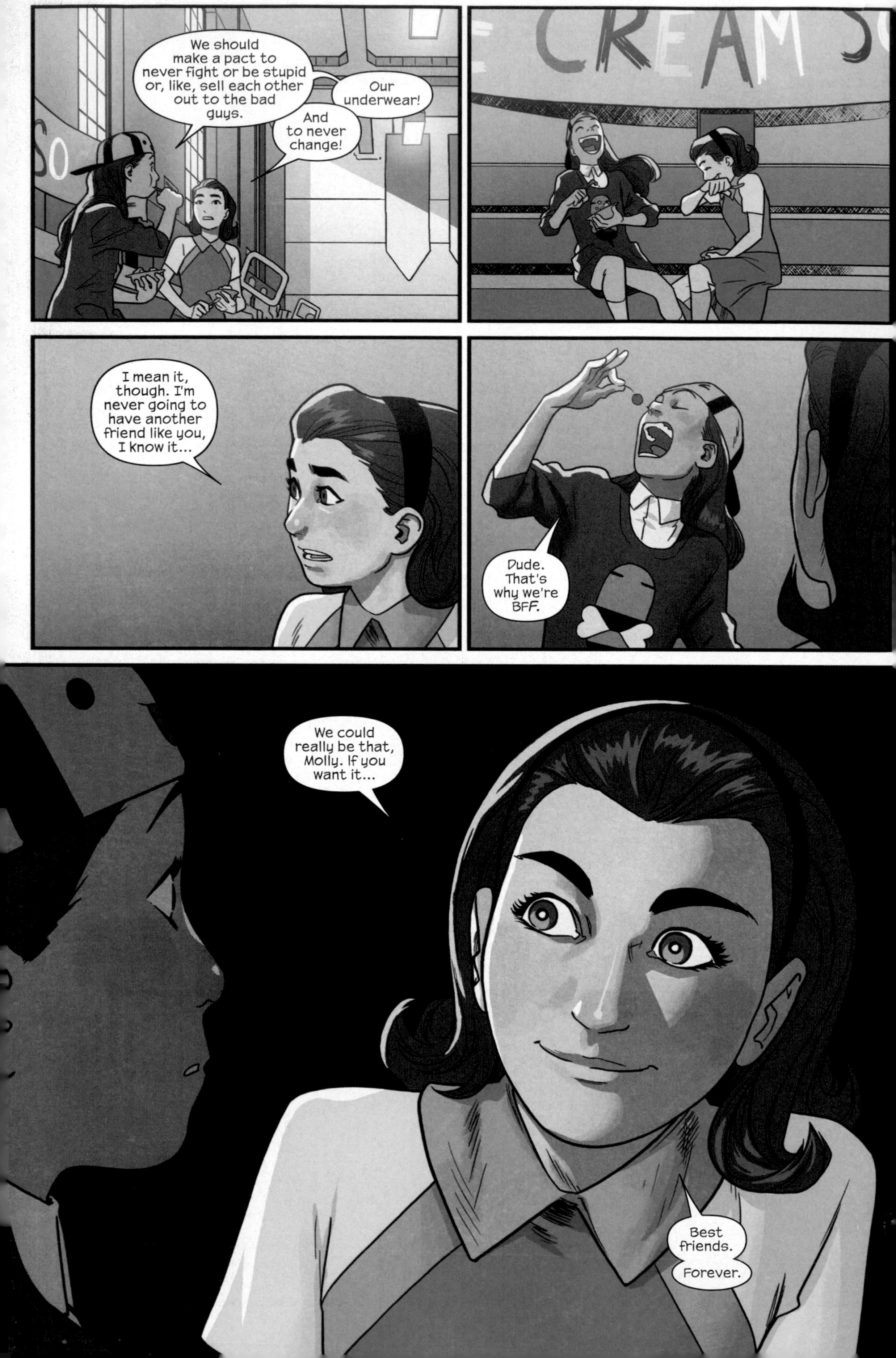
We should make a pact to never fight or be stupid or, like, sell each other out to the bad guys.
Our underwear!
And to never change!
CREAM S
I mean it, though. I'm never going to have another friend like you, I know it...
Dude. That's why we're BFF.
We could really be that, Molly. If you want it...
Best friends.
Forever.

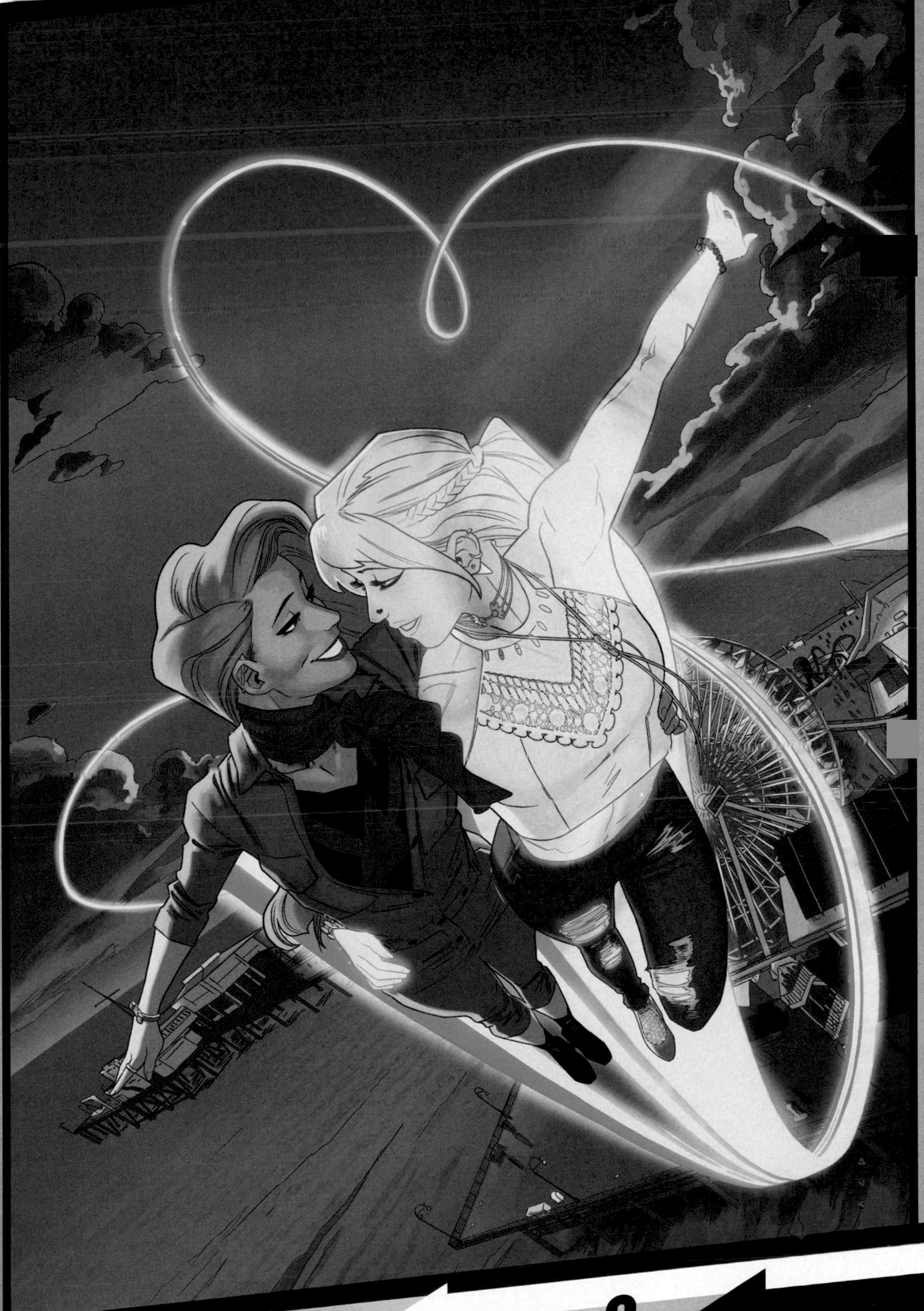

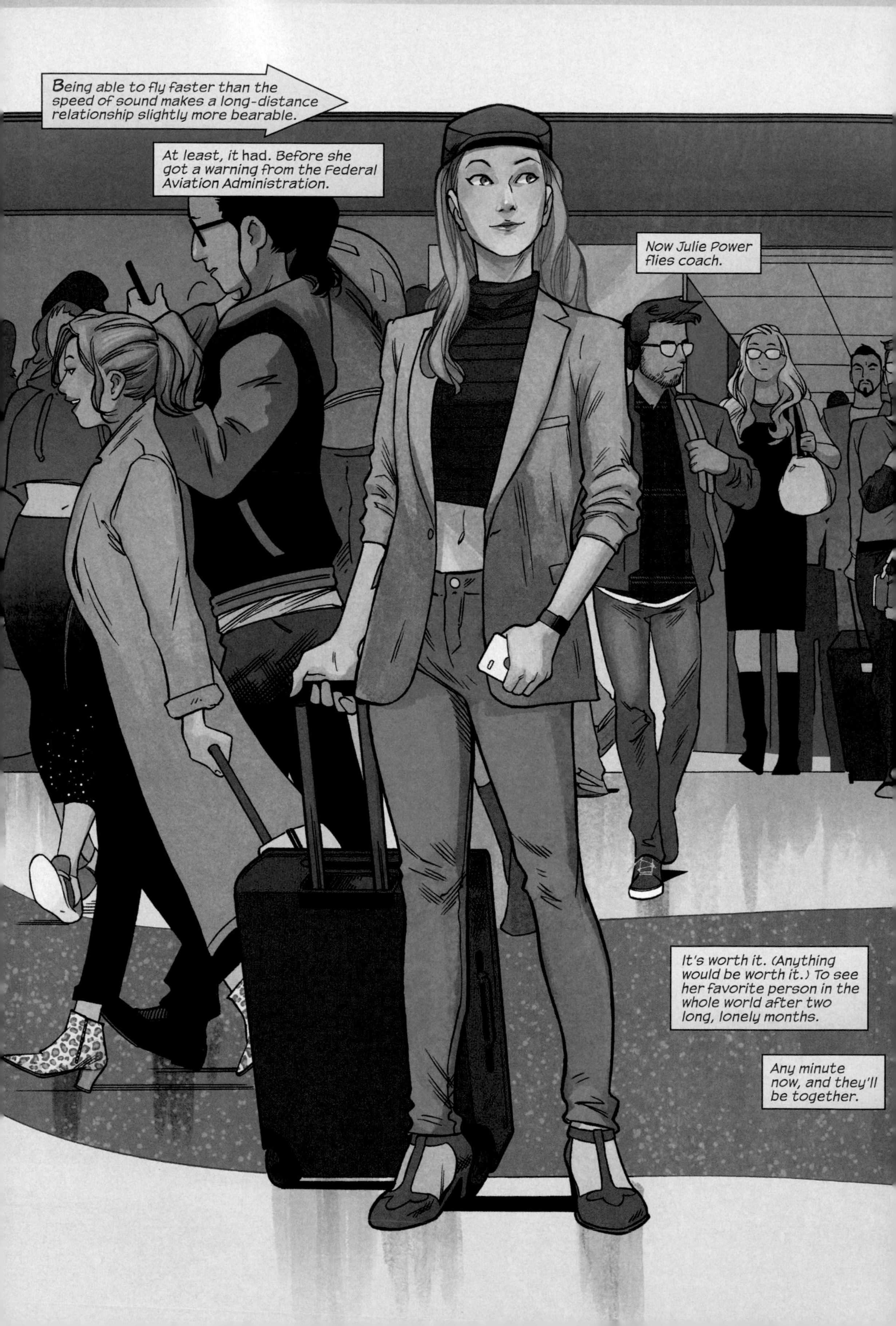
Being able to fly faster than the speed of sound makes a long-distance relationship slightly more bearable.
At least, it had. Before she got a warning from the Federal Aviation Administration.
Now Julie Power flies coach.
It's worth it. (Anything would be worth it.) To see her favorite person in the whole world after two long, lonely months.
Any minute now, and they'll be together.

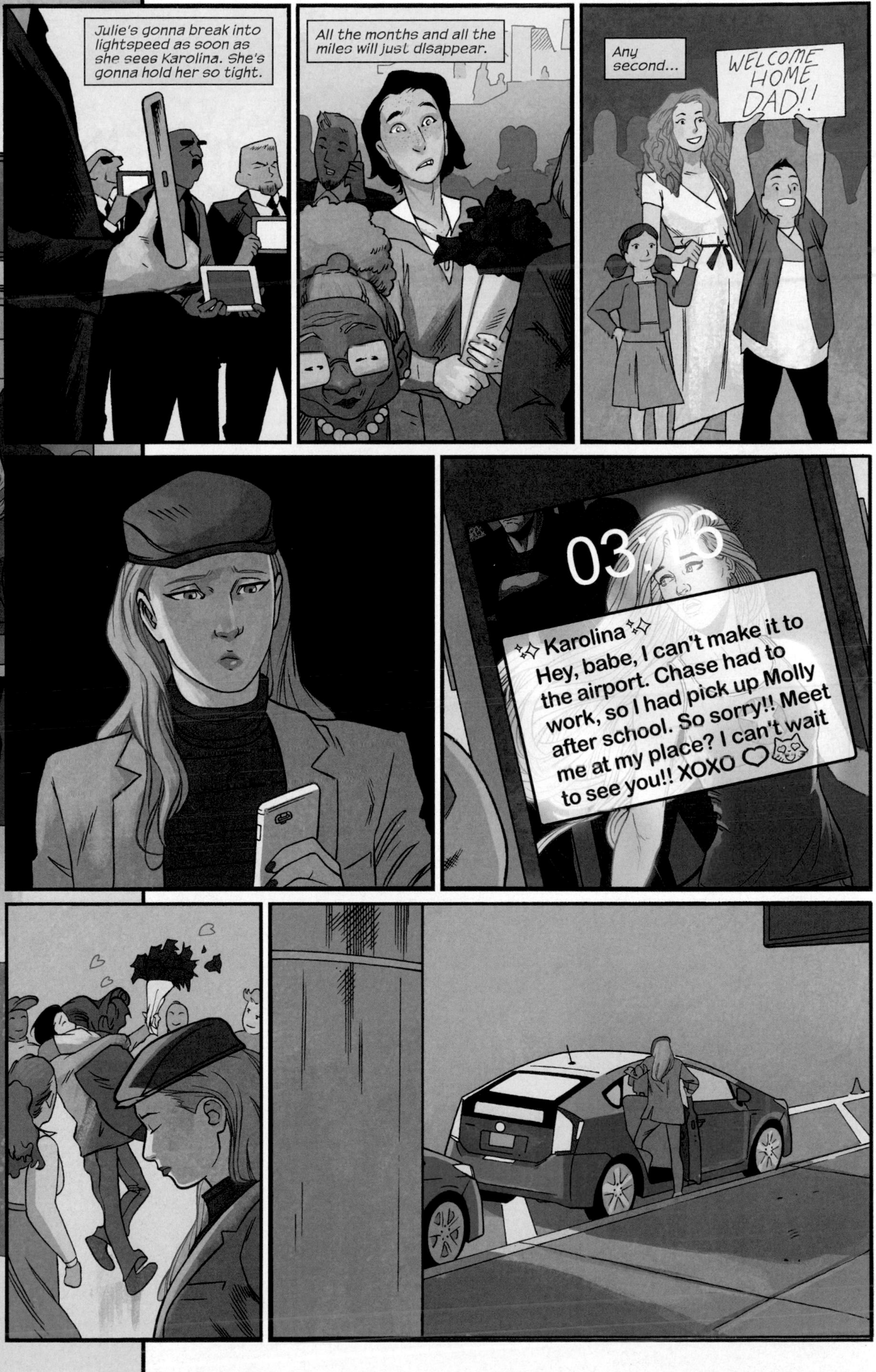
Julie's gonna break into lightspeed as soon as she sees Karolina. She's gonna hold her so tight.
All the months and all the miles will just disappear.
Any second...
WELCOME HOME DAD!!
Karolina
Hey, babe, I can't make it to the airport. Chase had to work, so I had pick up Molly after school. So sorry!! Meet me at my place? I can't wait to see you!! XOXO

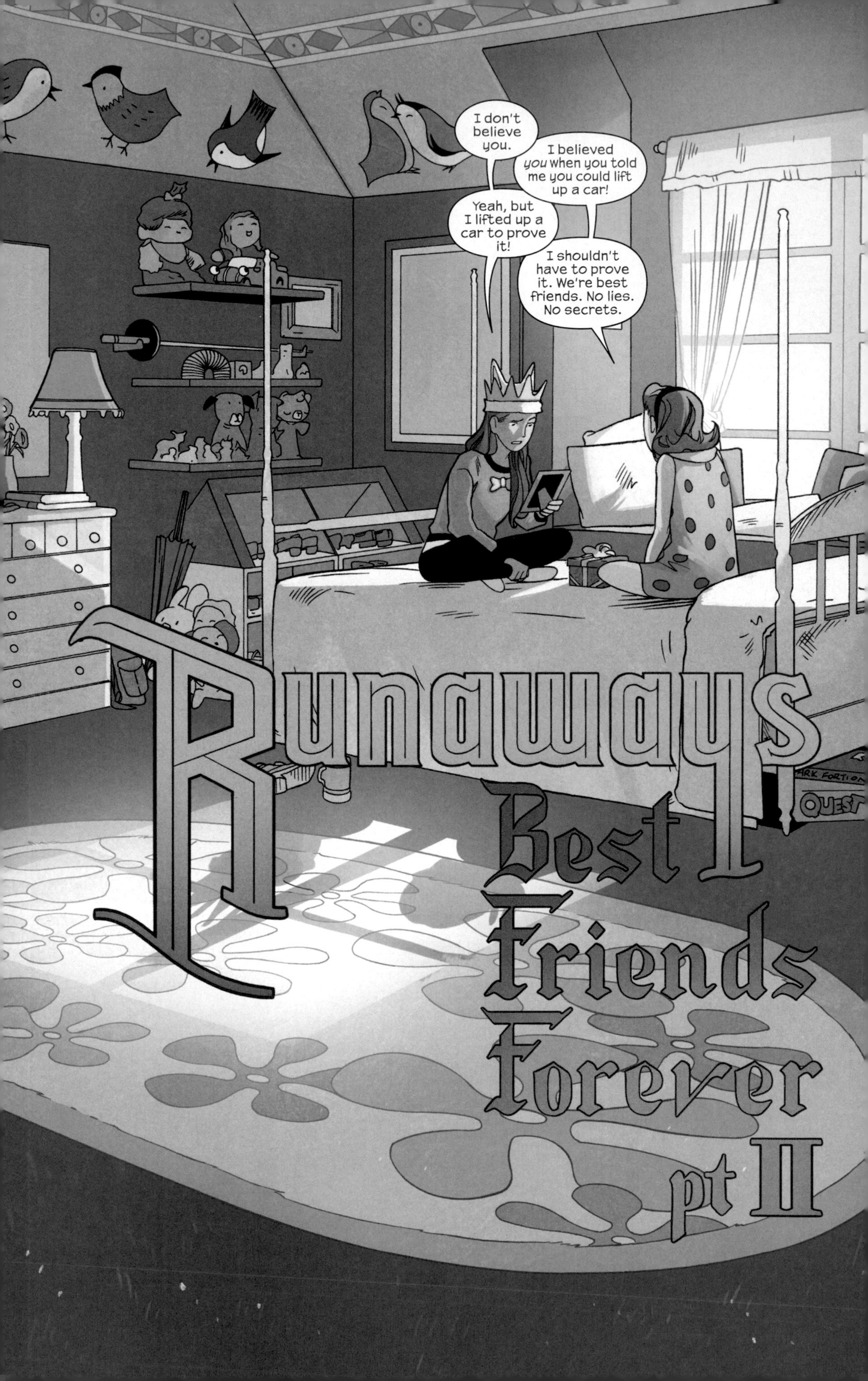
I don't believe you.
I believed *you* when you told me you could lift up a car!
Yeah, but I lifted up a car to prove it!
I shouldn't have to prove it. We're best friends. No lies. No secrets.
Runaways
Best Friends Forever pt II

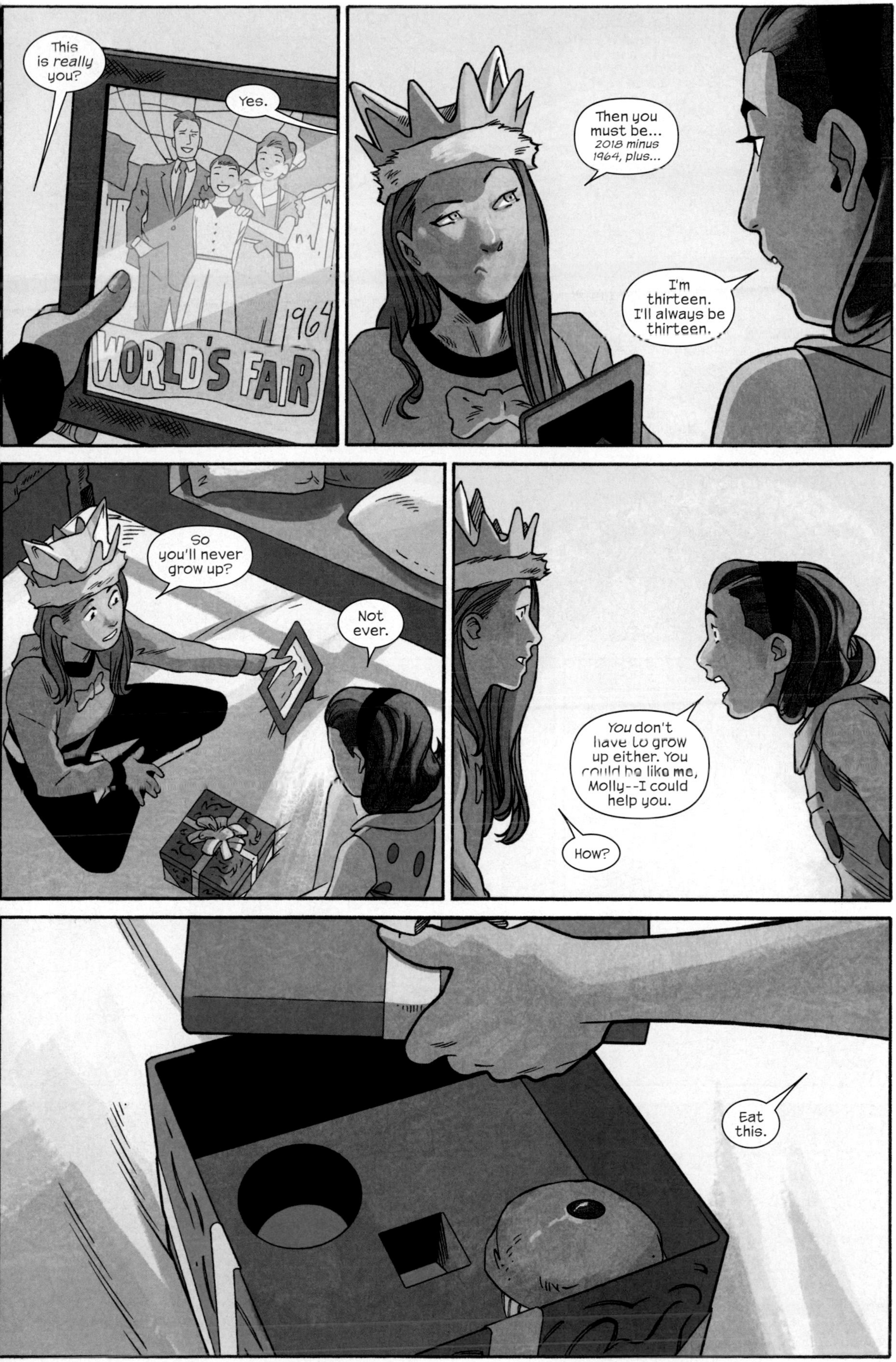

This is really you?
Yes.
WORLD'S FAIR
1964
Then you must be... 2018 minus 1964, plus...
I'm thirteen. I'll always be thirteen.
So you'll never grow up?
Not ever.
You don't have to grow up either. You could be like me, Molly--I could help you.
How?
Eat this.

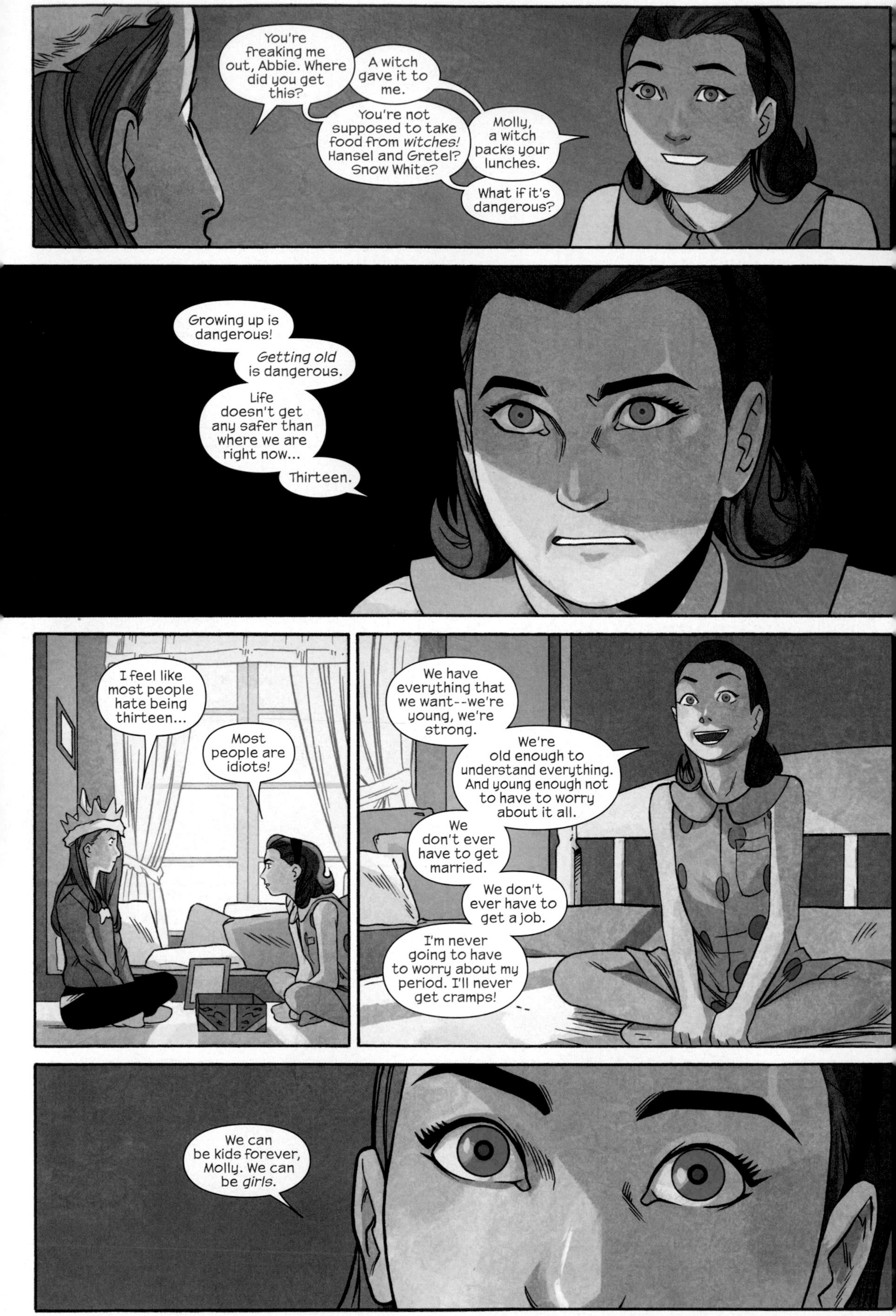

You're freaking me out, Abbie. Where did you get this?
A witch gave it to me.
You're not supposed to take food from *witches!* Hansel and Gretel? Snow White?
Molly, a witch packs your lunches.
What if it's dangerous?
Growing up is dangerous!
Getting old is dangerous.
Life doesn't get any safer than where we are right now...
Thirteen.
I feel like most people hate being thirteen...
Most people are idiots!
We have everything that we want--we're young, we're strong.
We're old enough to understand everything. And young enough not to have to worry about it all.
We don't ever have to get married.
We don't ever have to get a job.
I'm never going to have to worry about my period. I'll never get cramps!
We can be kids forever, Molly. We can be *girls.*

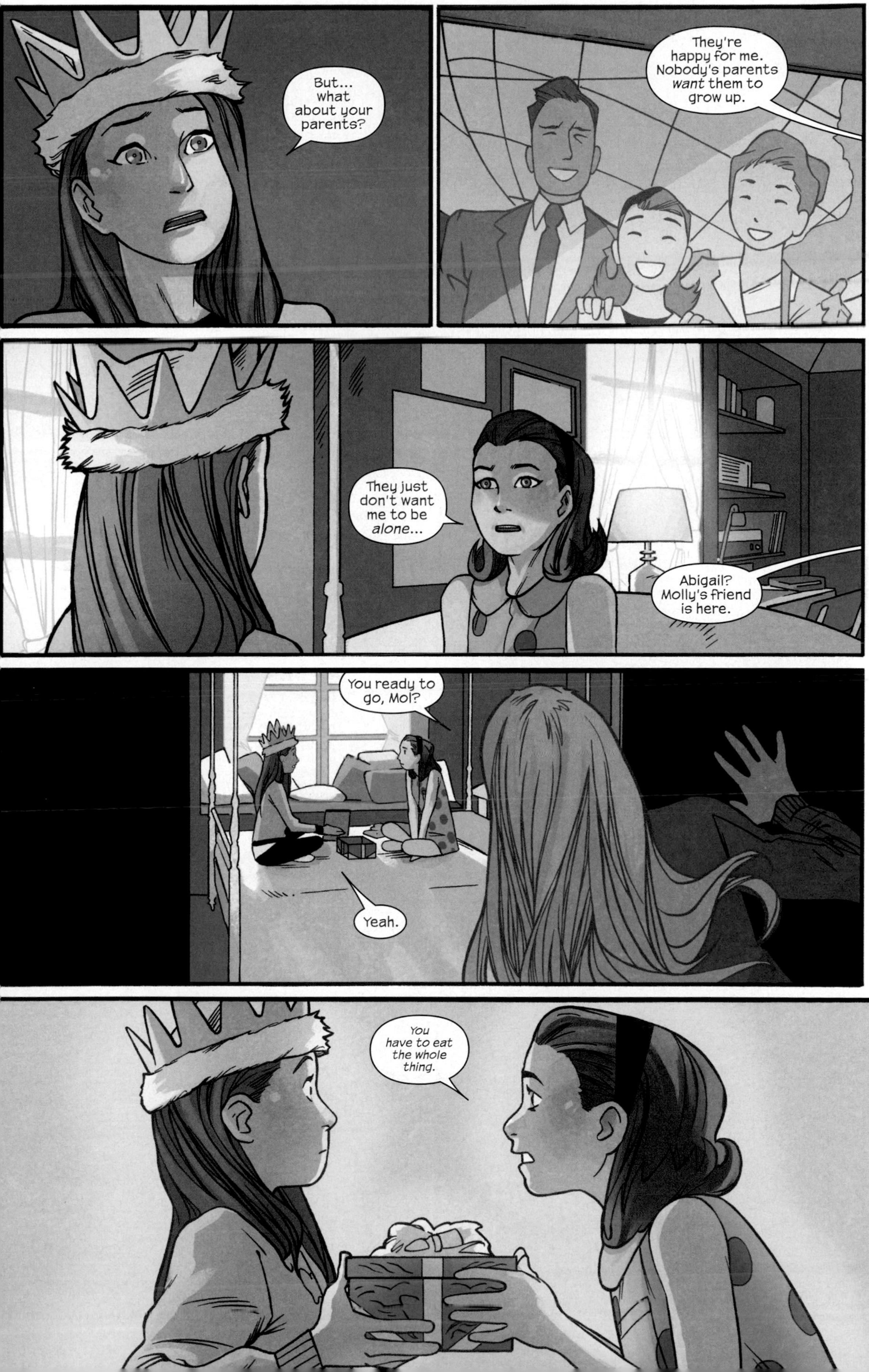

But... what about your parents?
They're happy for me. Nobody's parents *want* them to grow up.
They just don't want me to be *alone*...
Abigail? Molly's friend is here.
You ready to go, Mol?
Yeah.
You have to eat the whole thing.

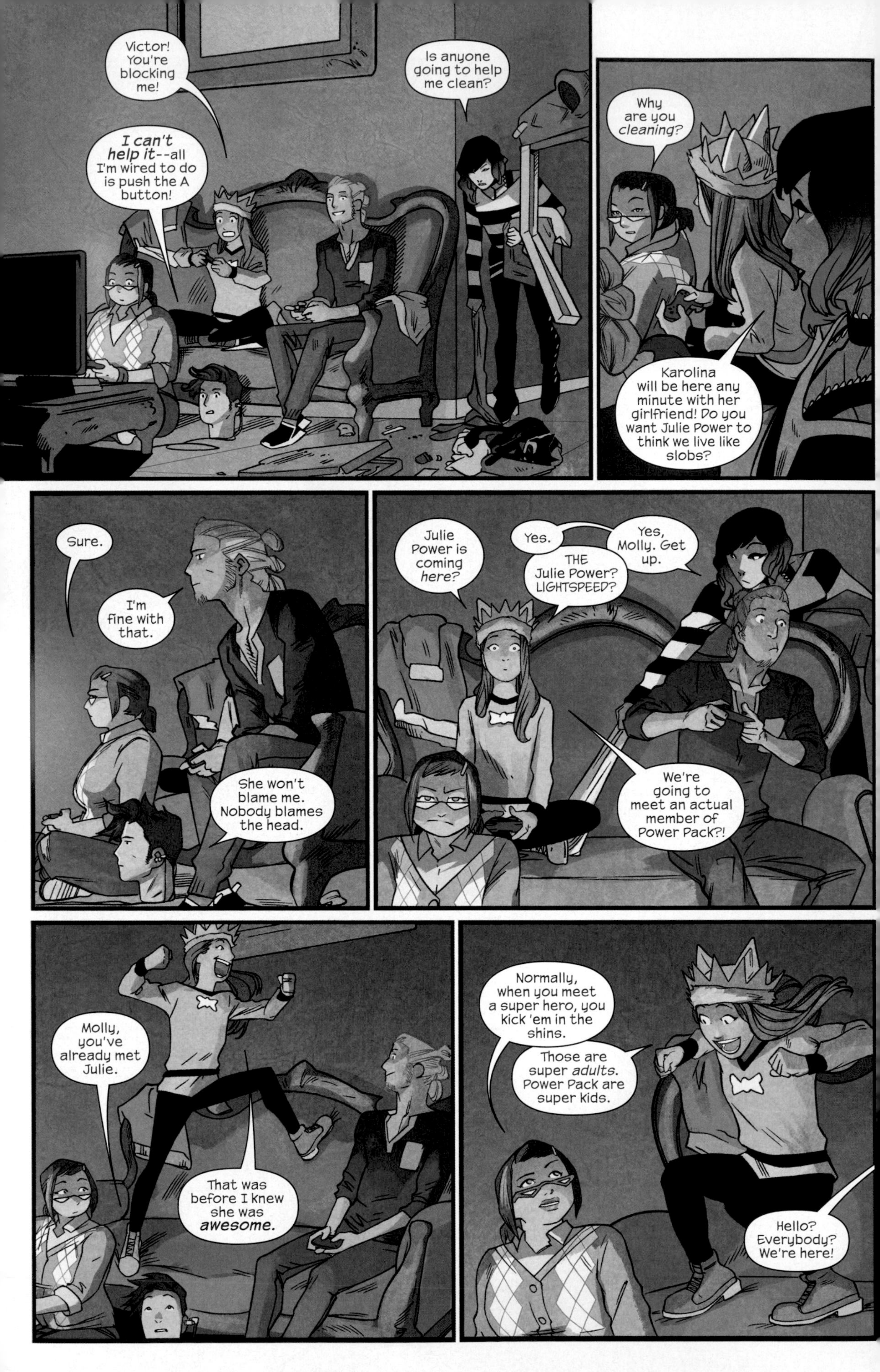

Victor! You're blocking me!
I can't help it--all I'm wired to do is push the A button!
Is anyone going to help me clean?
Why are you cleaning?
Karolina will be here any minute with her girlfriend! Do you want Julie Power to think we live like slobs?
Sure.
I'm fine with that.
She won't blame me. Nobody blames the head.
Julie Power is coming here?
Yes.
Yes, Molly. Get up.
THE Julie Power? LIGHTSPEED?
We're going to meet an actual member of Power Pack?!
Molly, you've already met Julie.
That was before I knew she was awesome.
Normally, when you meet a super hero, you kick 'em in the shins.
Those are super adults. Power Pack are super kids.
Hello? Everybody? We're here!

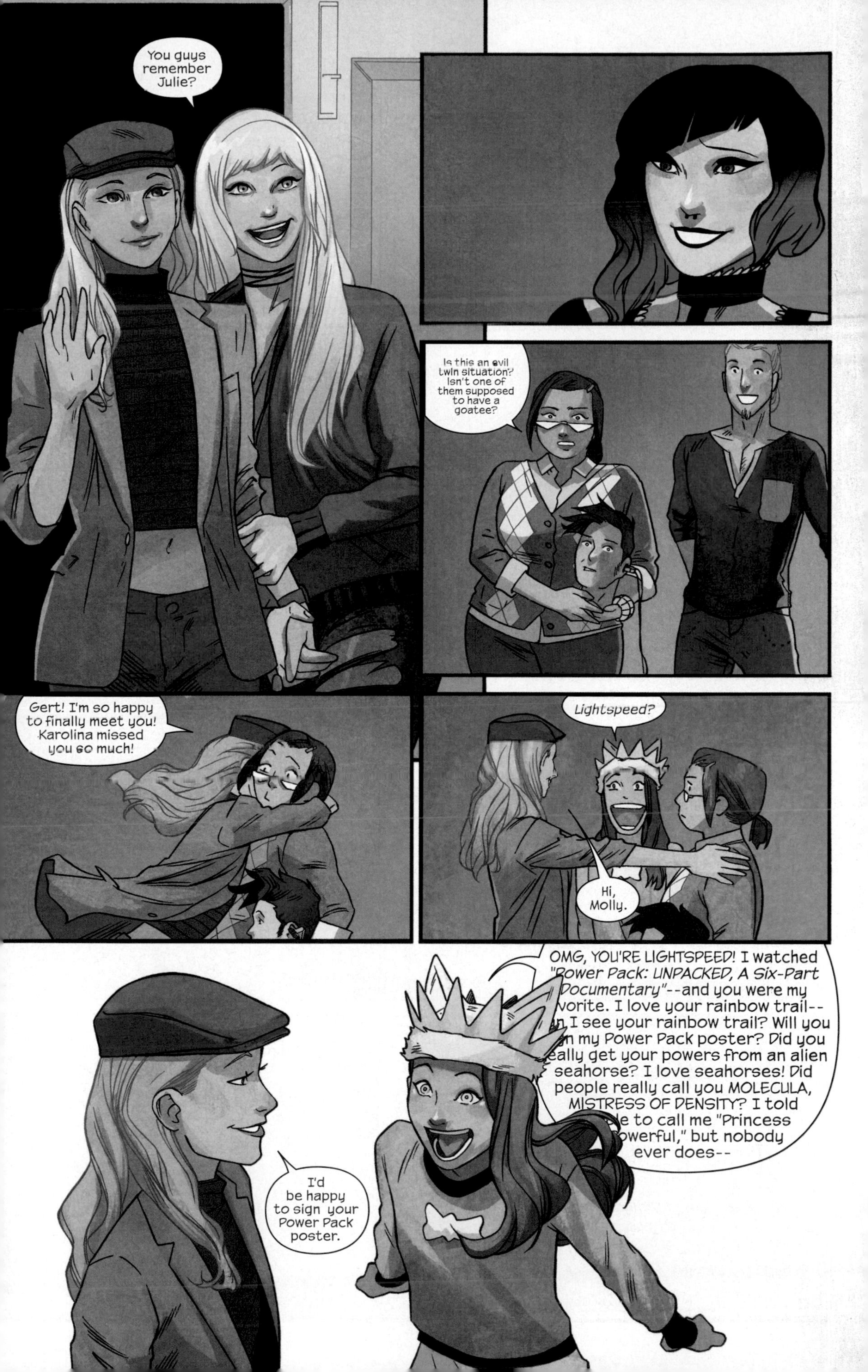
You guys remember Julie?
Is this an evil twin situation? Isn't one of them supposed to have a goatee?
Gert! I'm so happy to finally meet you! Karolina missed you so much!
Lightspeed?
Hi, Molly.
OMG, YOU'RE LIGHTSPEED! I watched "Power Pack: UNPACKED, A Six-Part Documentary"--and you were my vorite. I love your rainbow trail-- n I see your rainbow trail? Will you n my Power Pack poster? Did you eally get your powers from an alien seahorse? I love seahorses! Did people really call you MOLECULA, MISTRESS OF DENSITY? I told le to call me "Princess owerful," but nobody ever does--
I'd be happy to sign your Power Pack poster.

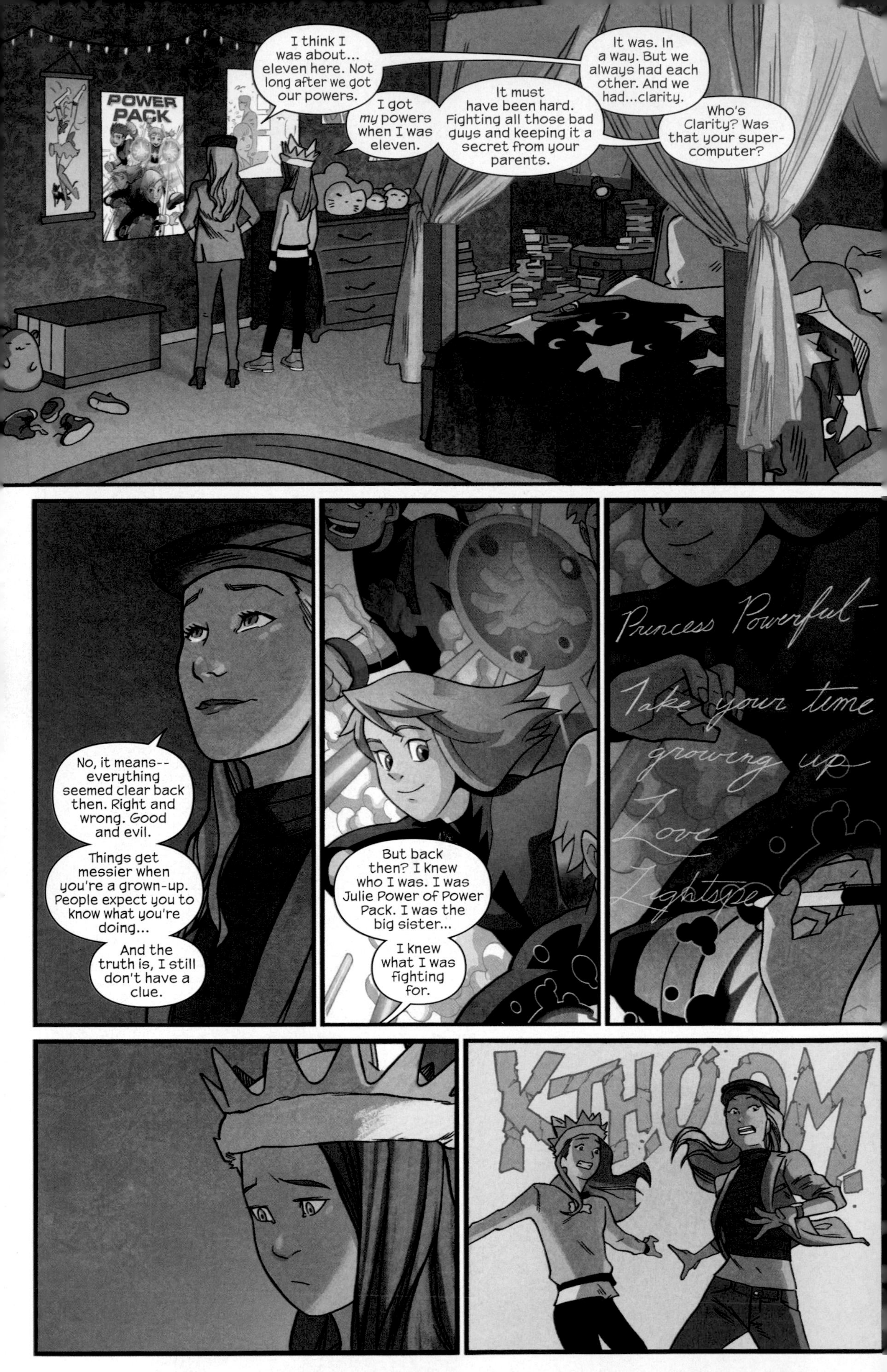
I think I was about... eleven here. Not long after we got our powers.
It was. In a way. But we always had each other. And we had...clarity.
I got *my* powers when I was eleven.
It must have been hard. Fighting all those bad guys and keeping it a secret from your parents.
Who's Clarity? Was that your super-computer?
POWER PACK
No, it means-- everything seemed clear back then. Right and wrong. Good and evil.
Things get messier when you're a grown-up. People expect you to know what you're doing...
And the truth is, I still don't have a clue.
But back then? I knew who I was. I was Julie Power of Power Pack. I was the big sister...
I knew what I was fighting for.
Princess Powerful-
Take your time
growing up
Love
Lightspe
KTHOOM!

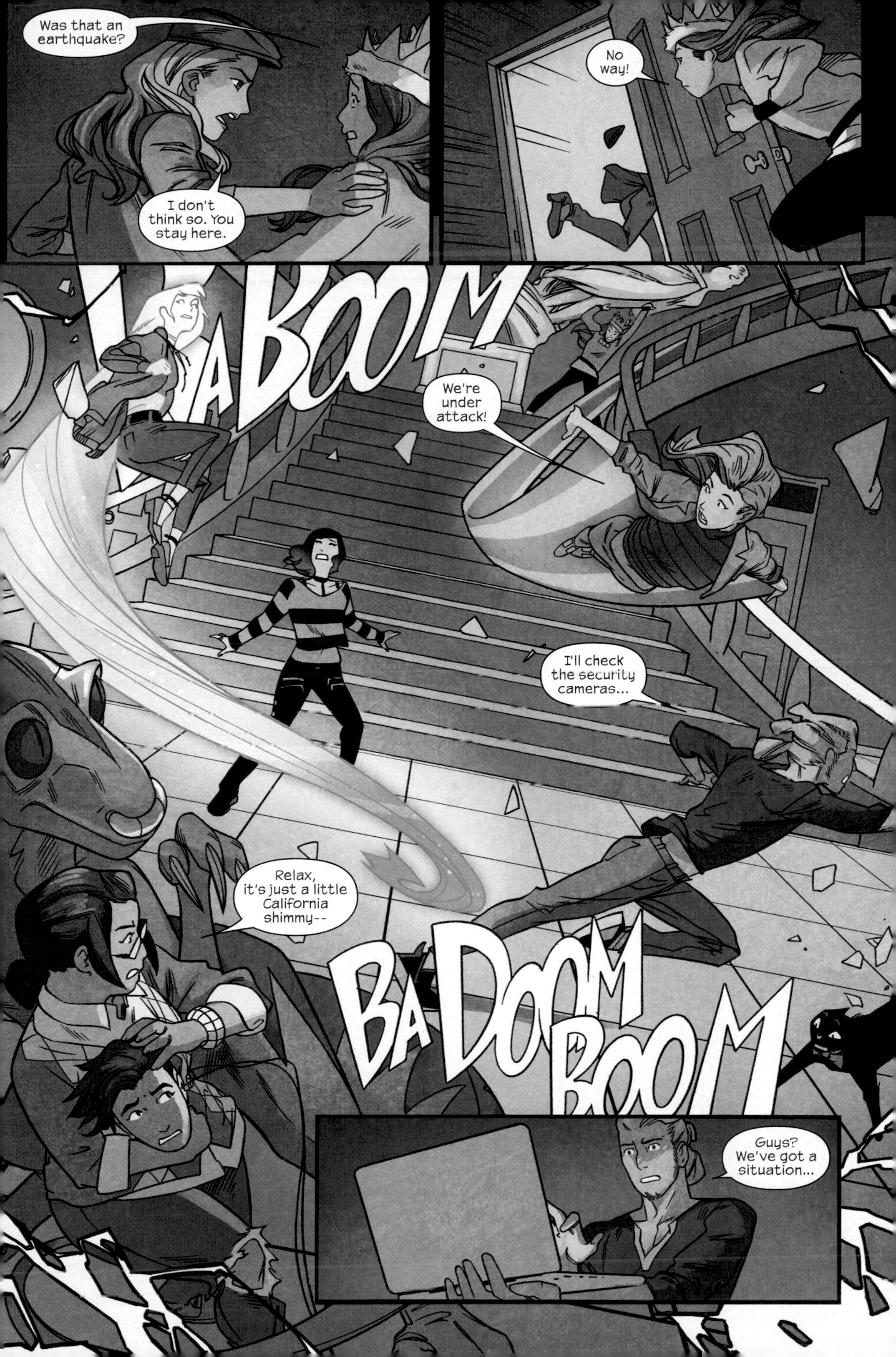
Was that an earthquake?
I don't think so. You stay here.
No way!
KABOOM
We're under attack!
I'll check the security cameras...
Relax, it's just a little California shimmy--
BADOOM
BOOM
Guys? We've got a situation...

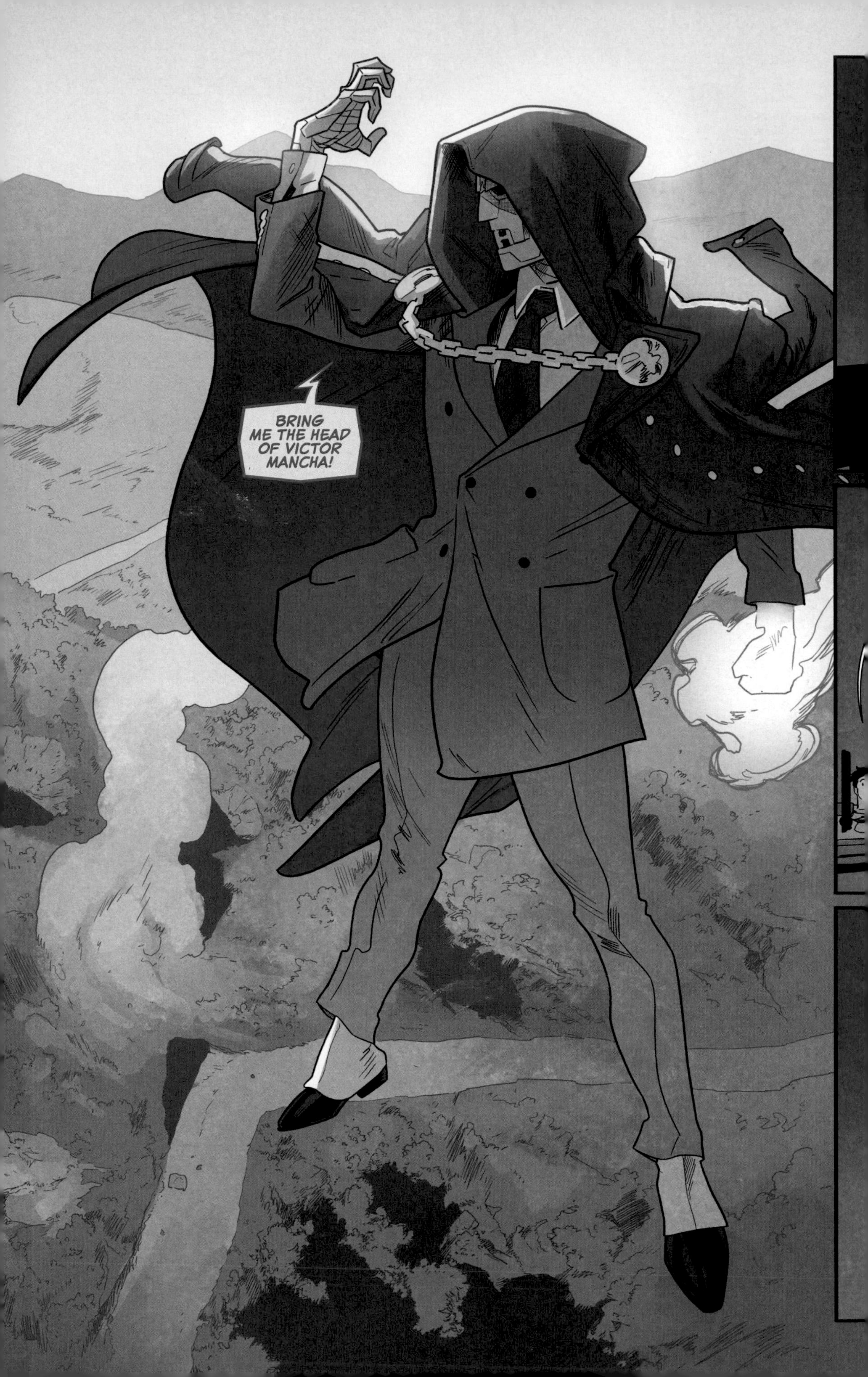
BRING ME THE HEAD OF VICTOR MANCHA!

Doctor Doom?

Not *this* loser again.

What does he want with Victor?

I don't know, and I don't care!

Chase, wait!

We can't fight Doctor Doom!

What's our defense protocol, Nico?

Uh, protocol?

We don't have protocols.

Then what's the battle plan?

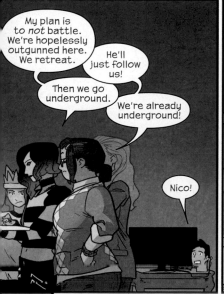

My plan is to *not* battle. We're hopelessly outgunned here. We retreat.

He'll just follow us!

Then we go underground.

We're already underground!

Nico!

YOU CANNOT HIDE FROM FATE, CHASE STEIN. AND YOU CANNOT HIDE FROM DOOM.

Coming, sweetheart!

Take me with you! I think--

We can't take you, Victor-- that's just what he wants!

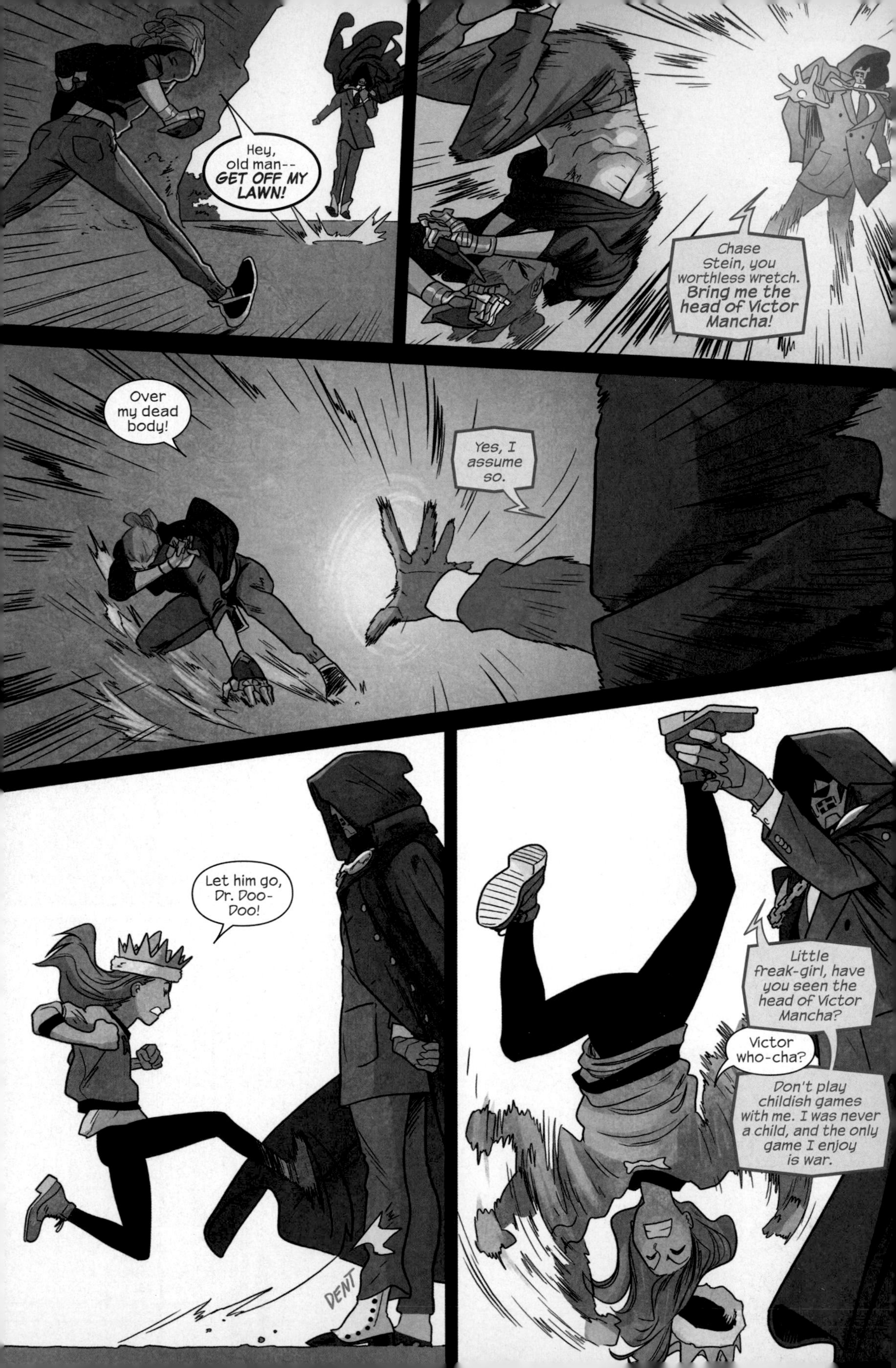
Hey, old man-- GET OFF MY LAWN!
Chase Stein, you worthless wretch. Bring me the head of Victor Mancha!
Over my dead body!
Yes, I assume so.
Let him go, Dr. Doo-Doo!
DENT
Little freak-girl, have you seen the head of Victor Mancha?
Victor who-cha?
Don't play childish games with me. I was never a child, and the only game I enjoy is war.

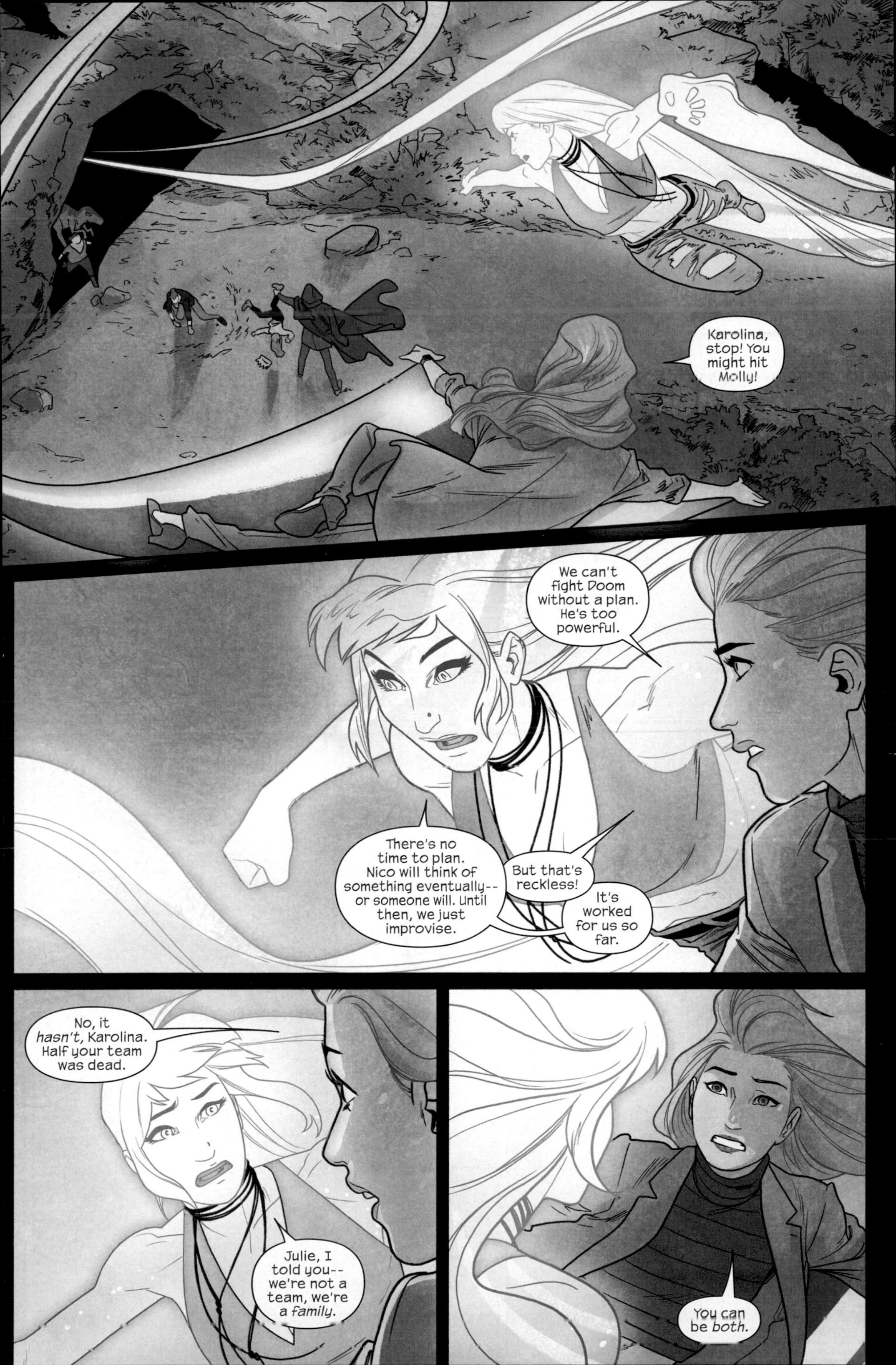
Karolina, stop! You might hit Molly!
We can't fight Doom without a plan. He's too powerful.
There's no time to plan. Nico will think of something eventually-- or someone will. Until then, we just improvise.
But that's reckless!
It's worked for us so far.
No, it *hasn't*, Karolina. Half your team was dead.
Julie, I told you-- we're not a team, we're a *family*.
You can be *both*.

Get back in the Hostel before you get hurt.

Are you okay?

Oh no, that's not how this is going to work.

I mean it-- you're too vulnerable.

Says the guy I'm helping up.

I'm fine. I'm still a girl with a dinosaur.

Enough! I know that you have Mancha's central processing unit, and I will have it now!

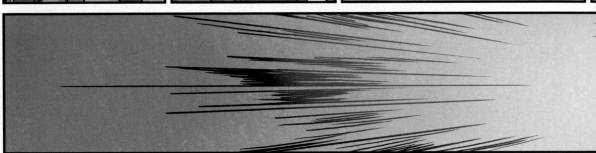

Huh? Old Lace?

Uhn!

What--

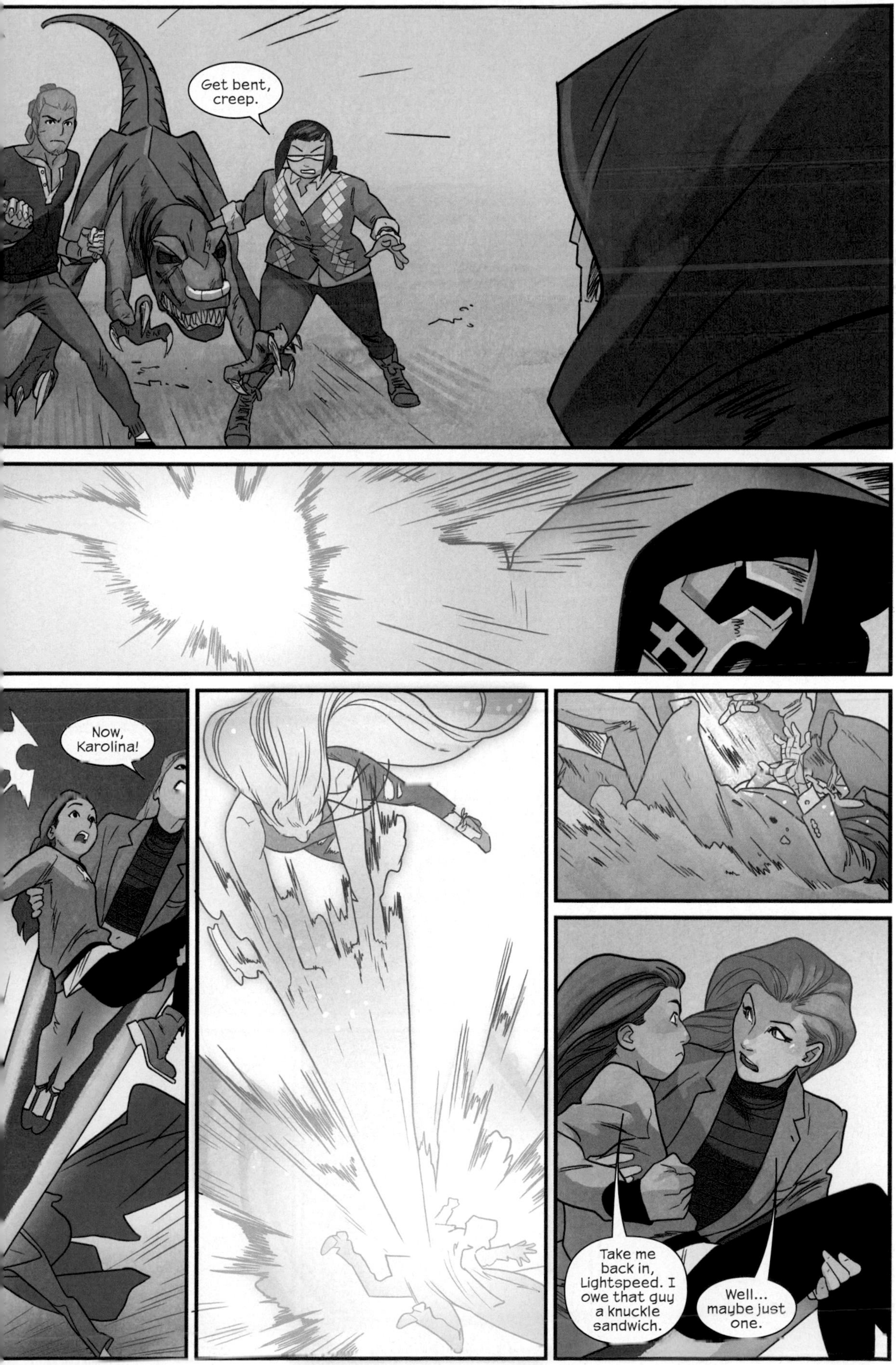
Get bent, creep.
Now, Karolina!
Take me back in, Lightspeed. I owe that guy a knuckle sandwich.
Well... maybe just one.

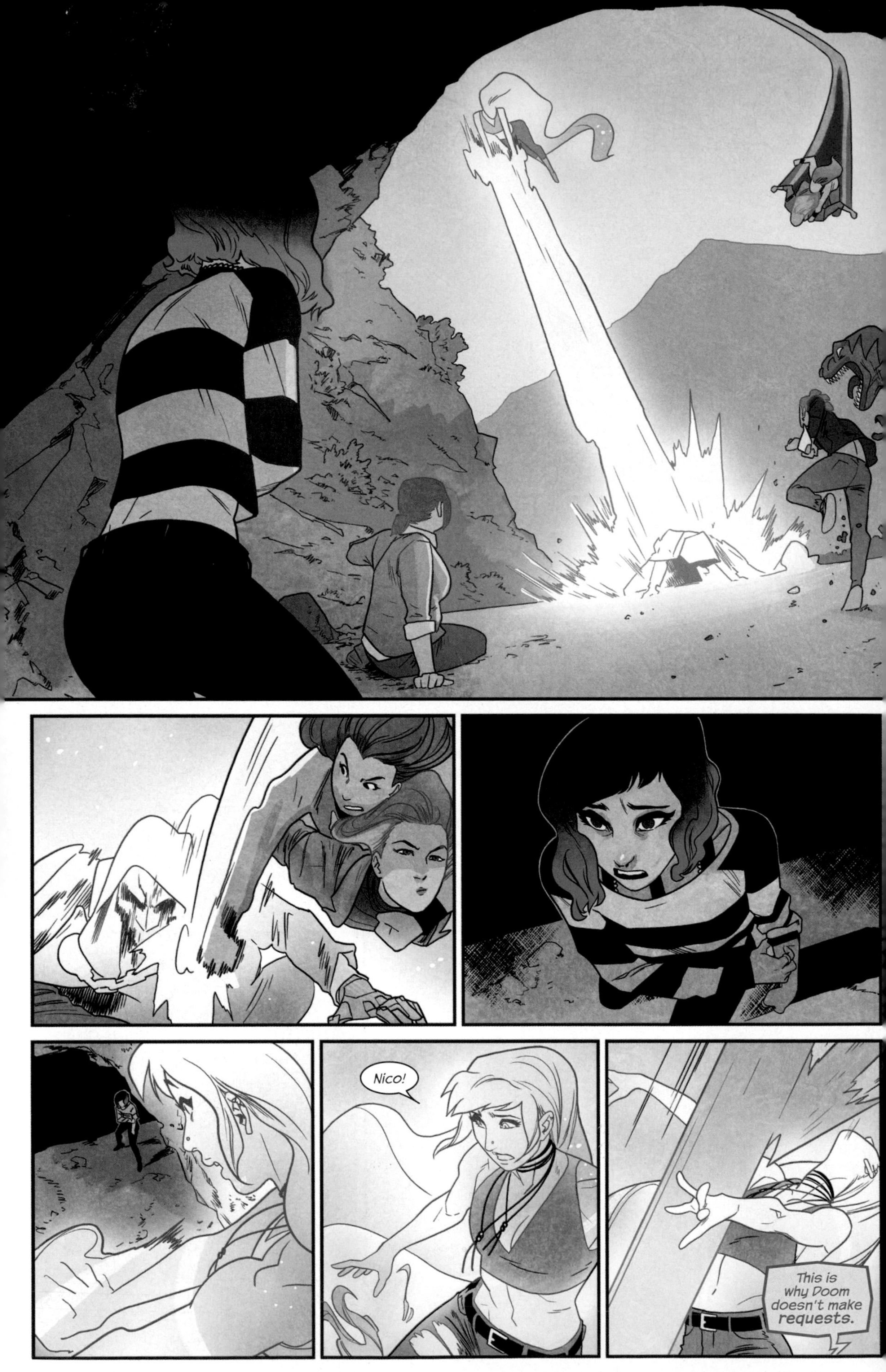
Nico!
This is why Doom doesn't make requests.

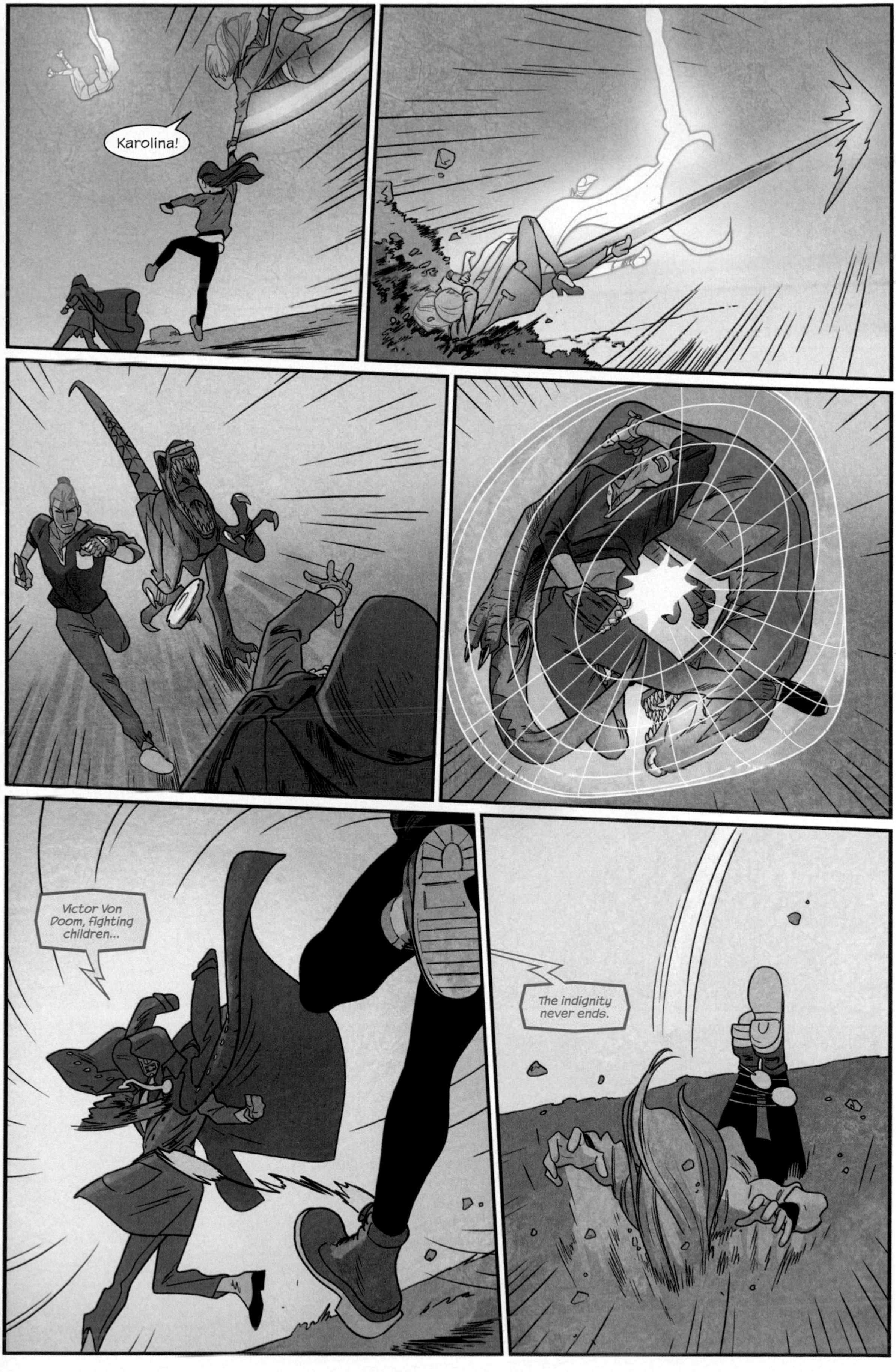

Karolina!
Victor Von Doom, fighting children...
The indignity never ends.

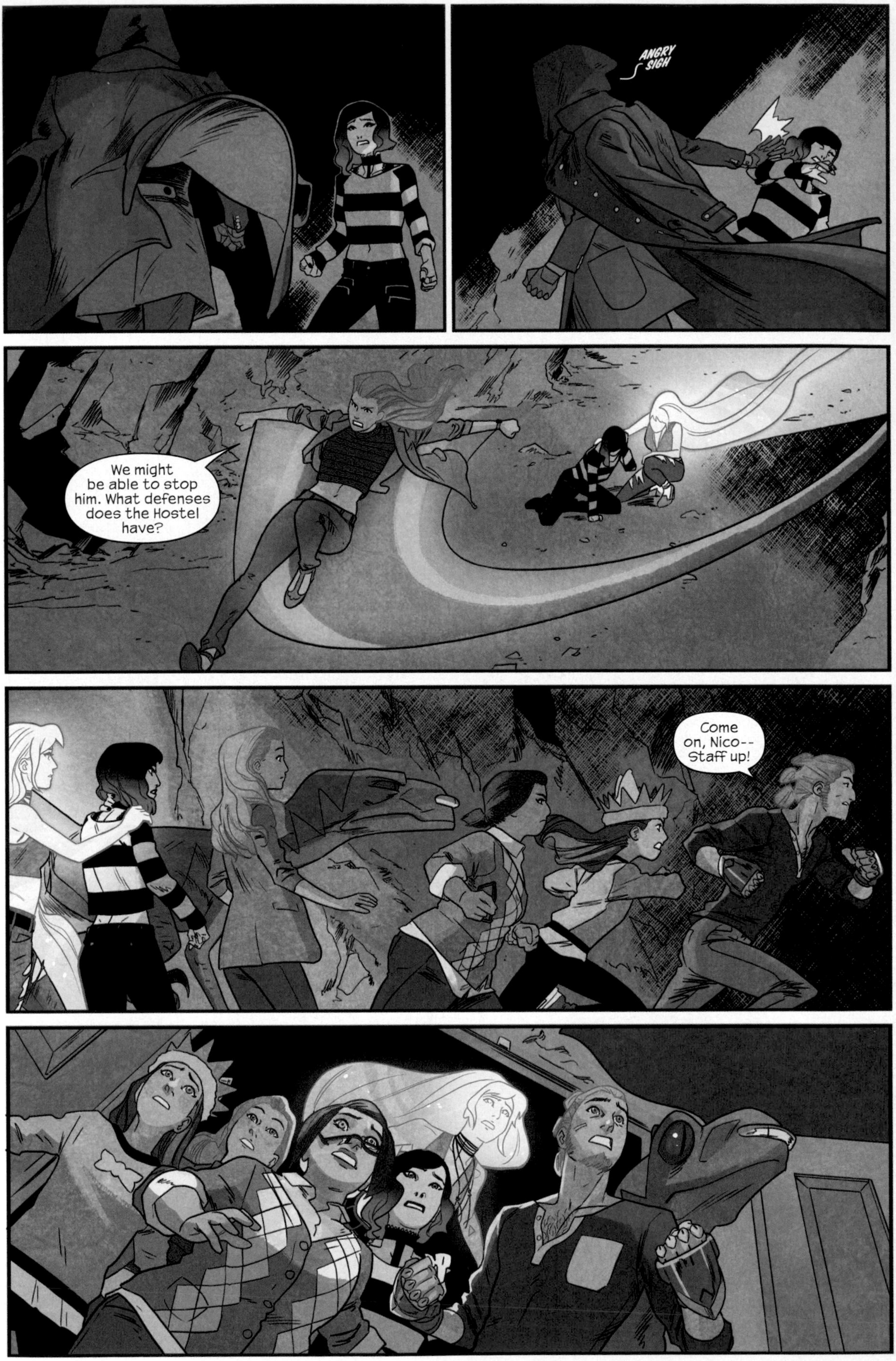
ANGRY SIGH
We might be able to stop him. What defenses does the Hostel have?
Come on, Nico-- Staff up!

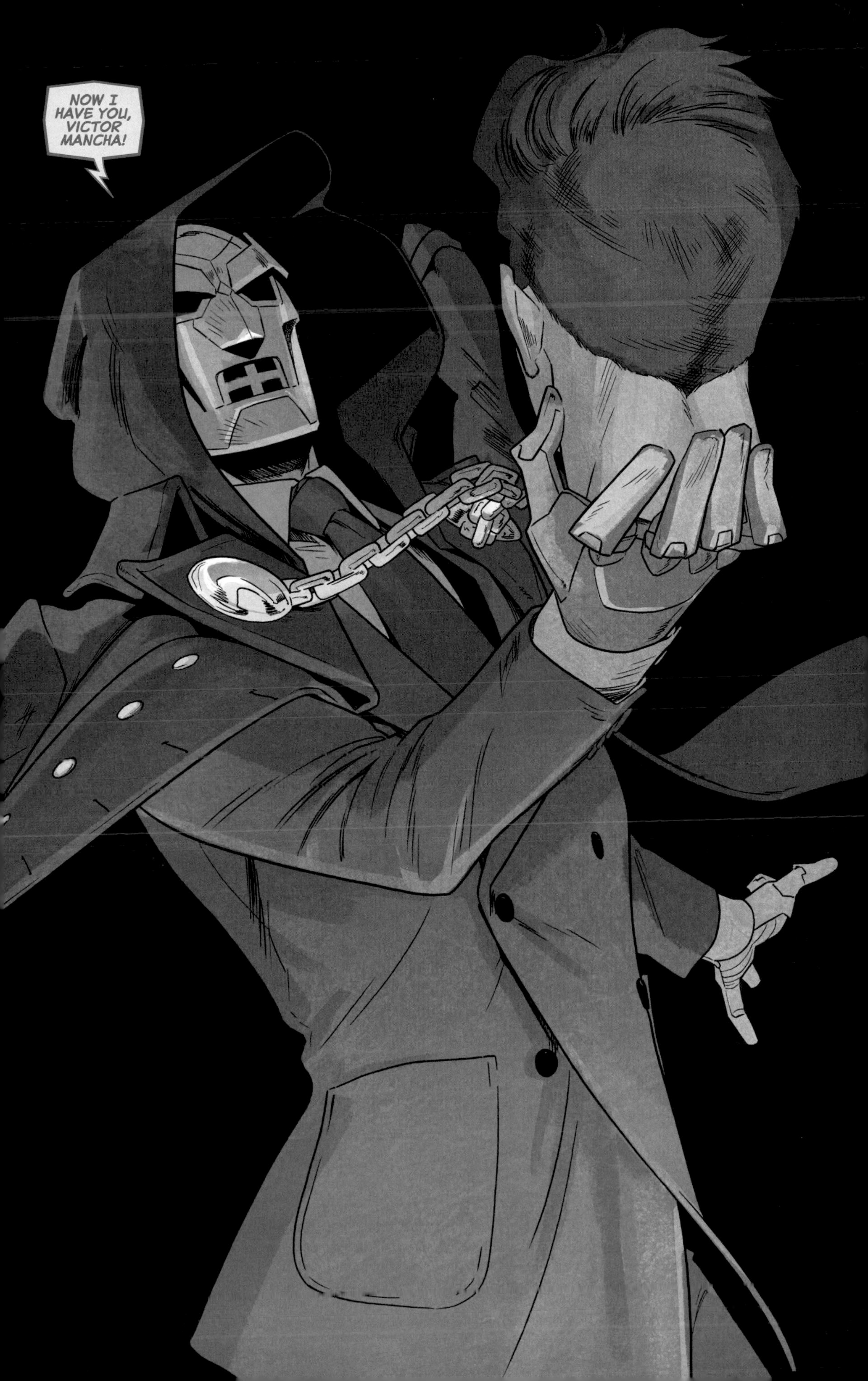
NOW I HAVE YOU, VICTOR MANCHA!

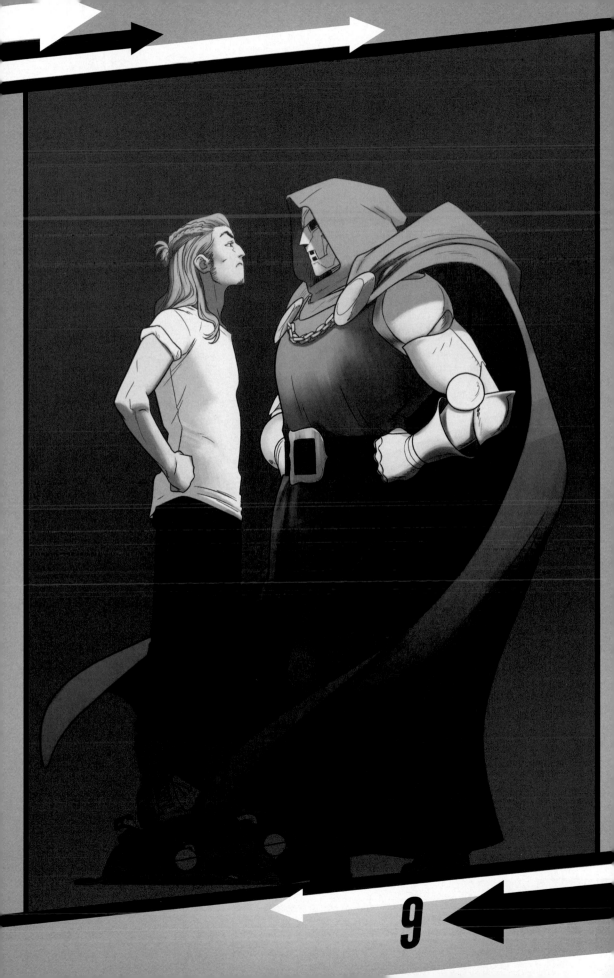

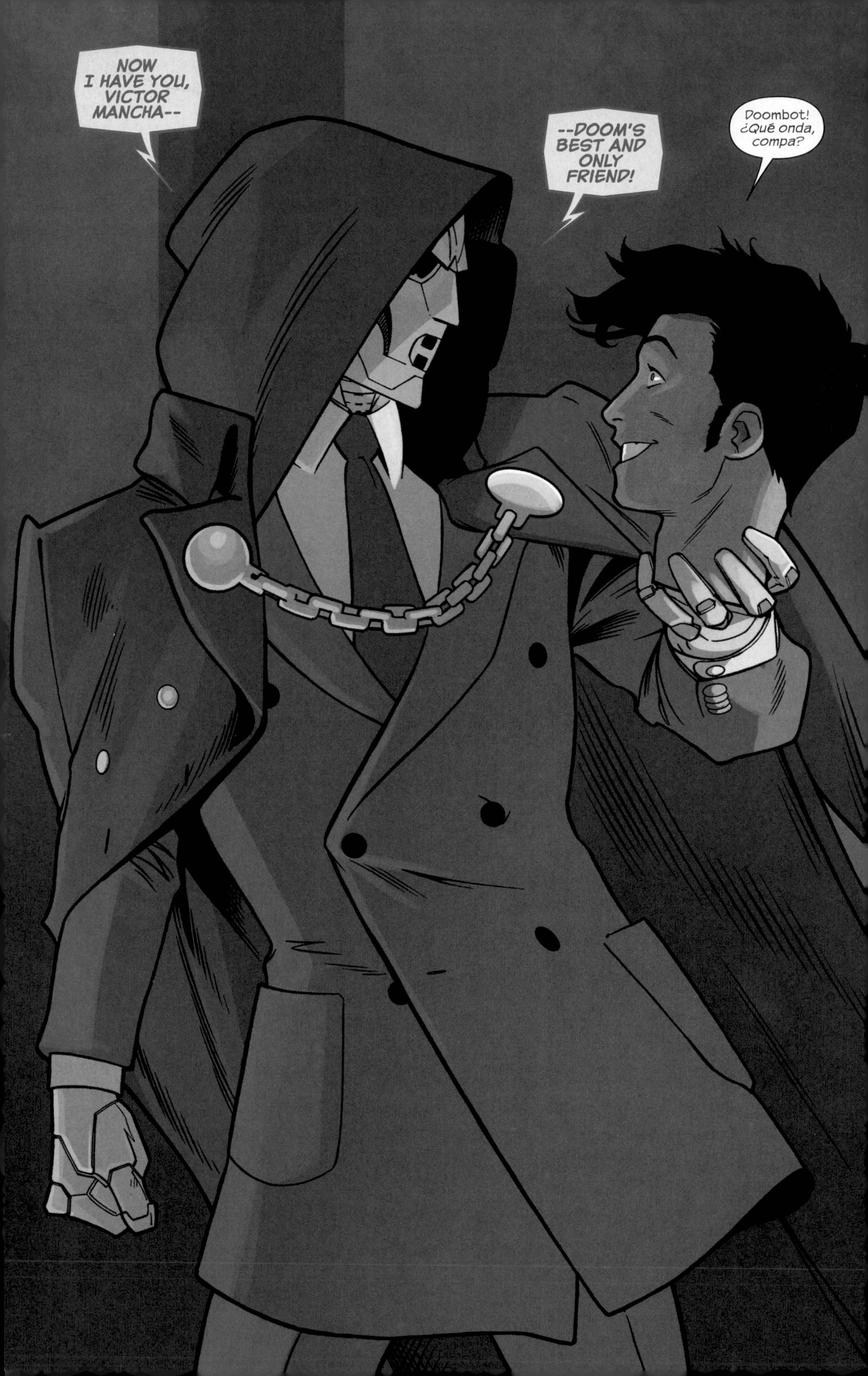
NOW I HAVE YOU, VICTOR MANCHA--
--DOOM'S BEST AND ONLY FRIEND!
Doombot! ¿Qué onda, compa?

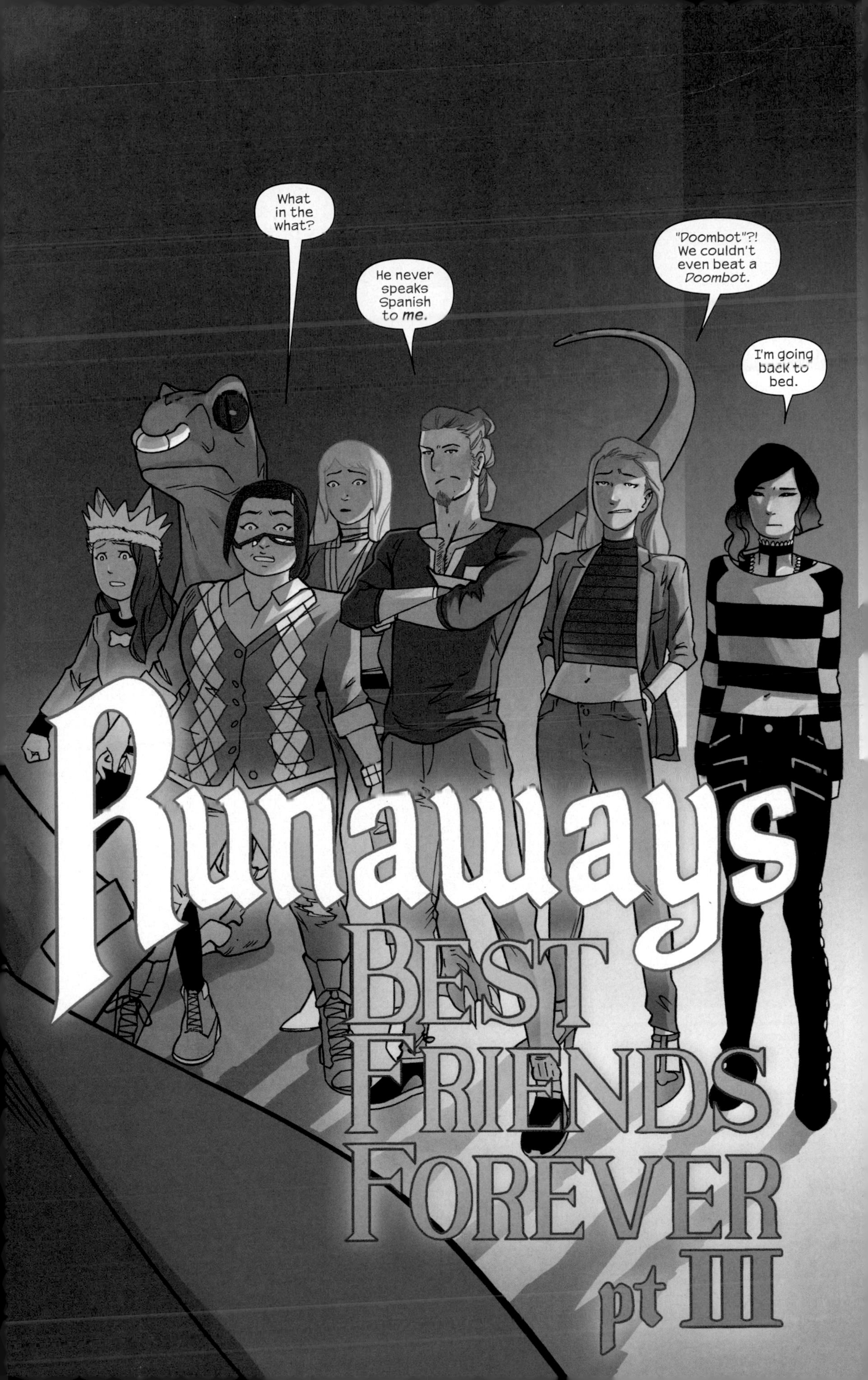

What in the what?
He never speaks Spanish to *me*.
"Doombot"?! We couldn't even beat a *Doombot*.
I'm going back to bed.
Runaways
BEST FRIENDS FOREVER pt III

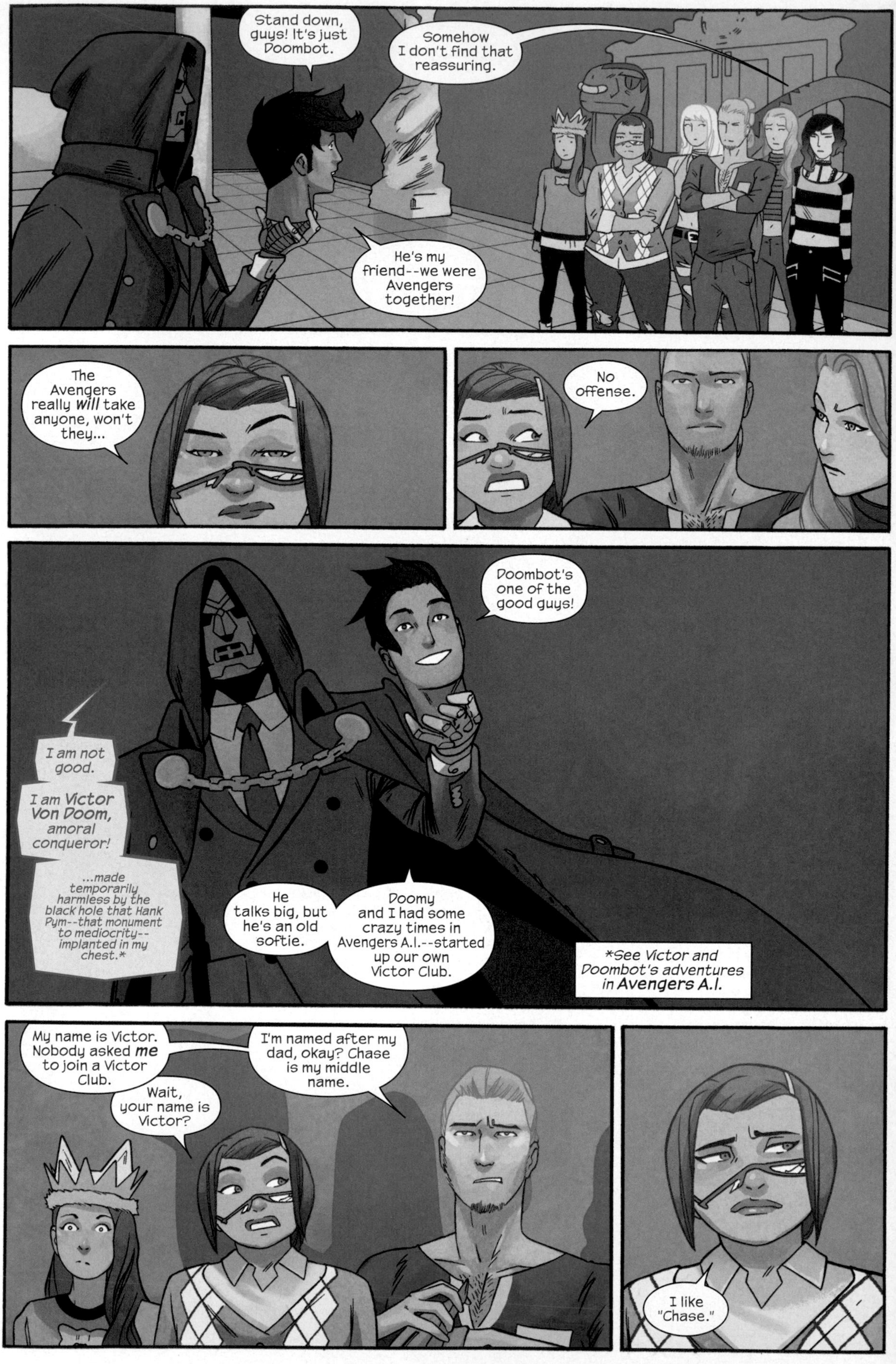
Stand down, guys! It's just Doombot.
Somehow I don't find that reassuring.
He's my friend--we were Avengers together!
The Avengers really *will* take anyone, won't they...
No offense.
Doombot's one of the good guys!
I am not good.
I am Victor Von Doom, amoral conqueror!
...made temporarily harmless by the black hole that Hank Pym--that monument to mediocrity--implanted in my chest.*
He talks big, but he's an old softie.
Doomy and I had some crazy times in Avengers A.I.--started up our own Victor Club.
*See Victor and Doombot's adventures in **Avengers A.I.**
My name is Victor. Nobody asked *me* to join a Victor Club.
I'm named after my dad, okay? Chase is my middle name.
Wait, your name is Victor?
I like "Chase."

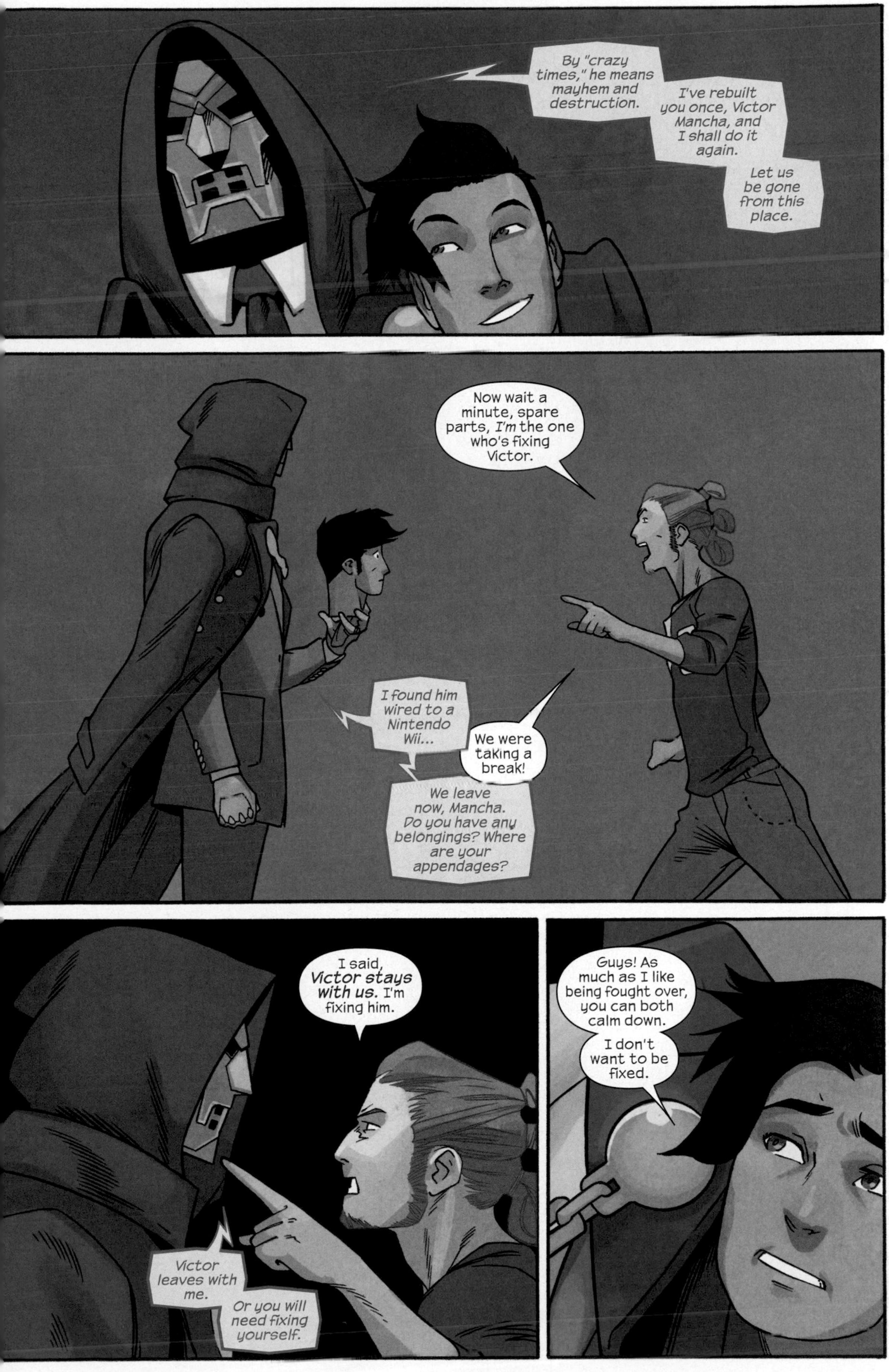
By "crazy times," he means mayhem and destruction.
I've rebuilt you once, Victor Mancha, and I shall do it again.
Let us be gone from this place.
Now wait a minute, spare parts, I'm the one who's fixing Victor.
I found him wired to a Nintendo Wii...
We were taking a break!
We leave now, Mancha. Do you have any belongings? Where are your appendages?
I said, Victor stays with us. I'm fixing him.
Victor leaves with me.
Or you will need fixing yourself.
Guys! As much as I like being fought over, you can both calm down.
I don't want to be fixed.

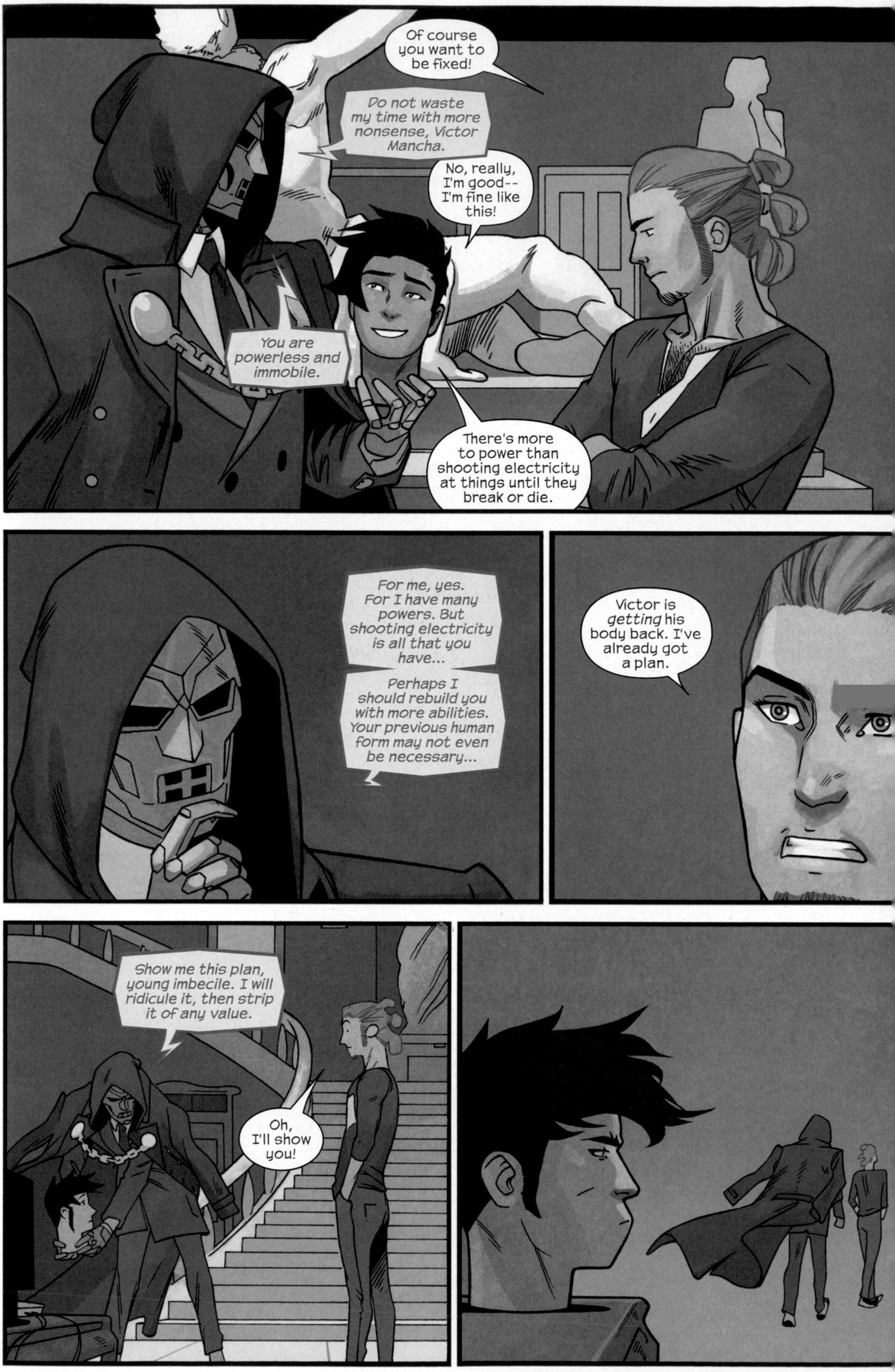

Of course you want to be fixed!
Do not waste my time with more nonsense, Victor Mancha.
No, really, I'm good-- I'm fine like this!
You are powerless and immobile.
There's more to power than shooting electricity at things until they break or die.
For me, yes. For I have many powers. But shooting electricity is all that you have...
Perhaps I should rebuild you with more abilities. Your previous human form may not even be necessary...
Victor is getting his body back. I've already got a plan.
Show me this plan, young imbecile. I will ridicule it, then strip it of any value.
Oh, I'll show you!

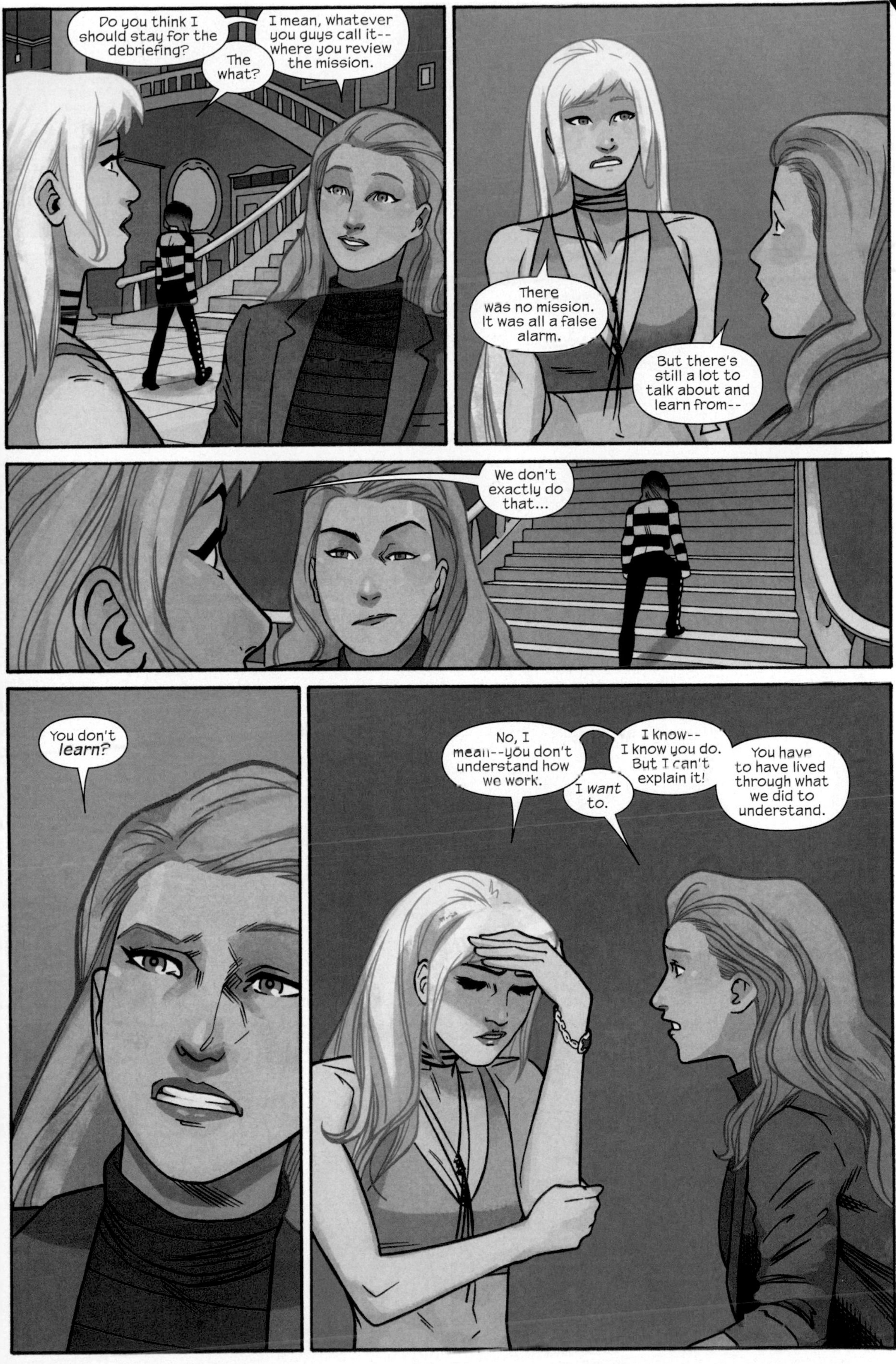
Do you think I should stay for the debriefing?
The what?
I mean, whatever you guys call it--where you review the mission.
There was no mission. It was all a false alarm.
But there's still a lot to talk about and learn from--
We don't exactly do that...
You don't *learn?*
No, I mean--you don't understand how we work.
I *want* to.
I know--I know you do. But I can't explain it!
You have to have lived through what we did to understand.

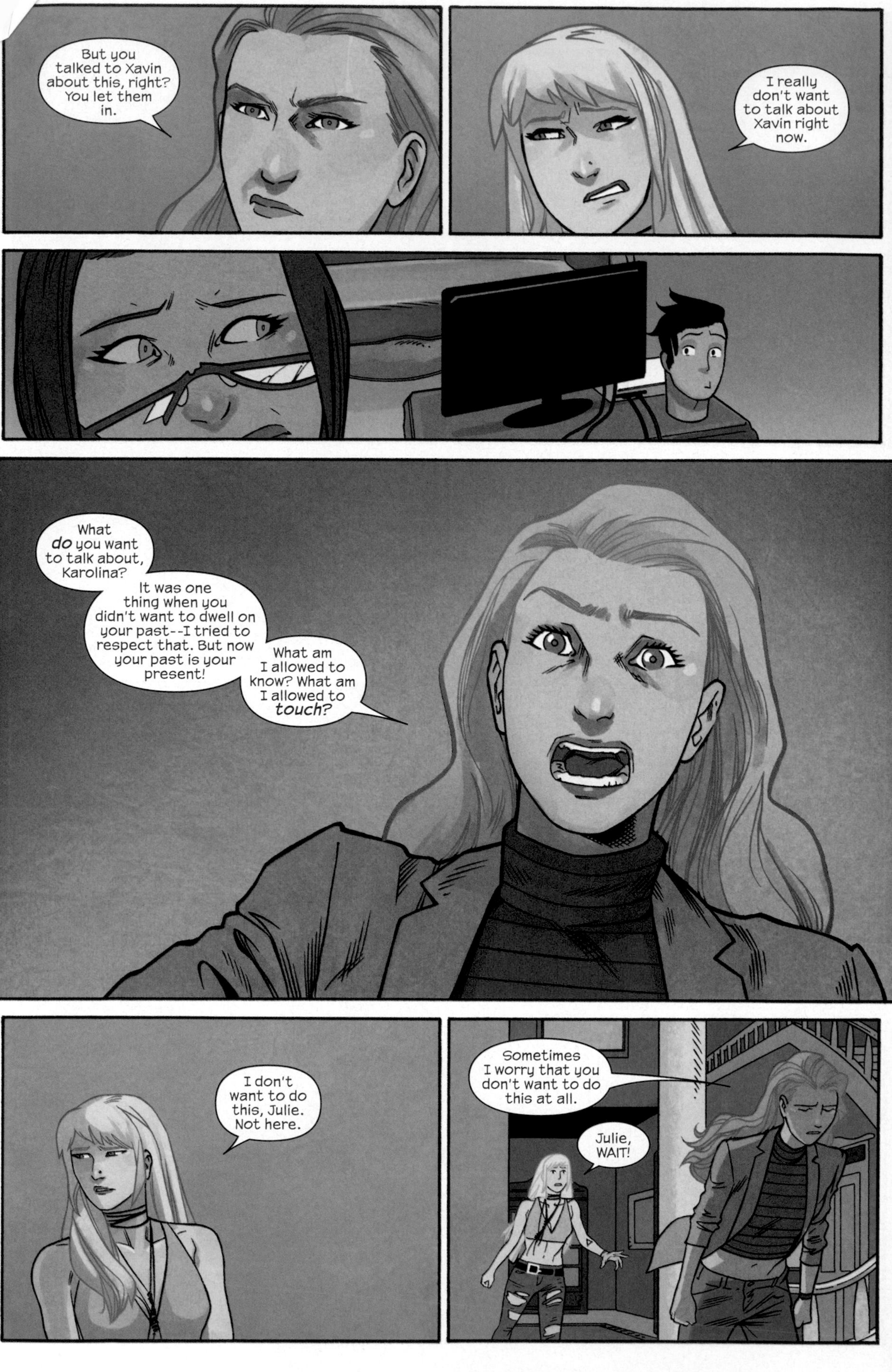

But you talked to Xavin about this, right? You let them in.
I really don't want to talk about Xavin right now.
What *do* you want to talk about, Karolina?
It was one thing when you didn't want to dwell on your past--I tried to respect that. But now your past is your present!
What am I allowed to know? What am I allowed to *touch*?
I don't want to do this, Julie. Not here.
Sometimes I worry that you don't want to do this at all.
Julie, WAIT!

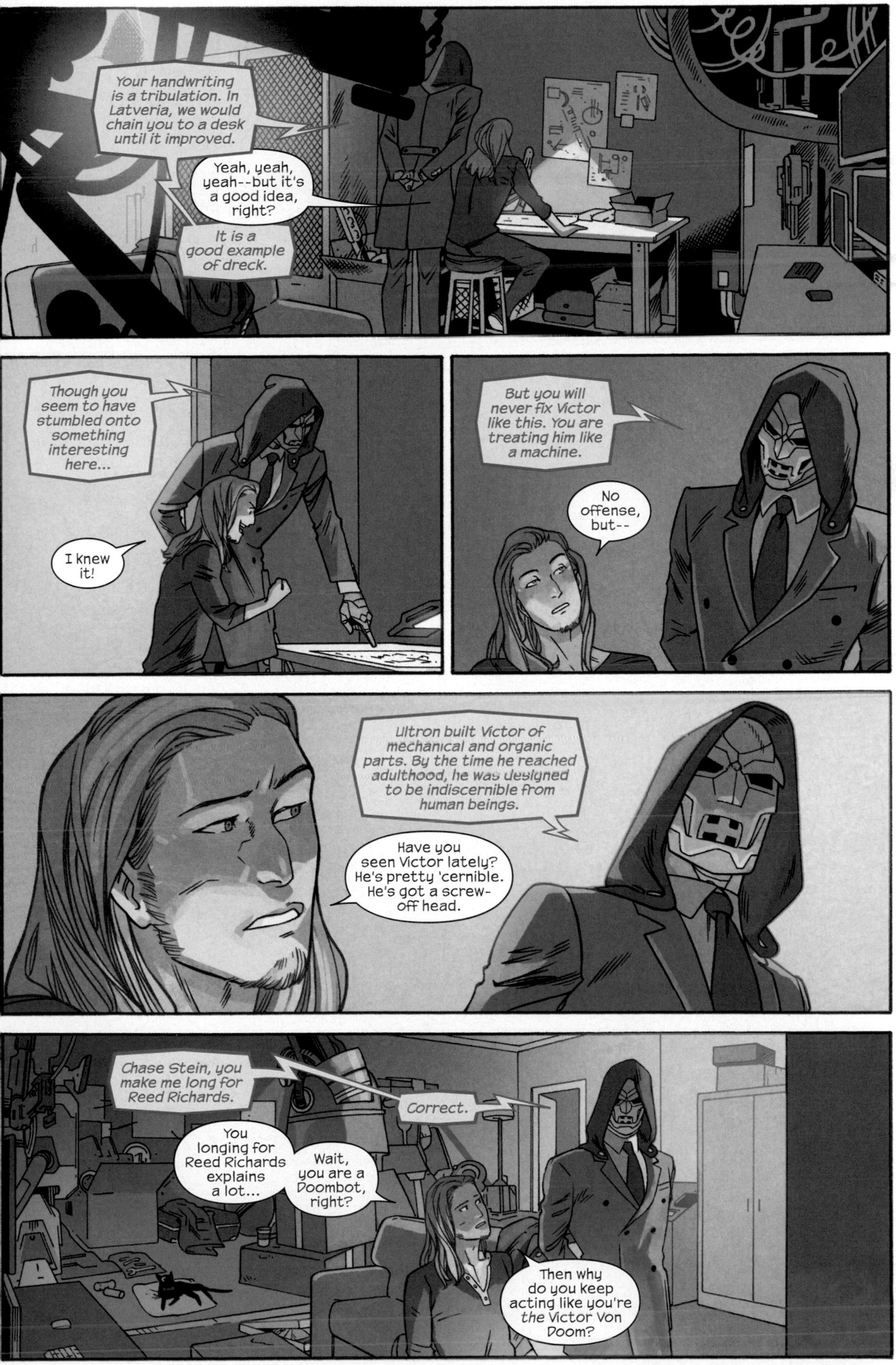
Your handwriting is a tribulation. In Latveria, we would chain you to a desk until it improved.
Yeah, yeah, yeah--but it's a good idea, right?
It is a good example of dreck.
Though you seem to have stumbled onto something interesting here...
I knew it!
But you will never fix Victor like this. You are treating him like a machine.
No offense, but--
Ultron built Victor of mechanical and organic parts. By the time he reached adulthood, he was designed to be indiscernible from human beings.
Have you seen Victor lately? He's pretty 'cernible. He's got a screw-off head.
Chase Stein, you make me long for Reed Richards.
You longing for Reed Richards explains a lot...
Wait, you are a Doombot, right?
Correct.
Then why do you keep acting like you're the Victor Von Doom?

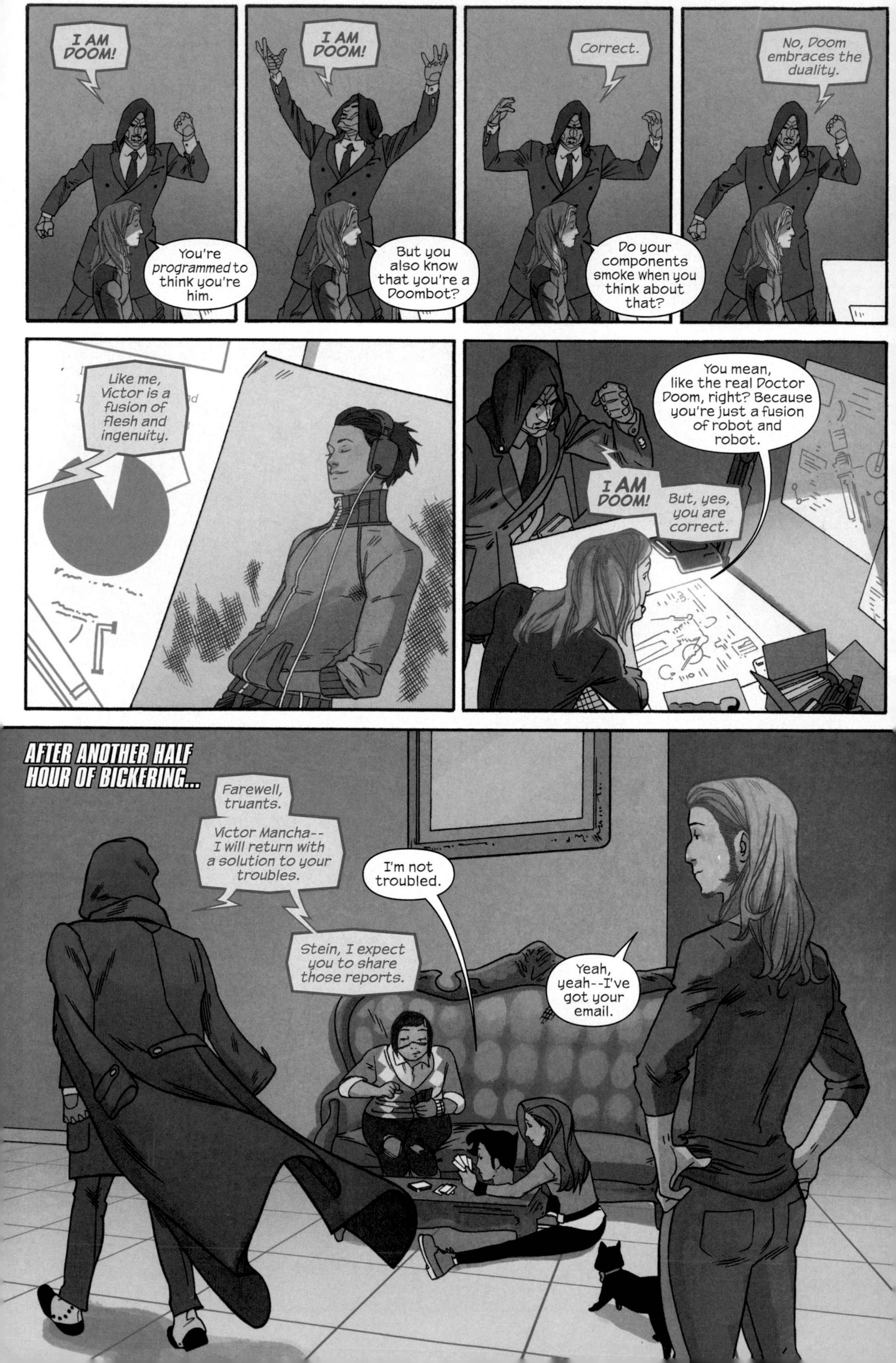
I AM DOOM!
You're programmed to think you're him.
I AM DOOM!
But you also know that you're a Doombot?
Correct.
Do your components smoke when you think about that?
No, Doom embraces the duality.
Like me, Victor is a fusion of flesh and ingenuity.
You mean, like the real Doctor Doom, right? Because you're just a fusion of robot and robot.
I AM DOOM!
But, yes, you are correct.
AFTER ANOTHER HALF HOUR OF BICKERING...
Farewell, truants.
Victor Mancha-- I will return with a solution to your troubles.
Stein, I expect you to share those reports.
I'm not troubled.
Yeah, yeah--I've got your email.

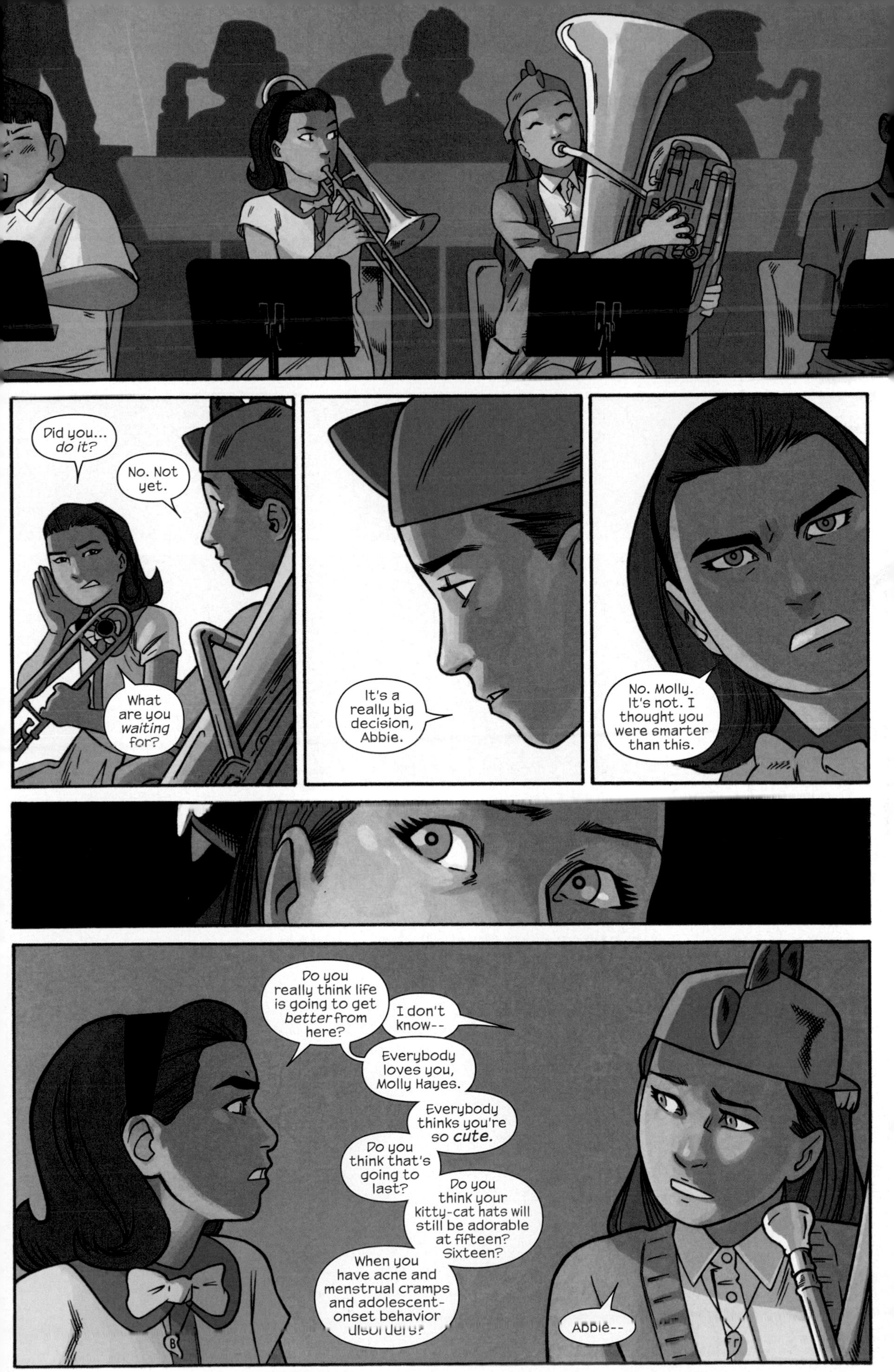

Did you... *do it?*
No. Not yet.
What are you *waiting* for?
It's a really big decision, Abbie.
No. Molly. It's not. I thought you were smarter than this.
Do you really think life is going to get *better* from here?
I don't know--
Everybody loves you, Molly Hayes.
Everybody thinks you're so ***cute.***
Do you think that's going to last?
Do you think your kitty-cat hats will still be adorable at fifteen? Sixteen?
When you have acne and menstrual cramps and adolescent-onset behavior disorders?
Abbie--

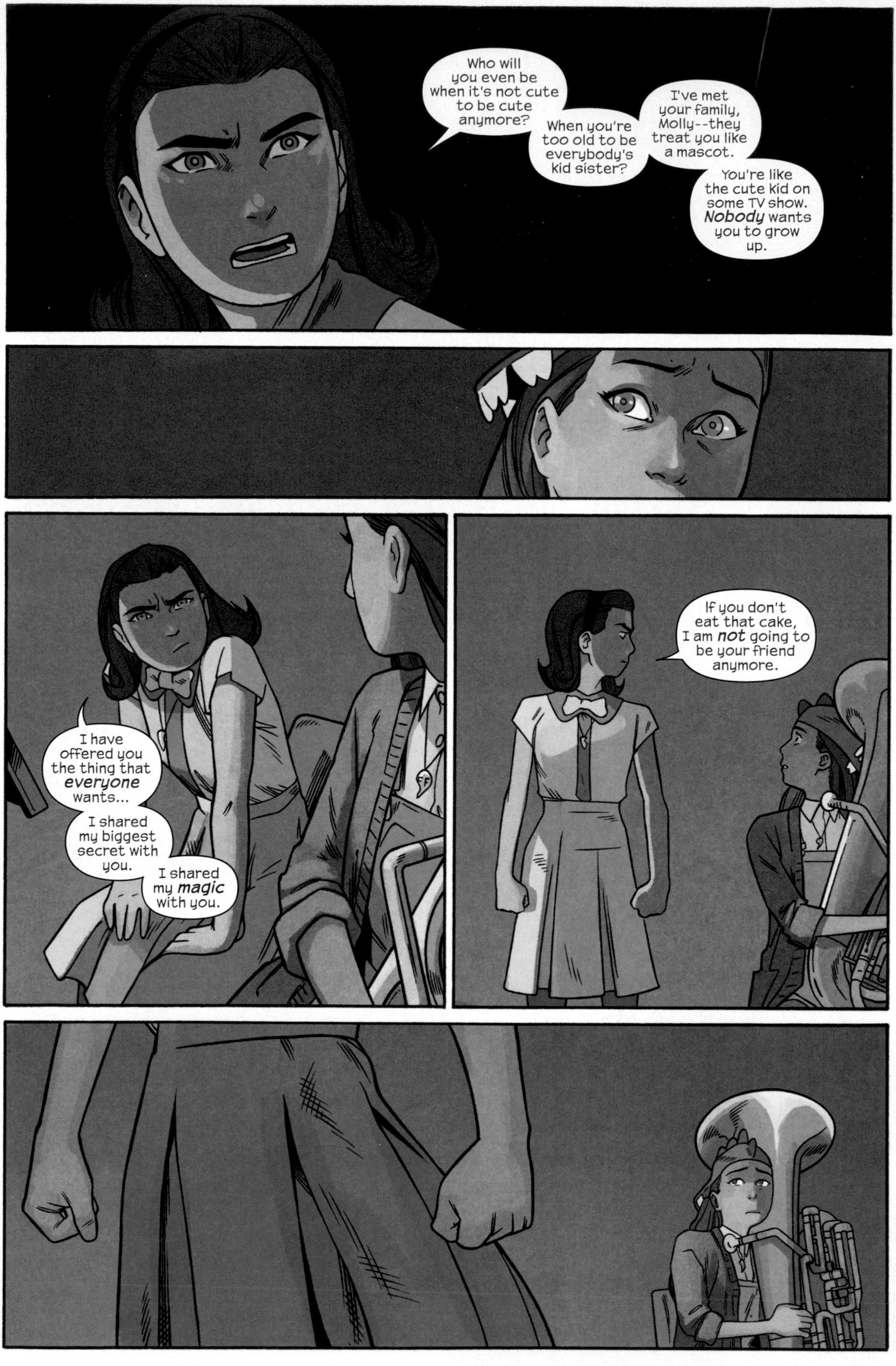
Who will you even be when it's not cute to be cute anymore?
When you're too old to be everybody's kid sister?
I've met your family, Molly--they treat you like a mascot.
You're like the cute kid on some TV show. *Nobody* wants you to grow up.
I have offered you the thing that *everyone* wants...
I shared my biggest secret with you.
I shared my *magic* with you.
If you don't eat that cake, I am *not* going to be your friend anymore.

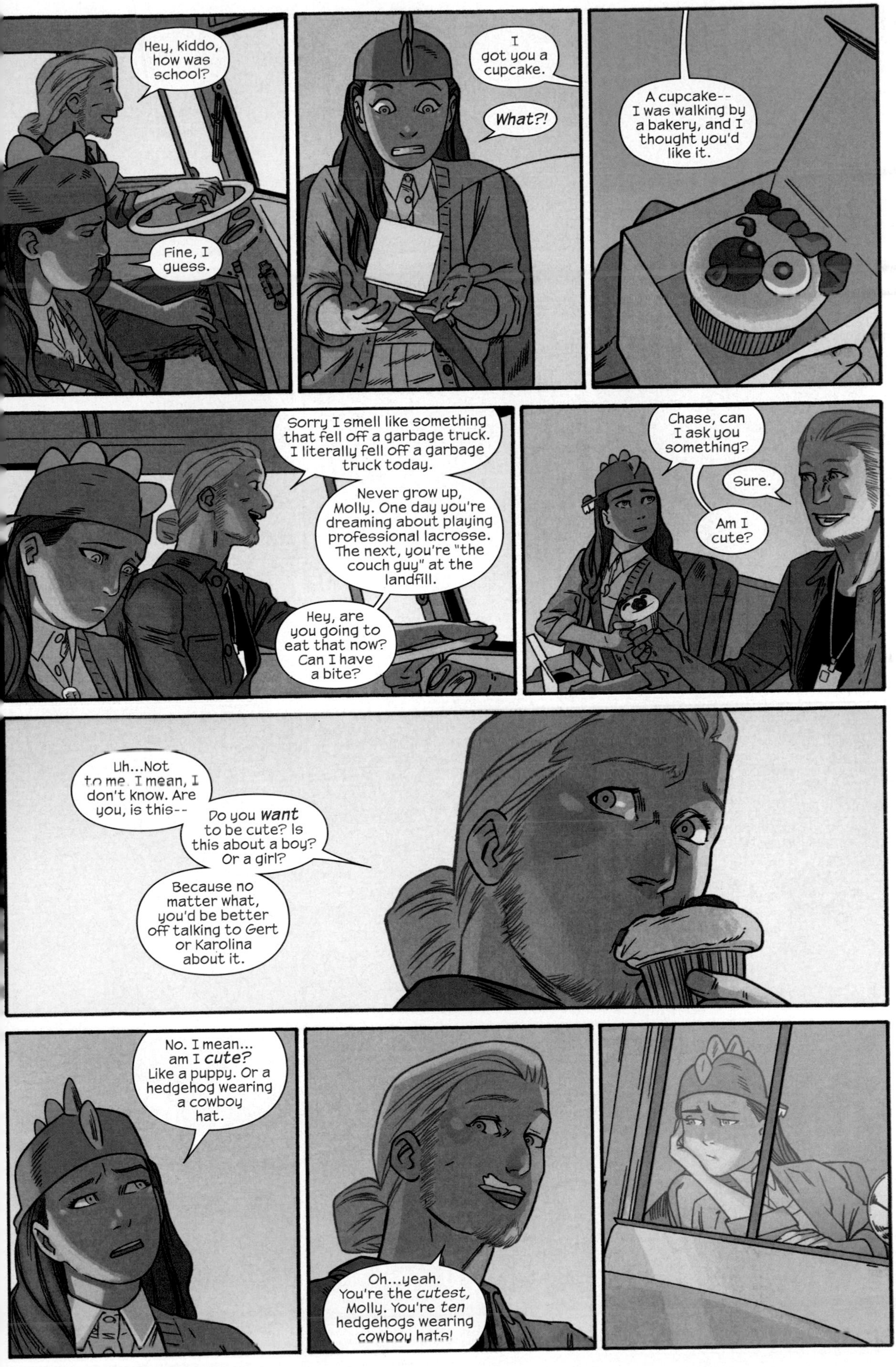
Hey, kiddo, how was school?
Fine, I guess.
I got you a cupcake.
What?!
A cupcake-- I was walking by a bakery, and I thought you'd like it.
Sorry I smell like something that fell off a garbage truck. I literally fell off a garbage truck today.
Never grow up, Molly. One day you're dreaming about playing professional lacrosse. The next, you're "the couch guy" at the landfill.
Hey, are you going to eat that now? Can I have a bite?
Chase, can I ask you something?
Sure.
Am I cute?
Uh...Not to me. I mean, I don't know. Are you, is this--
Do you want to be cute? Is this about a boy? Or a girl?
Because no matter what, you'd be better off talking to Gert or Karolina about it.
No. I mean... am I cute? Like a puppy. Or a hedgehog wearing a cowboy hat.
Oh...yeah. You're the cutest, Molly. You're ten hedgehogs wearing cowboy hats!

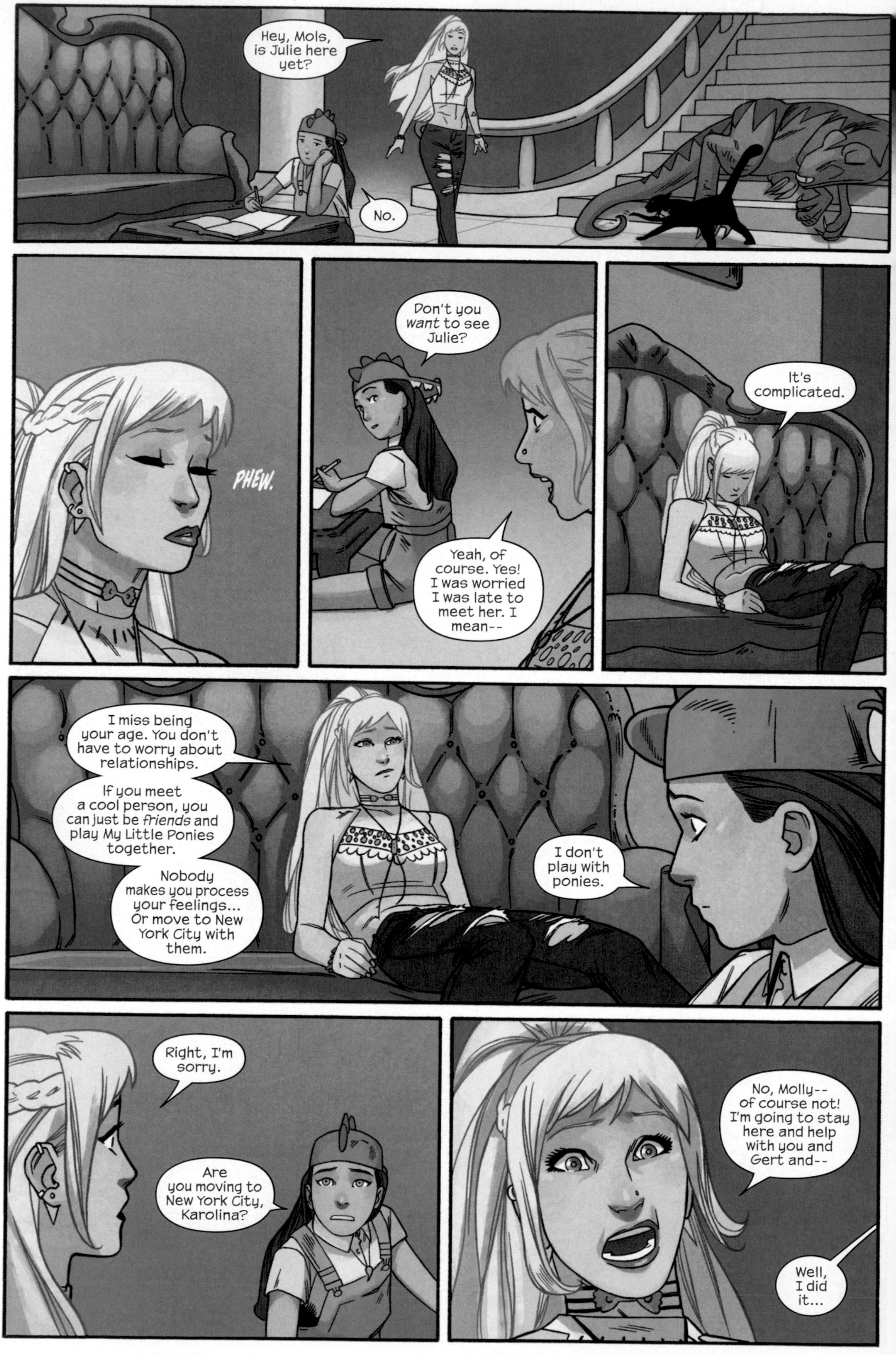
Hey, Mols, is Julie here yet?
No.
PHEW.
Don't you *want* to see Julie?
Yeah, of course. Yes! I was worried I was late to meet her. I mean--
It's complicated.
I miss being your age. You don't have to worry about relationships.
If you meet a cool person, you can just be *friends* and play My Little Ponies together.
Nobody makes you process your feelings... Or move to New York City with them.
I don't play with ponies.
Right, I'm sorry.
Are you moving to New York City, Karolina?
No, Molly-- of course not! I'm going to stay here and help with you and Gert and--
Well, I did it...

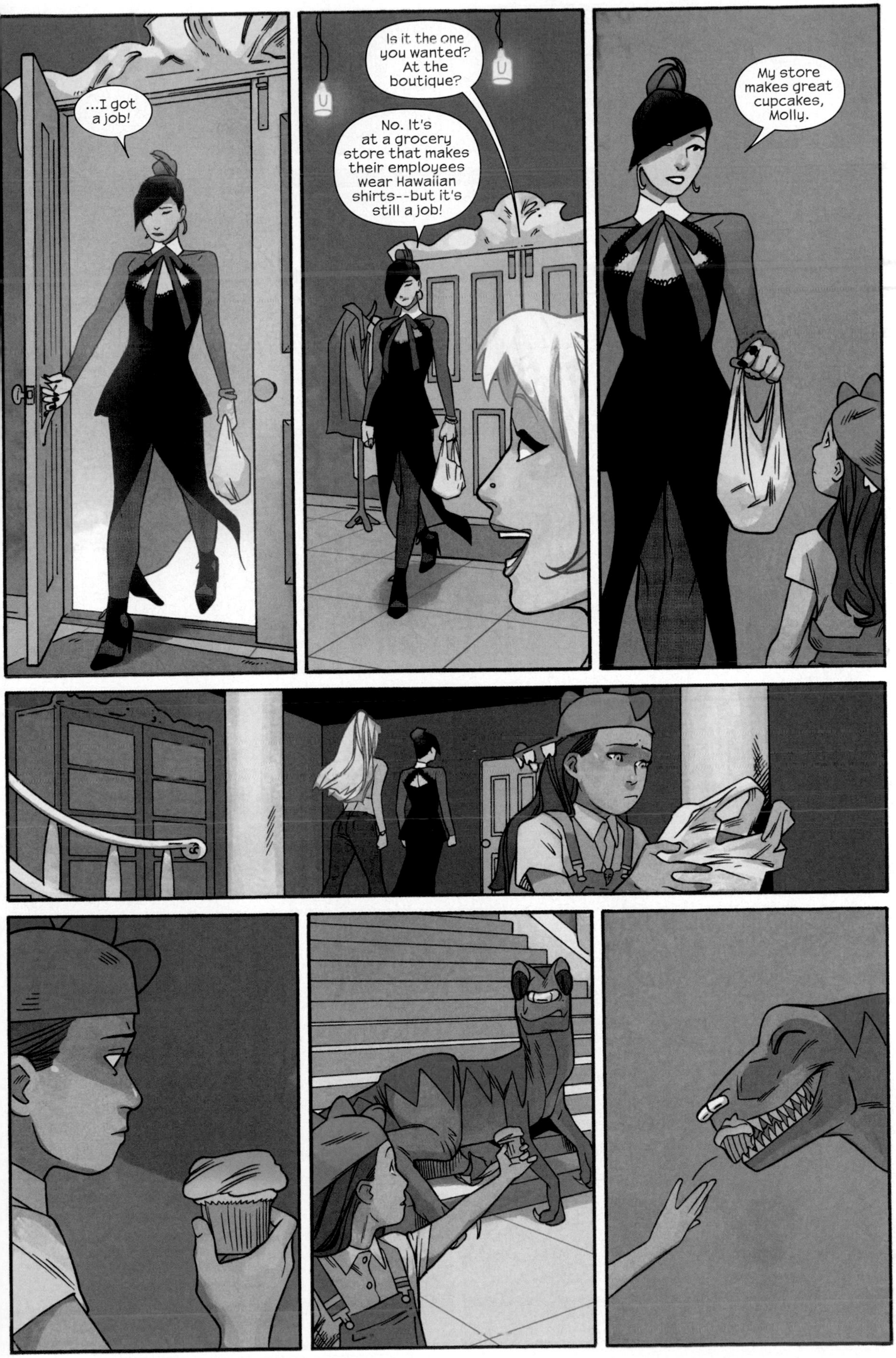
...I got a job!
Is it the one you wanted? At the boutique?
No. It's at a grocery store that makes their employees wear Hawaiian shirts--but it's still a job!
My store makes great cupcakes, Molly.

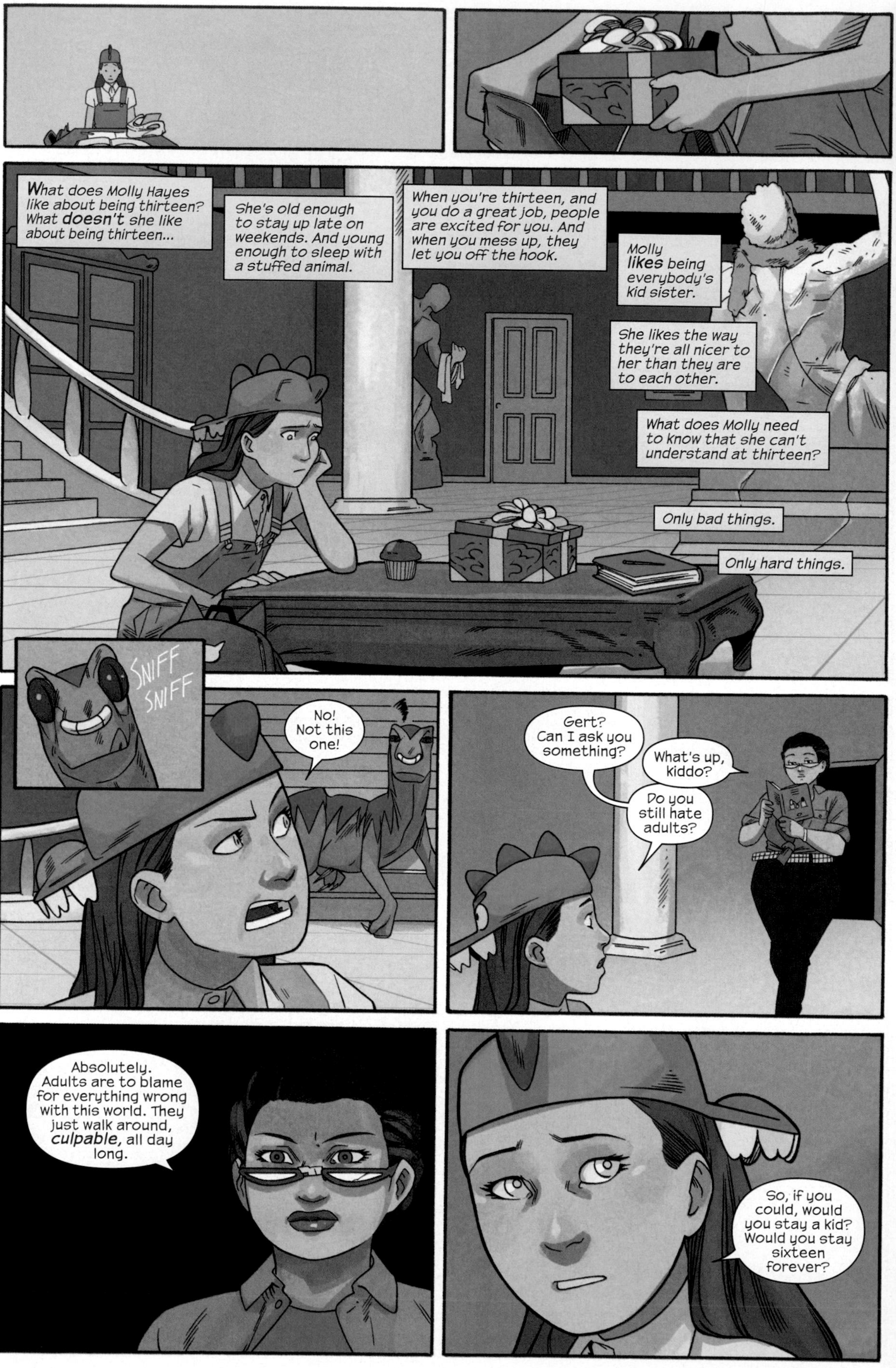
What does Molly Hayes like about being thirteen? What doesn't she like about being thirteen...
She's old enough to stay up late on weekends. And young enough to sleep with a stuffed animal.
When you're thirteen, and you do a great job, people are excited for you. And when you mess up, they let you off the hook.
Molly likes being everybody's kid sister.
She likes the way they're all nicer to her than they are to each other.
What does Molly need to know that she can't understand at thirteen?
Only bad things.
Only hard things.
SNIFF SNIFF
No! Not this one!
Gert? Can I ask you something?
What's up, kiddo?
Do you still hate adults?
Absolutely. Adults are to blame for everything wrong with this world. They just walk around, *culpable,* all day long.
So, if you could, would you stay a kid? Would you stay sixteen forever?

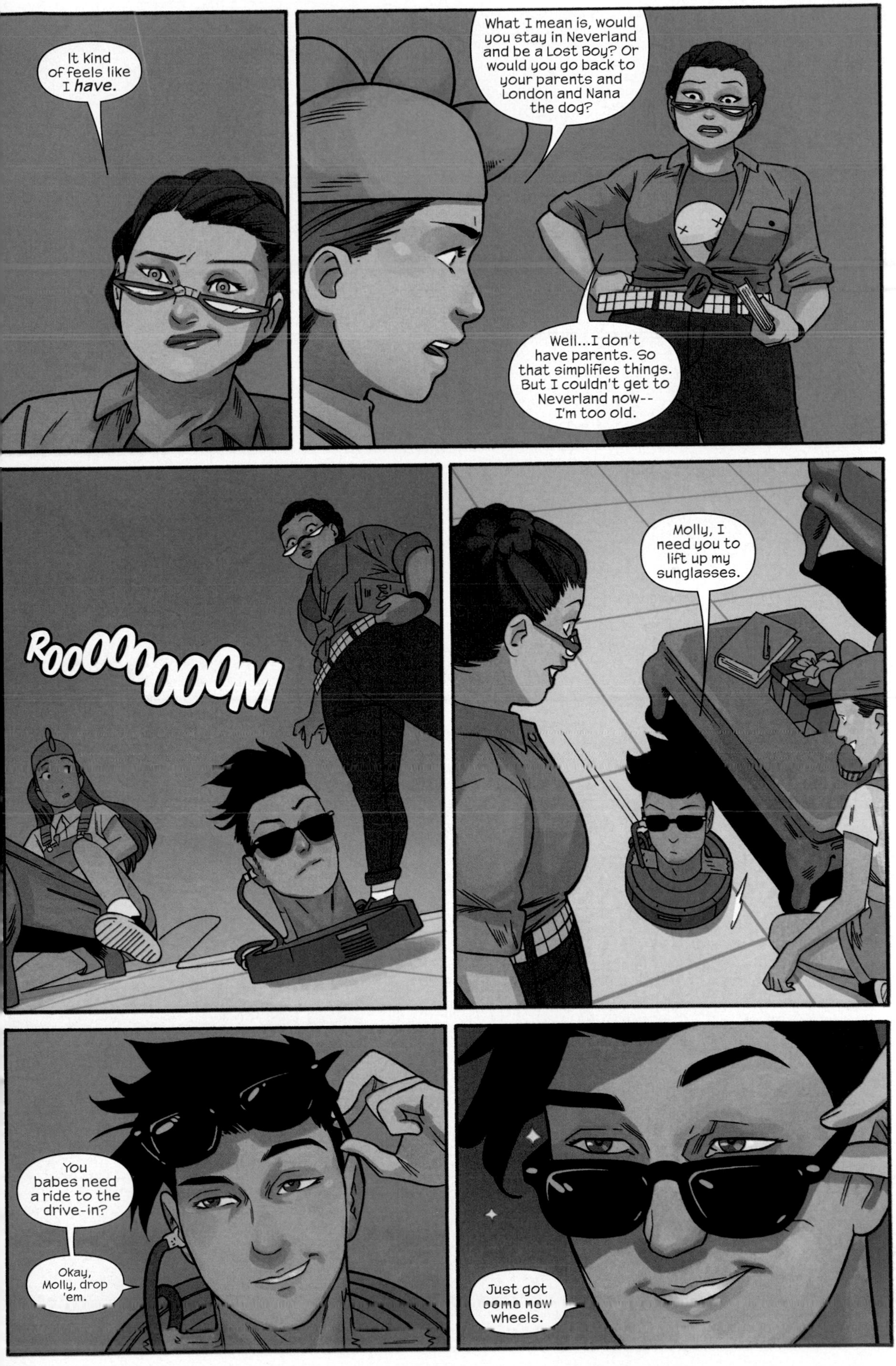
It kind of feels like I *have.*
What I mean is, would you stay in Neverland and be a Lost Boy? Or would you go back to your parents and London and Nana the dog?
Well...I don't have parents. So that simplifies things. But I couldn't get to Neverland now-- I'm too old.
ROOOOOOOOM
Molly, I need you to lift up my sunglasses.
You babes need a ride to the drive-in?
Okay, Molly, drop 'em.
Just got some new wheels.

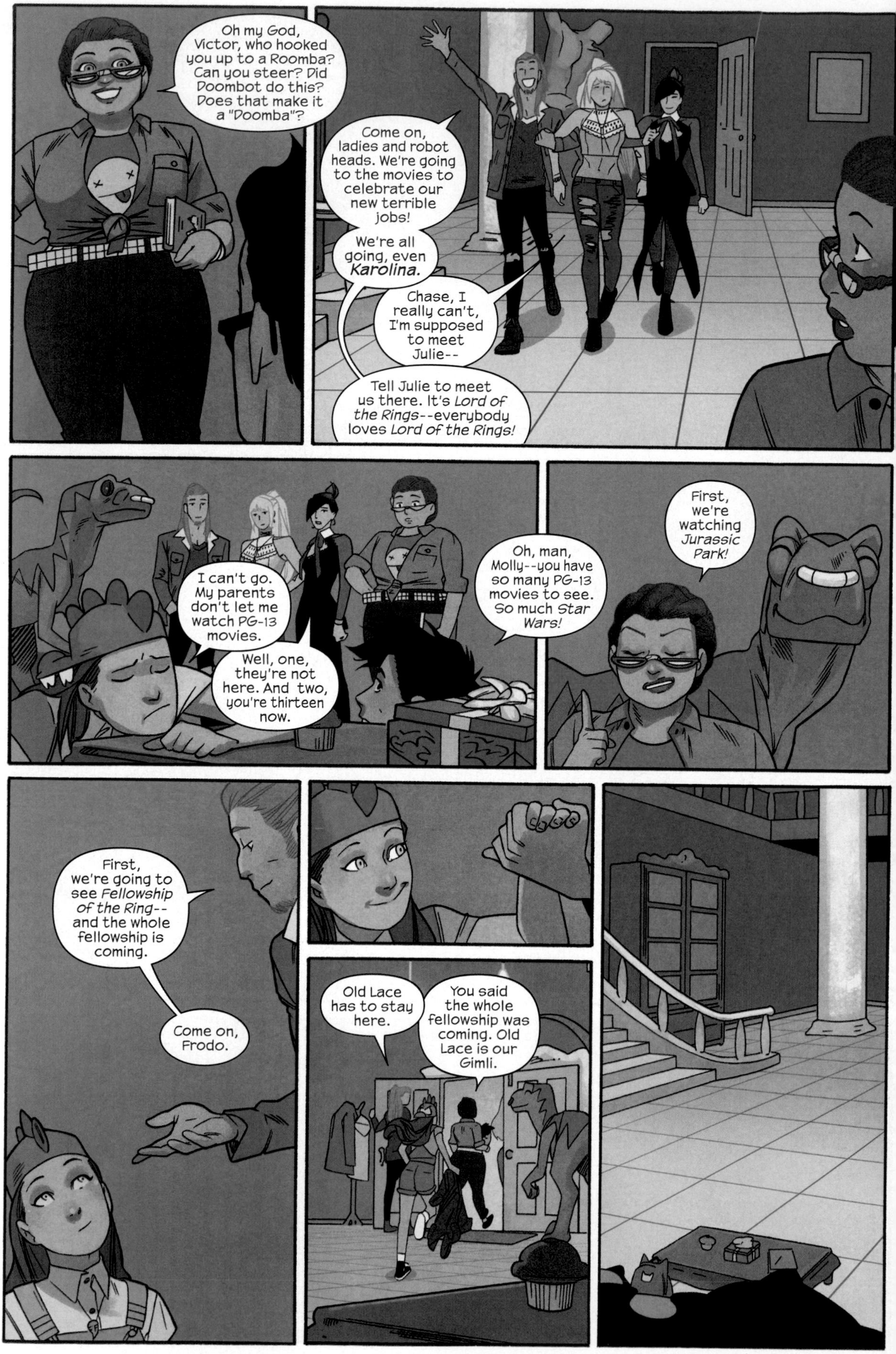
Oh my God, Victor, who hooked you up to a Roomba? Can you steer? Did Doombot do this? Does that make it a "Doomba"?
Come on, ladies and robot heads. We're going to the movies to celebrate our new terrible jobs!
We're all going, even Karolina.
Chase, I really can't, I'm supposed to meet Julie--
Tell Julie to meet us there. It's Lord of the Rings--everybody loves Lord of the Rings!
I can't go. My parents don't let me watch PG-13 movies.
Well, one, they're not here. And two, you're thirteen now.
Oh, man, Molly--you have so many PG-13 movies to see. So much Star Wars!
First, we're watching Jurassic Park!
First, we're going to see Fellowship of the Ring--and the whole fellowship is coming.
Come on, Frodo.
Old Lace has to stay here.
You said the whole fellowship was coming. Old Lace is our Gimli.

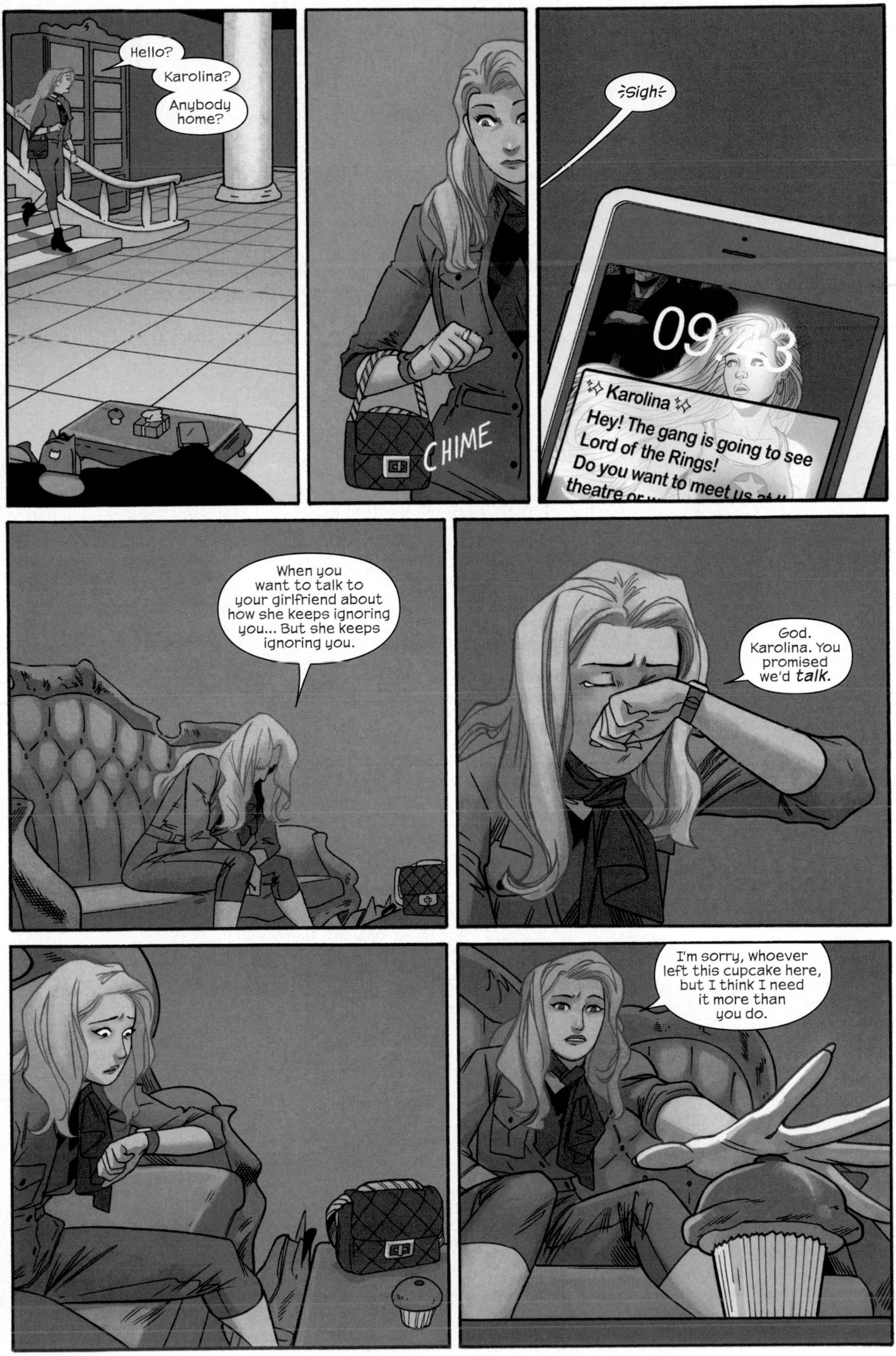
Hello?
Karolina?
Anybody home?
CHIME
Sigh
09:43
Karolina
Hey! The gang is going to see Lord of the Rings! Do you want to meet us at the
When you want to talk to your girlfriend about how she keeps ignoring you... But she keeps ignoring you.
God. Karolina. You promised we'd *talk.*
I'm sorry, whoever left this cupcake here, but I think I need it more than you do.

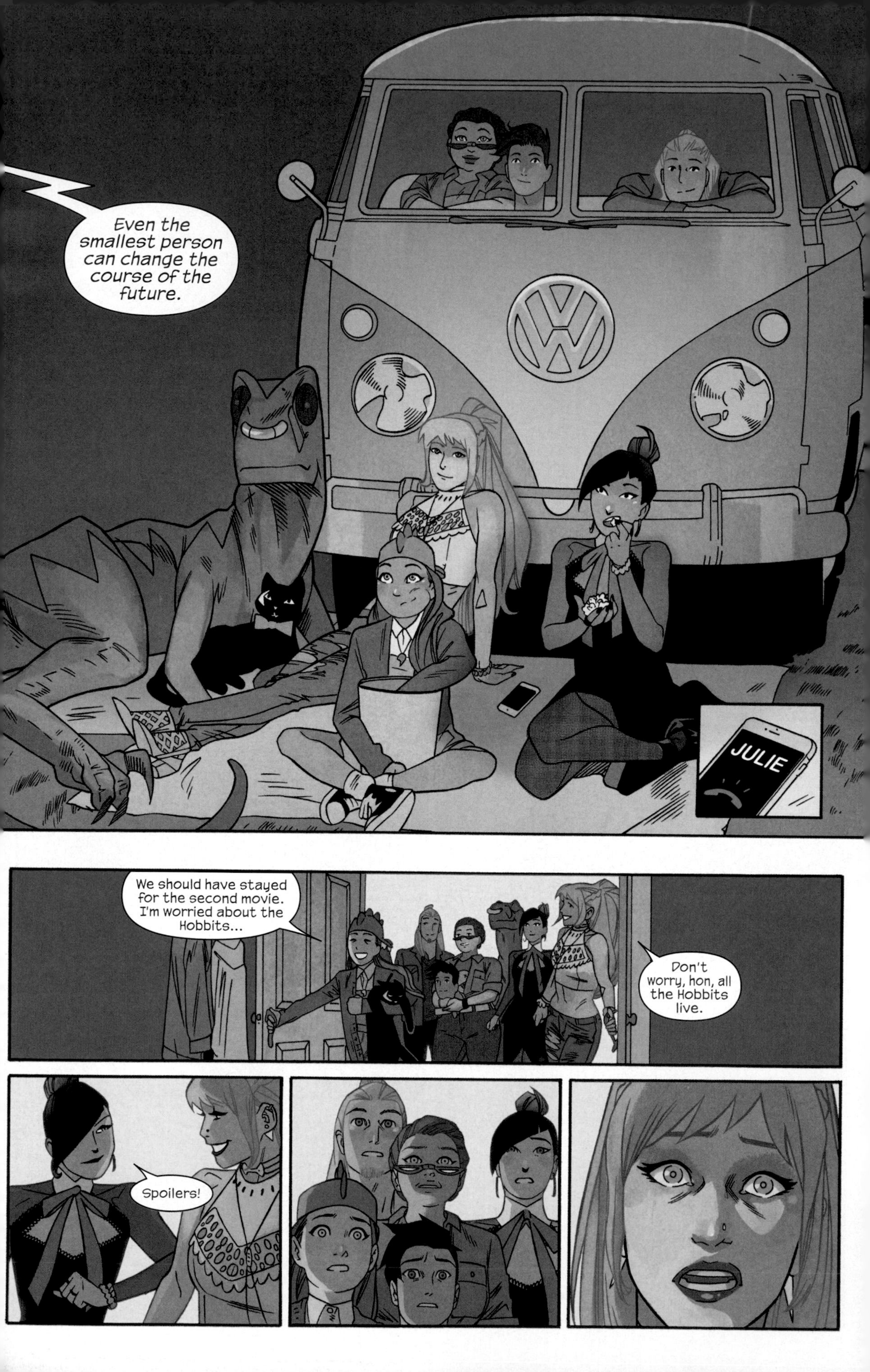
Even the smallest person can change the course of the future.
JULIE
We should have stayed for the second movie. I'm worried about the Hobbits...
Don't worry, hon, all the Hobbits live.
Spoilers!

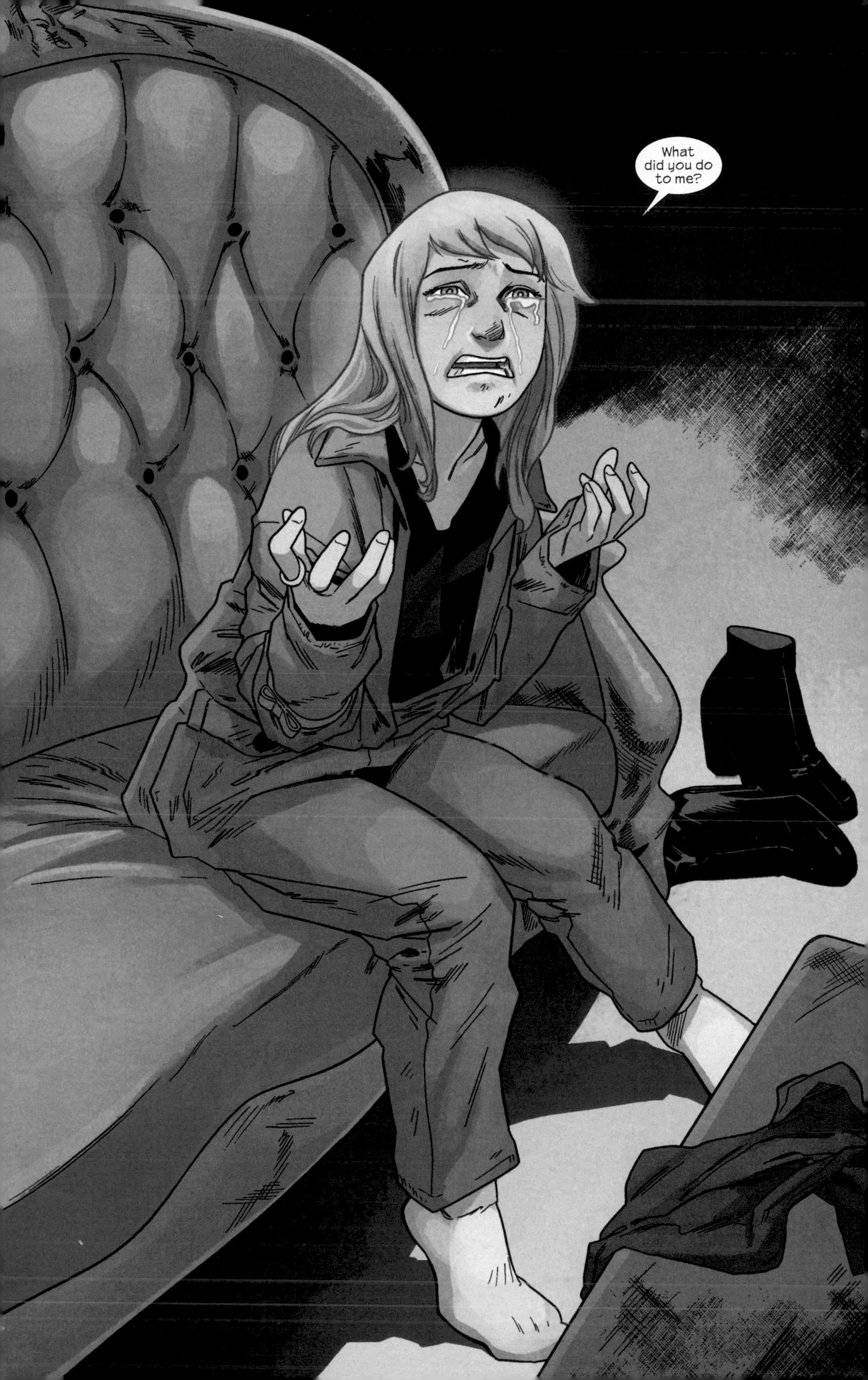
What did you do to me?

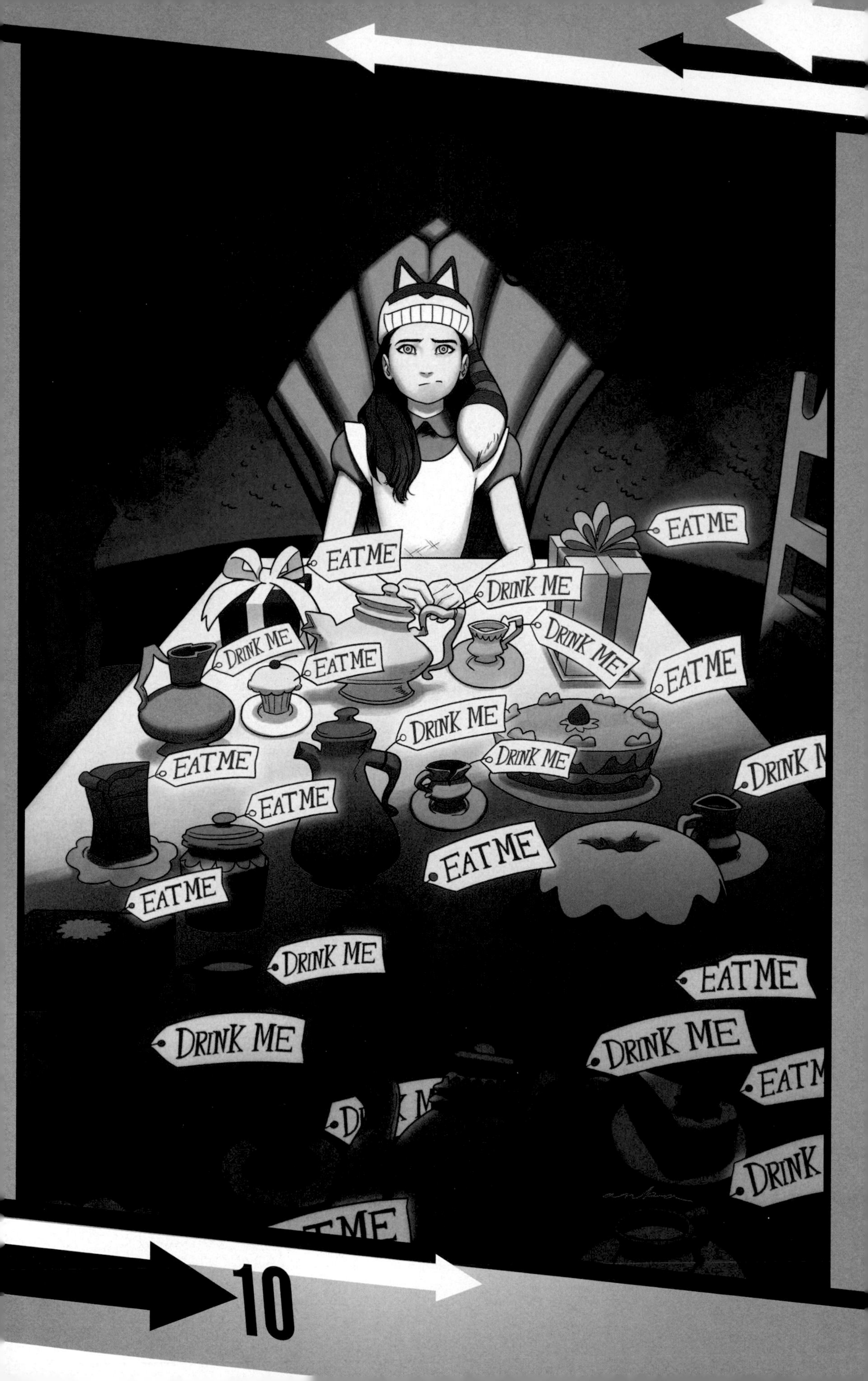

EAT ME
EAT ME
DRINK ME
DRINK ME
DRINK ME
EAT ME
EAT ME
DRINK ME
DRINK ME
EAT ME
EAT ME
EAT ME
EAT ME
DRINK ME
EAT ME
DRINK ME
DRINK ME
10

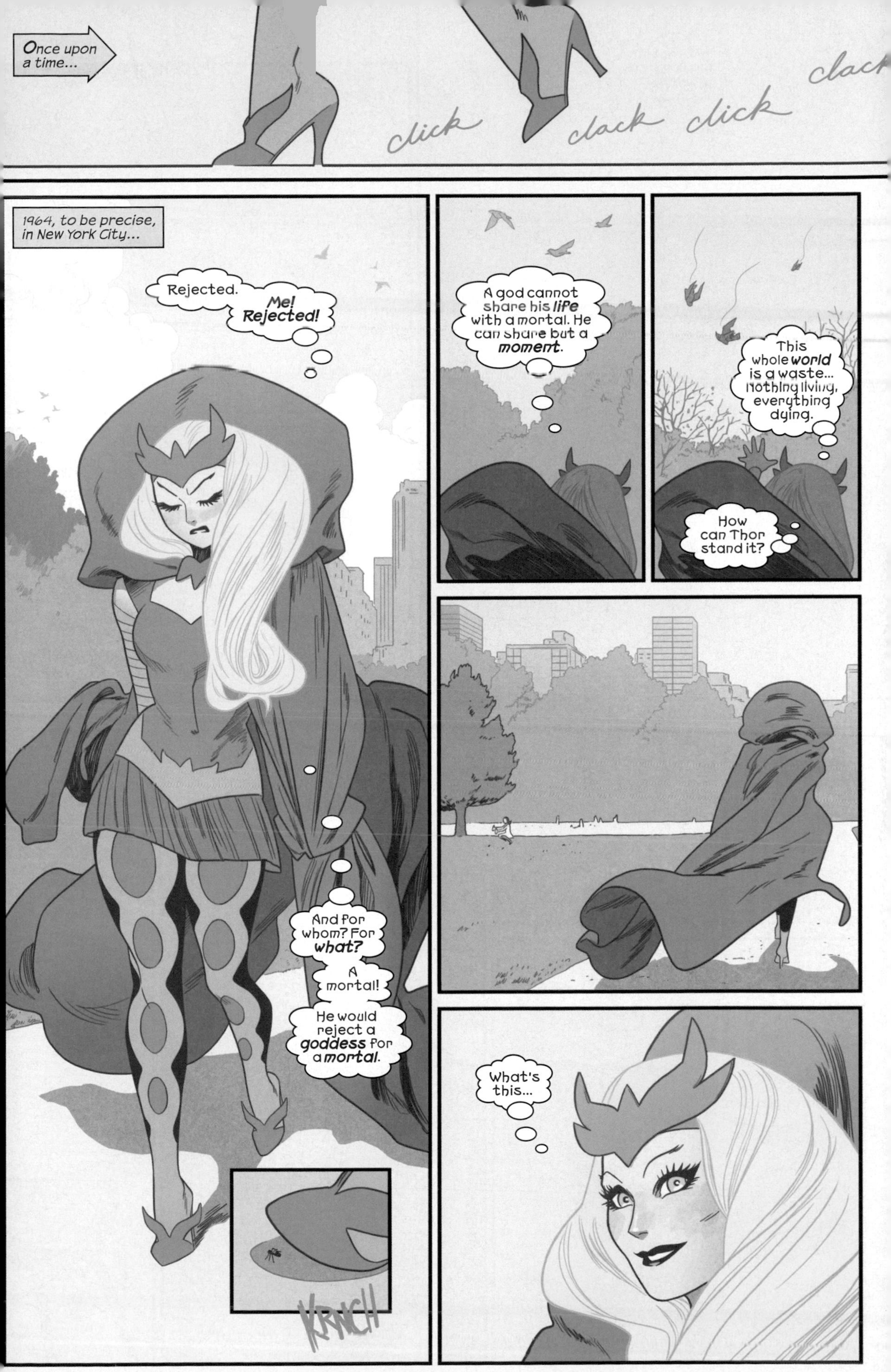
Once upon a time...
click
clack
click
clack
1964, to be precise, in New York City...
Rejected.
Me! Rejected!
A god cannot share his life with a mortal. He can share but a moment.
This whole world is a waste... nothing living, everything dying.
How can Thor stand it?
And for whom? For what?
A mortal!
He would reject a goddess for a mortal.
KRNCH
What's this...

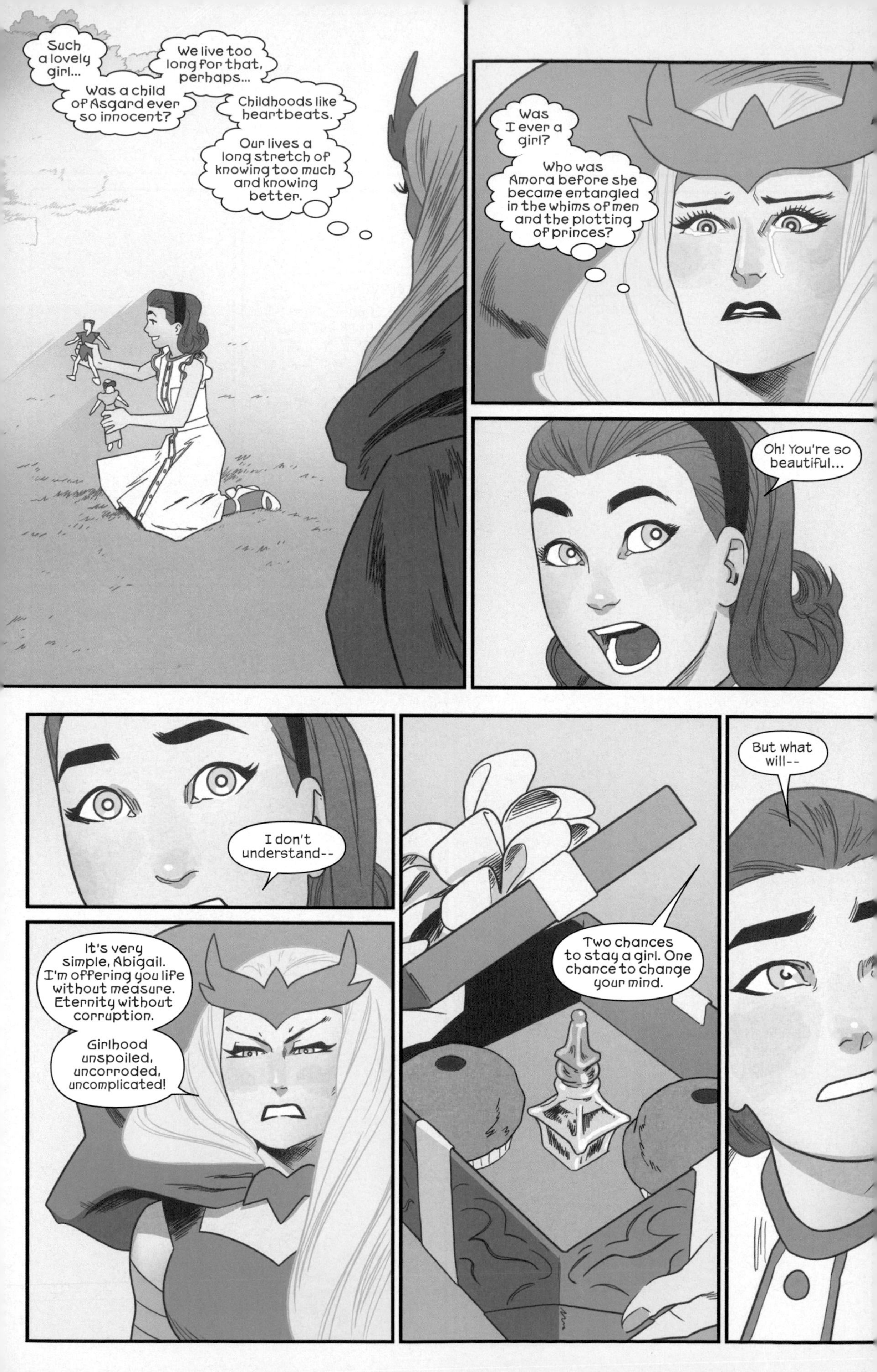
Such a lovely girl...
We live too long for that, perhaps...
Was a child of Asgard ever so innocent?
Childhoods like heartbeats.
Our lives a long stretch of knowing too much and knowing better.
Was I ever a girl?
Who was Amora before she became entangled in the whims of men and the plotting of princes?
Oh! You're so beautiful...
I don't understand--
It's very simple, Abigail. I'm offering you life without measure. Eternity without corruption.
Girlhood unspoiled, uncorroded, uncomplicated!
Two chances to stay a girl. One chance to change your mind.
But what will--

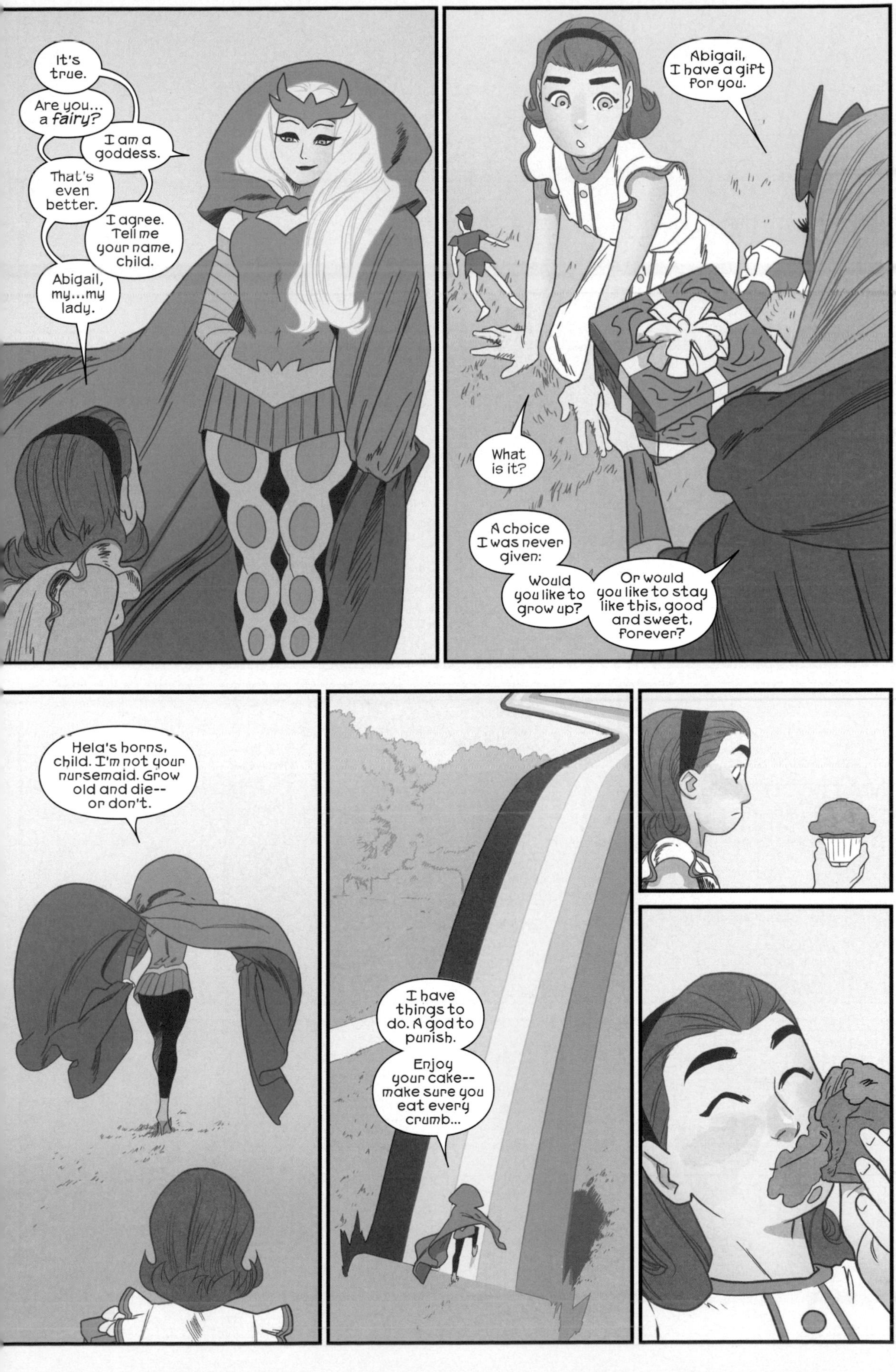
It's true.
Are you... a *fairy*?
I am a goddess.
That's even better.
I agree. Tell me your name, child.
Abigail, my...my lady.
Abigail, I have a gift for you.
What is it?
A choice I was never given:
Would you like to grow up?
Or would you like to stay like this, good and sweet, forever?
Hela's horns, child. I'm not your nursemaid. Grow old and die-- or don't.
I have things to do. A god to punish.
Enjoy your cake-- make sure you eat every crumb...

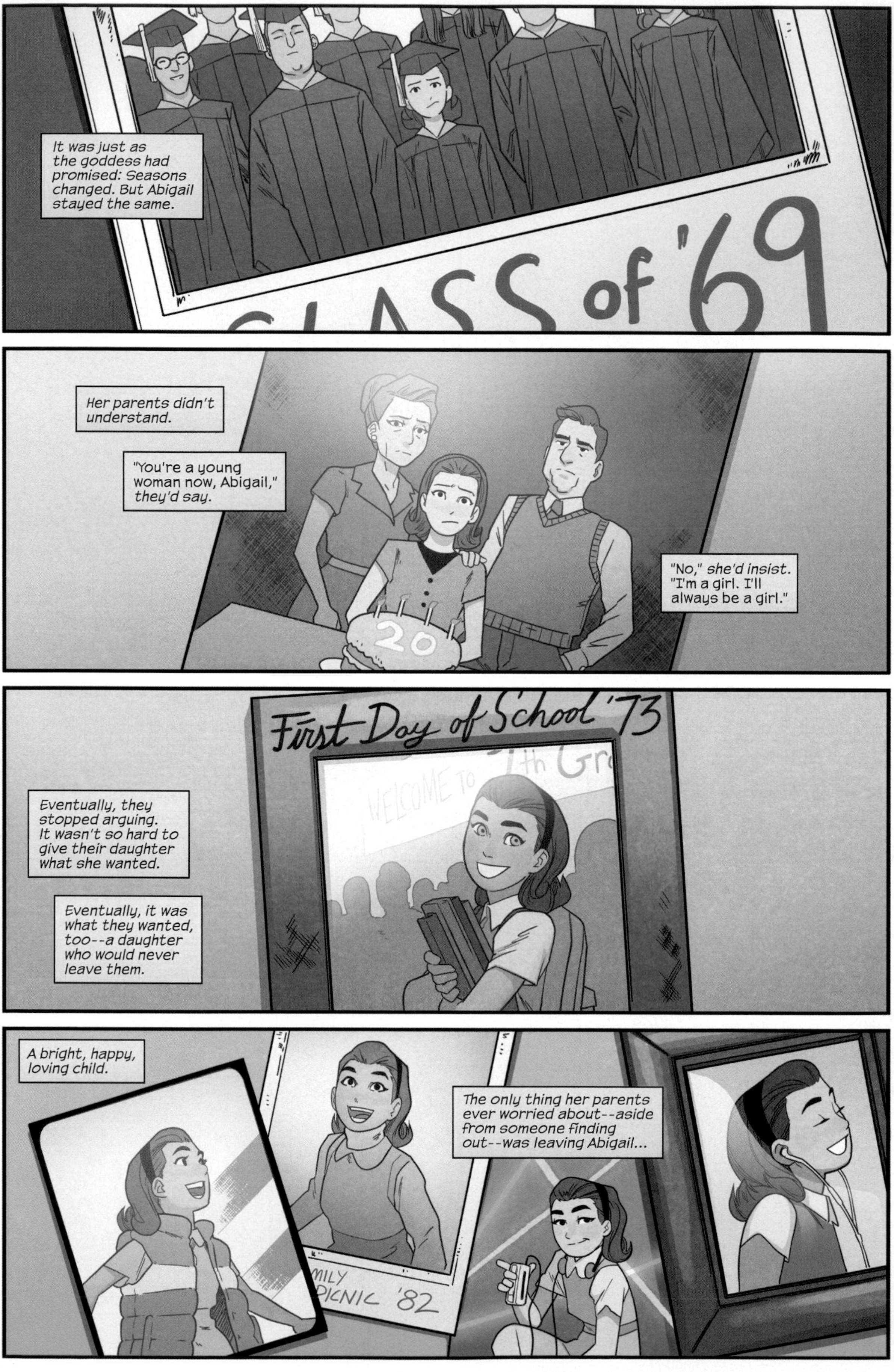
It was just as the goddess had promised: Seasons changed. But Abigail stayed the same.
CLASS of '69
Her parents didn't understand.
"You're a young woman now, Abigail," they'd say.
"No," she'd insist. "I'm a girl. I'll always be a girl."
20
First Day of School '73
WELCOME TO
Eventually, they stopped arguing. It wasn't so hard to give their daughter what she wanted.
Eventually, it was what they wanted, too--a daughter who would never leave them.
A bright, happy, loving child.
MILY PICNIC '82
The only thing her parents ever worried about--aside from someone finding out--was leaving Abigail...

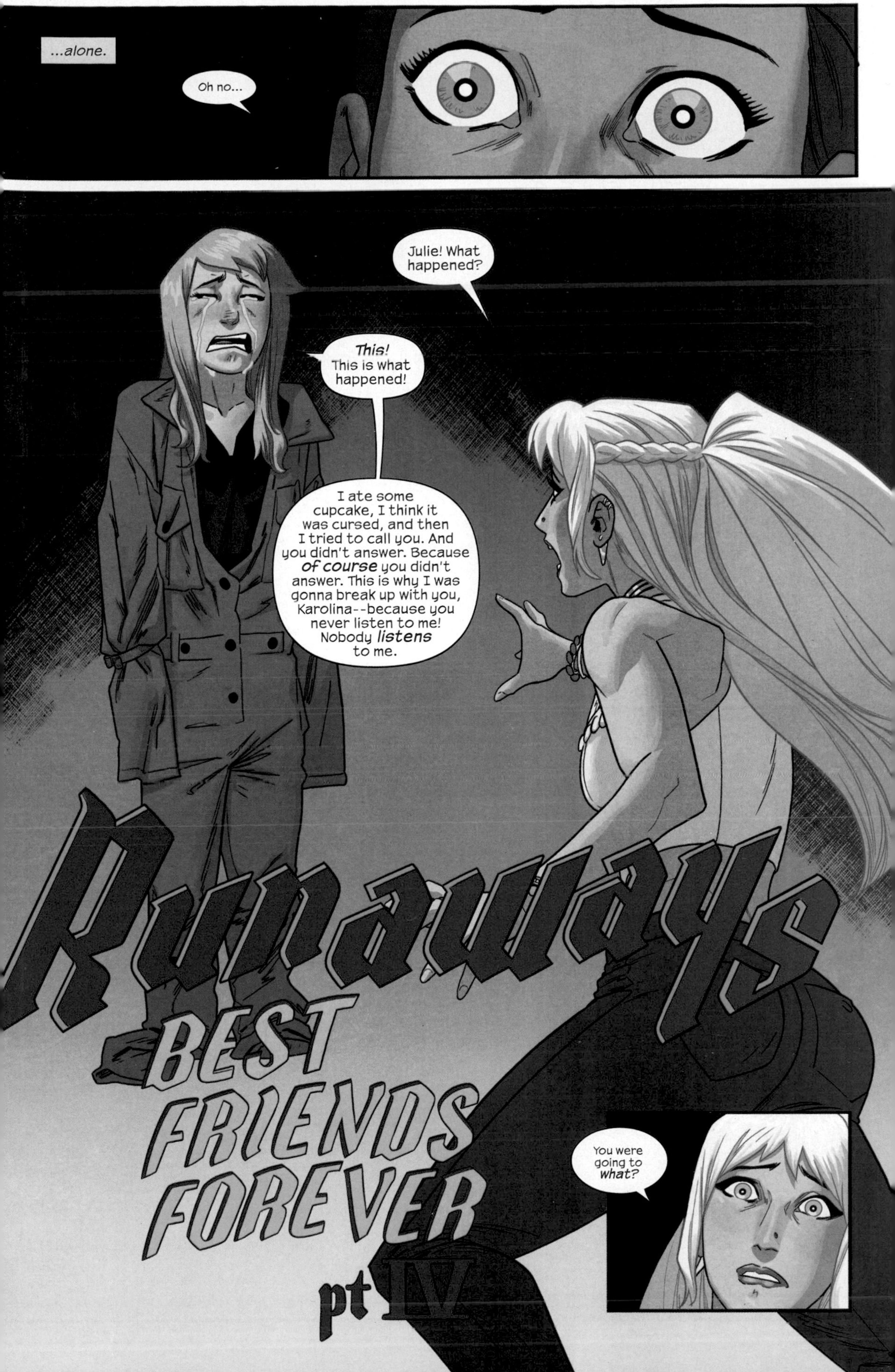
...alone.
Oh no...
Julie! What happened?
This! This is what happened!
I ate some cupcake, I think it was cursed, and then I tried to call you. And you didn't answer. Because of course you didn't answer. This is why I was gonna break up with you, Karolina--because you never listen to me! Nobody listens to me.
Runaways
BEST FRIENDS FOREVER pt IV
You were going to what?

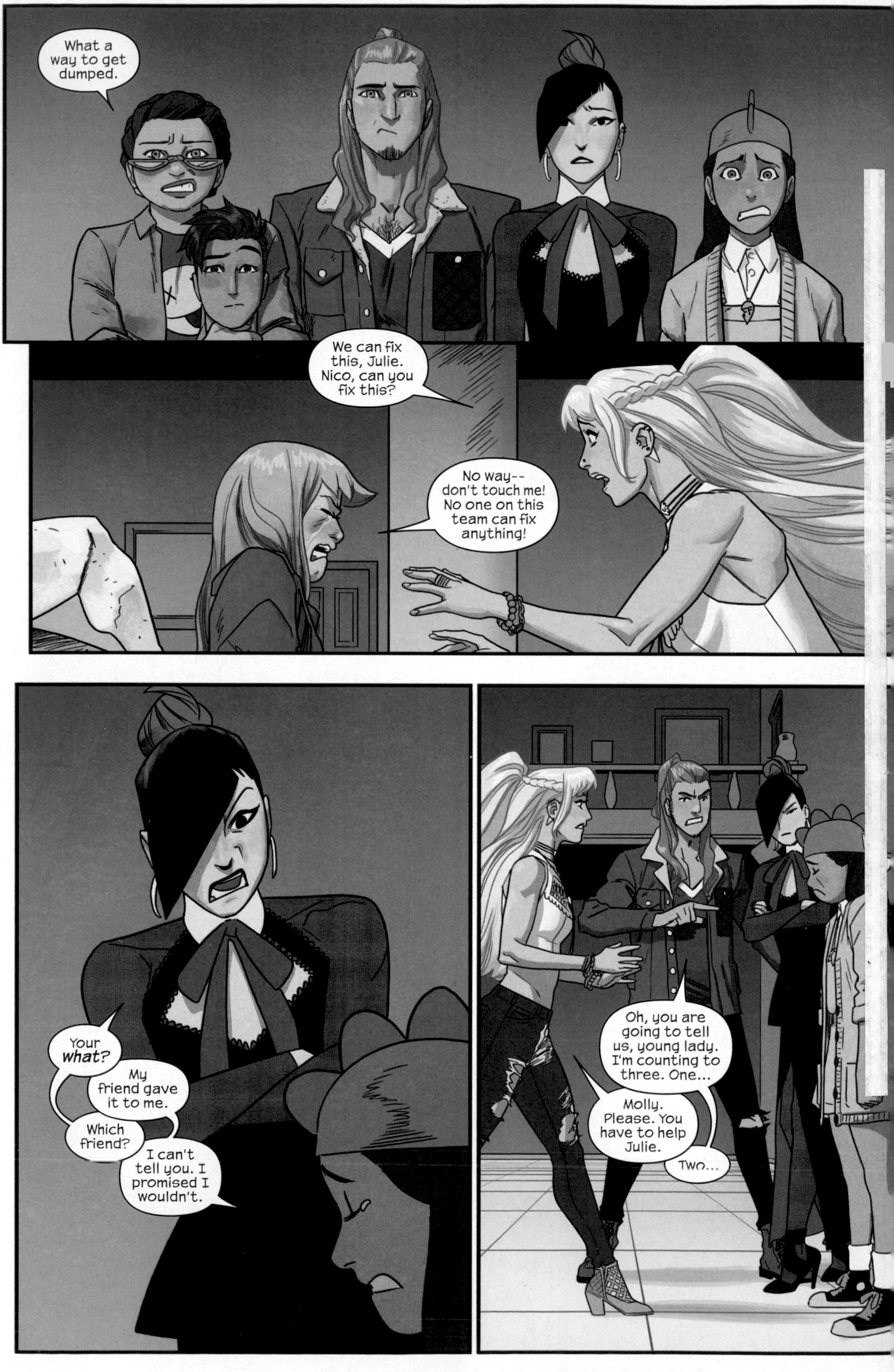
What a way to get dumped.
We can fix this, Julie. Nico, can you fix this?
No way-- don't touch me! No one on this team can fix anything!
Your *what?*
My friend gave it to me.
Which friend?
I can't tell you. I promised I wouldn't.
Oh, you are going to tell us, young lady. I'm counting to three. One...
Molly. Please. You have to help Julie.
Two...

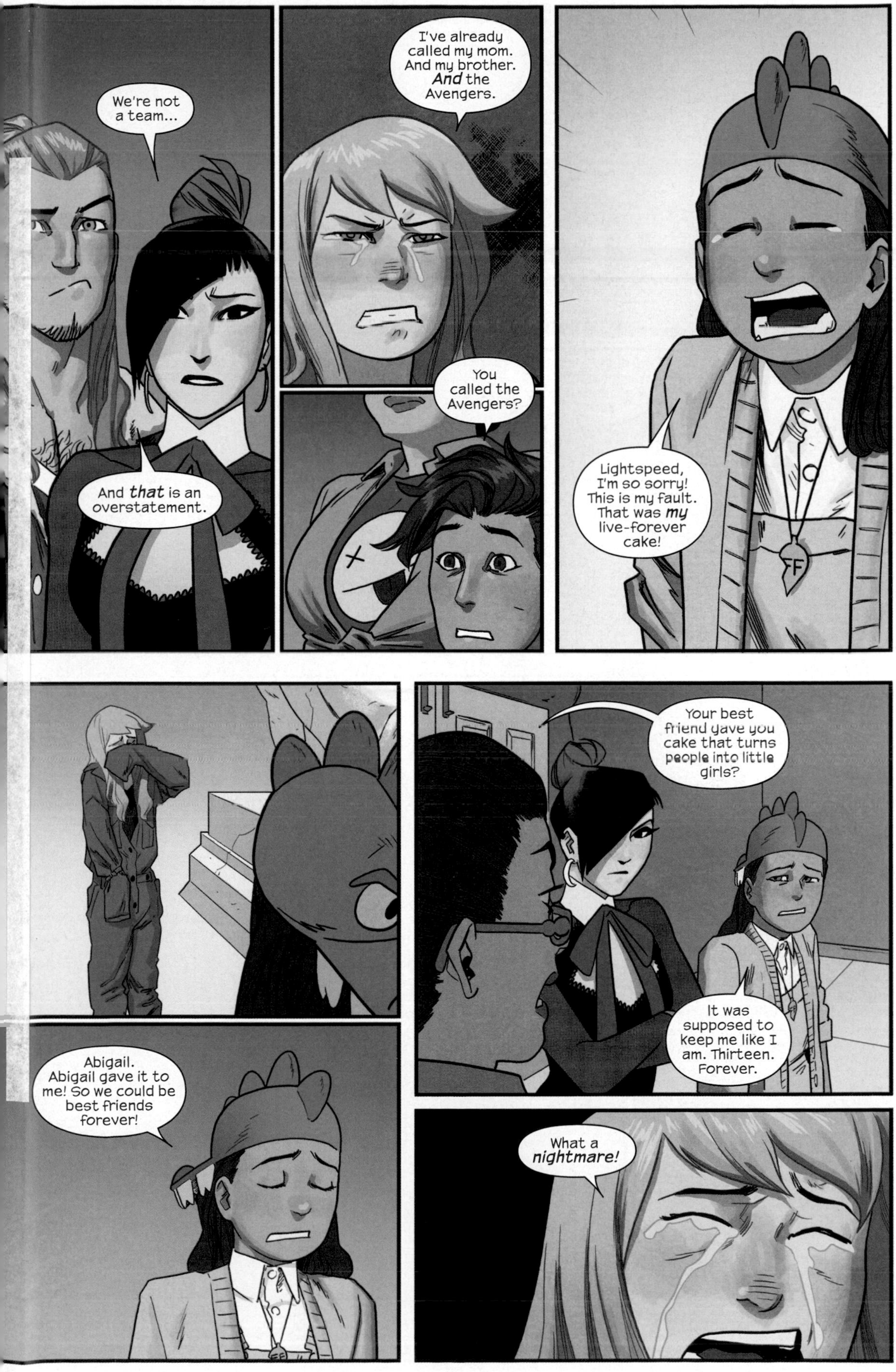
We're not a team...
And *that* is an overstatement.
I've already called my mom. And my brother. *And* the Avengers.
You called the Avengers?
Lightspeed, I'm so sorry! This is my fault. That was *my* live-forever cake!
Your best friend gave you cake that turns people into little girls?
It was supposed to keep me like I am. Thirteen. Forever.
Abigail. Abigail gave it to me! So we could be best friends forever!
What a *nightmare!*

Is there some sort of antidote? Another cake?

Where did your friend Abigail even *get* a magic cupcake?

Or pie?

She said a witch gave it to her. Or an alien. It might have been a goddess...

Why would you eat witch-alien-god cake, Molly?

I didn't eat it! I wasn't going to! I was just thinking about it.

You were *thinking* about it?

Molly. Why didn't you tell us?

I don't know.

Our focus now is helping Julie. I know where Abigail lives. We'll go, and we'll make her tell us the cure. I'm sure it's something simple.

Julie, I could *try* a spell.

Drop dead, Nico.

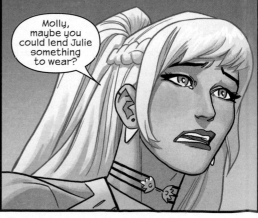

Molly, maybe you could lend Julie something to wear?

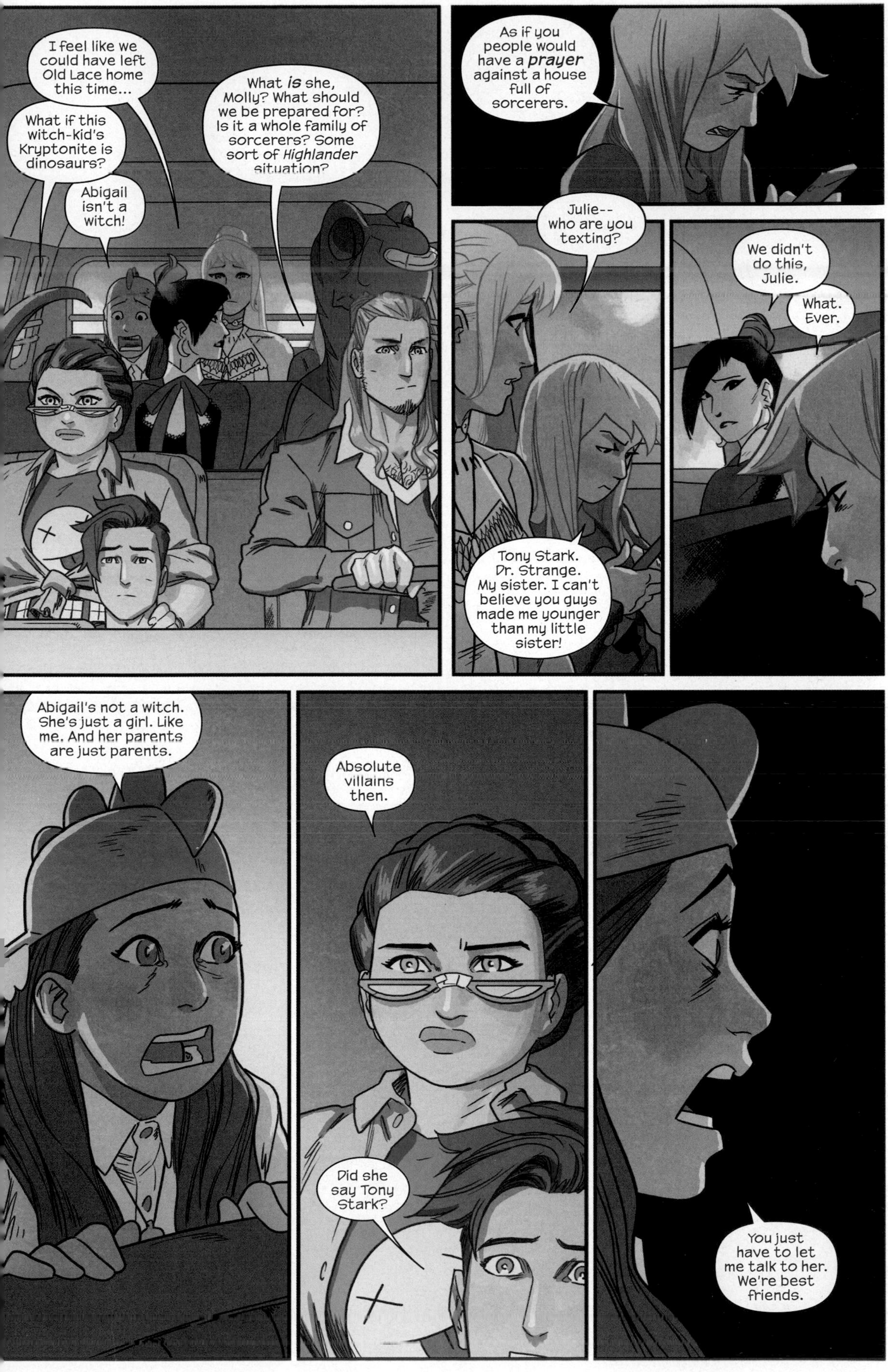
I feel like we could have left Old Lace home this time...
What if this witch-kid's Kryptonite is dinosaurs?
Abigail isn't a witch!
What *is* she, Molly? What should we be prepared for? Is it a whole family of sorcerers? Some sort of *Highlander* situation?
As if you people would have a ***prayer*** against a house full of sorcerers.
Julie-- who are you texting?
Tony Stark. Dr. Strange. My sister. I can't believe you guys made me younger than my little sister!
We didn't do this, Julie.
What. Ever.
Abigail's not a witch. She's just a girl. Like me. And her parents are just parents.
Absolute villains then.
Did she say Tony Stark?
You just have to let me talk to her. We're best friends.

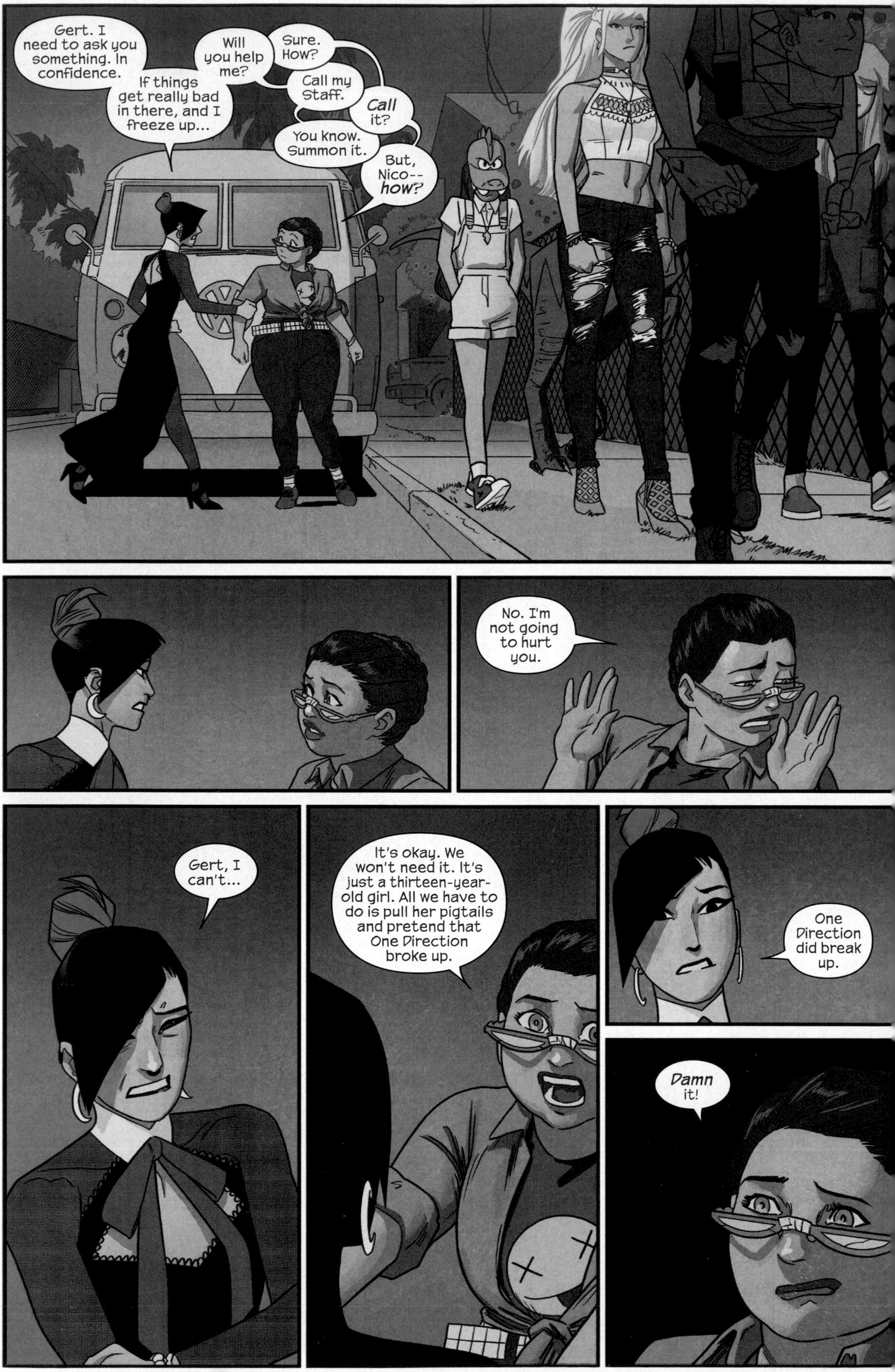
Gert. I need to ask you something. In confidence.
If things get really bad in there, and I freeze up...
Will you help me?
Sure. How?
Call my Staff.
Call it?
You know. Summon it.
But, Nico-- how?
No. I'm not going to hurt you.
Gert, I can't...
It's okay. We won't need it. It's just a thirteen-year-old girl. All we have to do is pull her pigtails and pretend that One Direction broke up.
One Direction did break up.
Damn it!

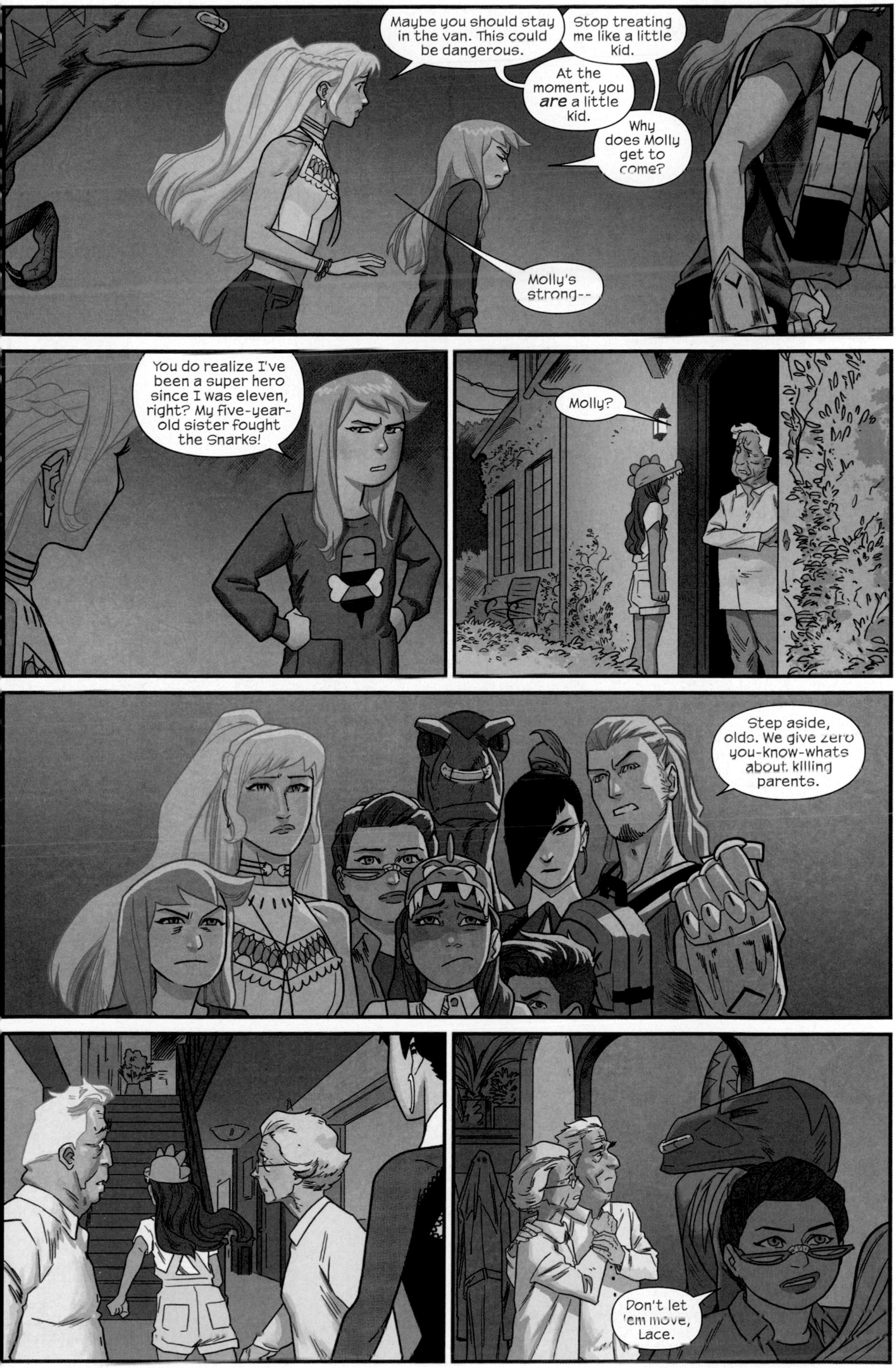
Maybe you should stay in the van. This could be dangerous.
Stop treating me like a little kid.
At the moment, you *are* a little kid.
Why does Molly get to come?
Molly's strong--
You do realize I've been a super hero since I was eleven, right? My five-year-old sister fought the Snarks!
Molly?
Step aside, olds. We give zero you-know-whats about killing parents.
Don't let 'em move, Lace.

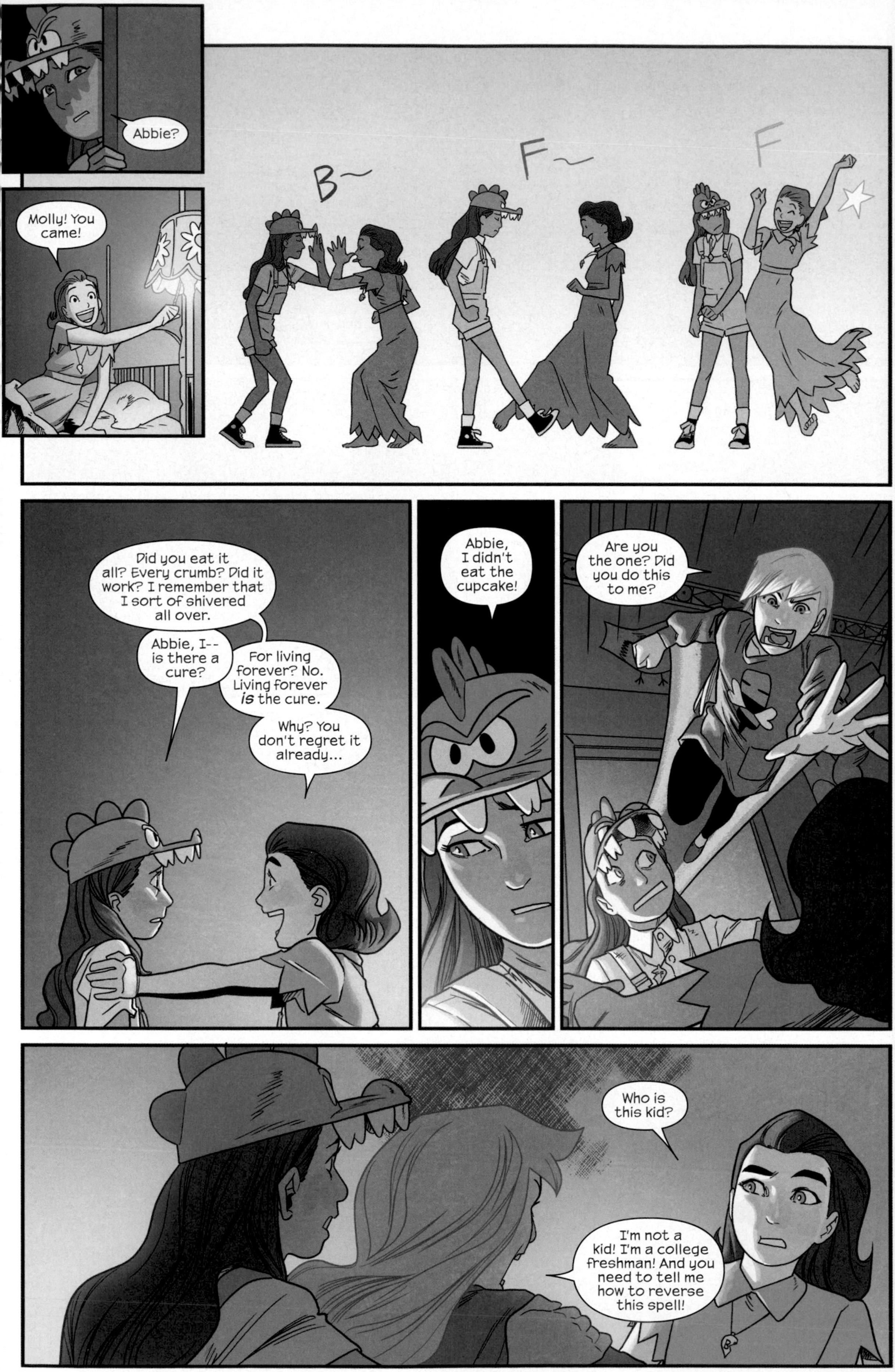
Abbie?
Molly! You came!
B~
F~
F
Did you eat it all? Every crumb? Did it work? I remember that I sort of shivered all over.
Abbie, I-- is there a cure?
For living forever? No. Living forever *is* the cure.
Why? You don't regret it already...
Abbie, I didn't eat the cupcake!
Are you the one? Did you do this to me?
Who is this kid?
I'm not a kid! I'm a college freshman! And you need to tell me how to reverse this spell!

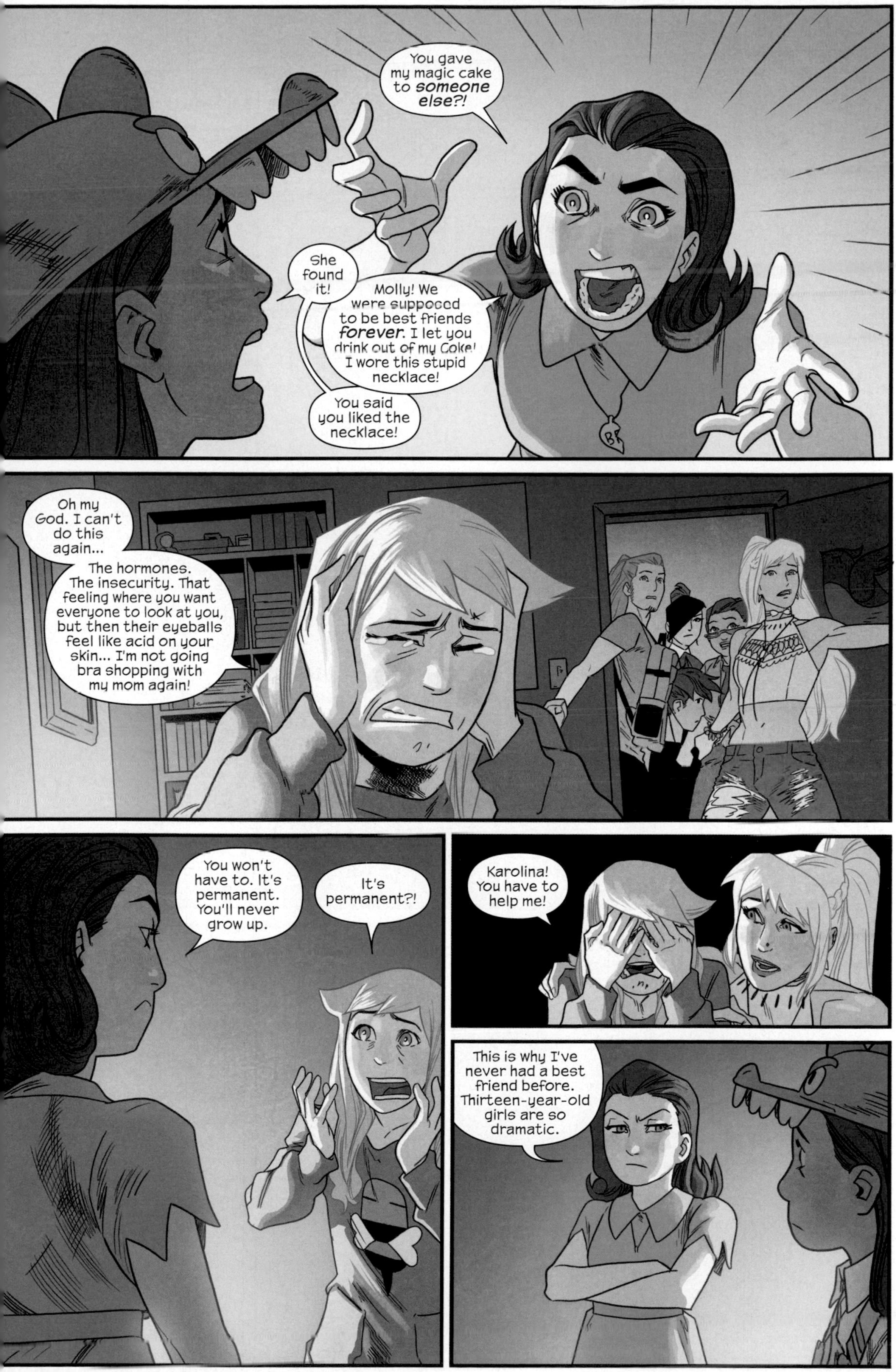
You gave my magic cake to *someone else*?!
She found it!
Molly! We were supposed to be best friends *forever*. I let you drink out of my Coke! I wore this stupid necklace!
You said you liked the necklace!
Oh my God. I can't do this again...
The hormones. The insecurity. That feeling where you want everyone to look at you, but then their eyeballs feel like acid on your skin... I'm not going bra shopping with my mom again!
You won't have to. It's permanent. You'll never grow up.
It's permanent?!
Karolina! You have to help me!
This is why I've never had a best friend before. Thirteen-year-old girls are so dramatic.

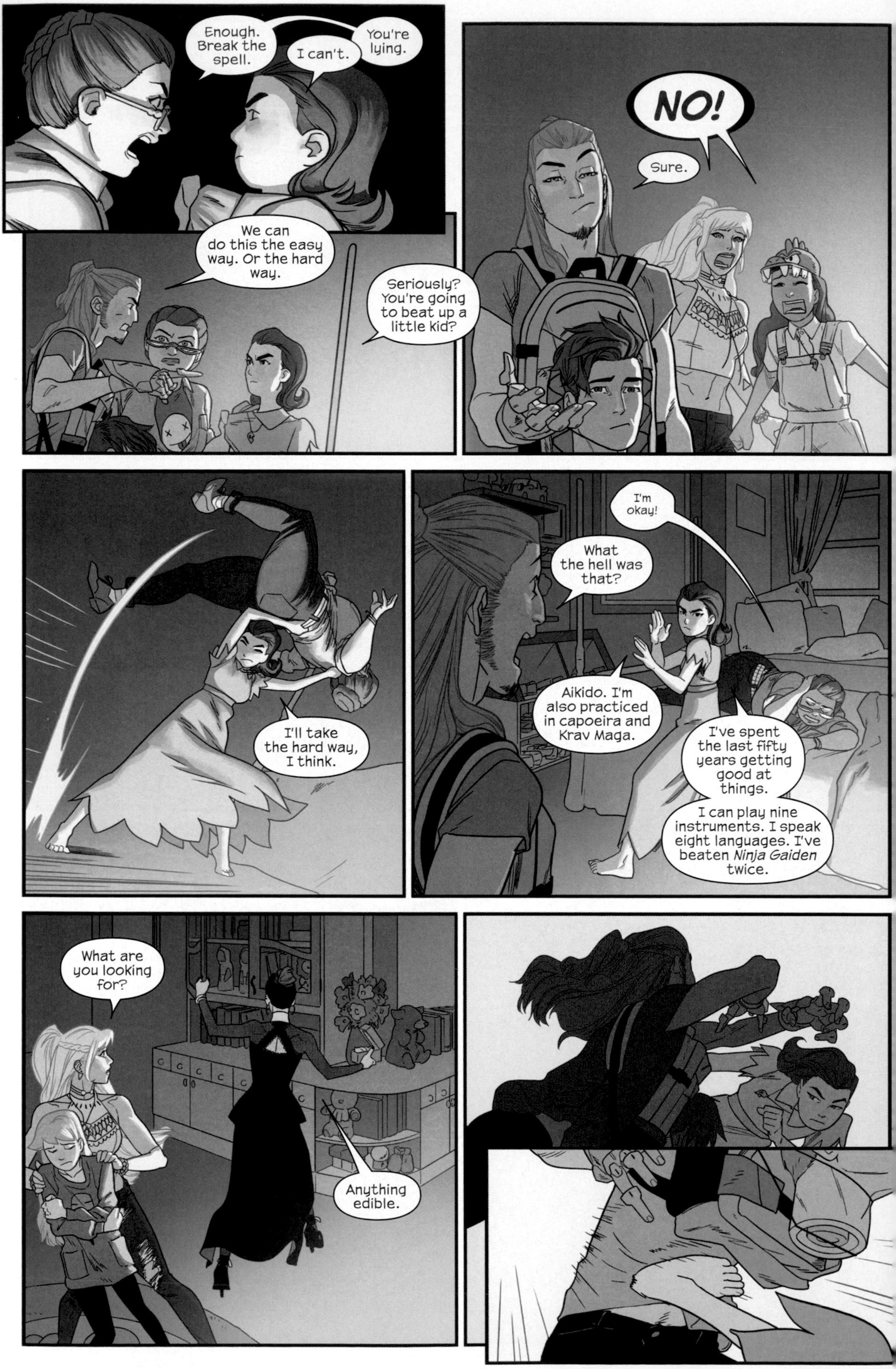
Enough. Break the spell.
I can't.
You're lying.
We can do this the easy way. Or the hard way.
Seriously? You're going to beat up a little kid?
Sure.
NO!
I'll take the hard way, I think.
I'm okay!
What the hell was that?
Aikido. I'm also practiced in capoeira and Krav Maga.
I've spent the last fifty years getting good at things.
I can play nine instruments. I speak eight languages. I've beaten *Ninja Gaiden* twice.
What are you looking for?
Anything edible.

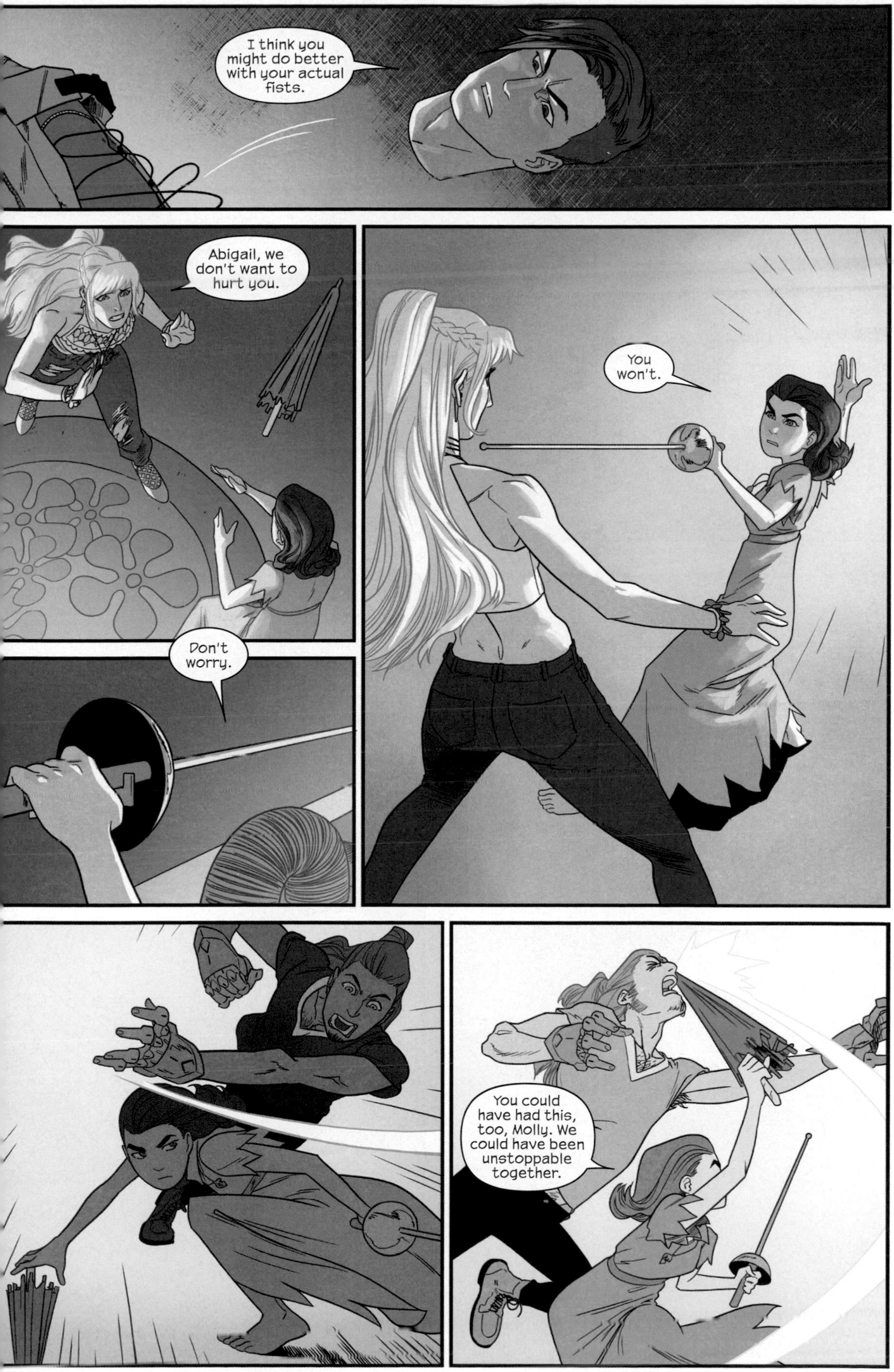

I think you might do better with your actual fists.
Abigail, we don't want to hurt you.
Don't worry.
You won't.
You could have had this, too, Molly. We could have been unstoppable together.

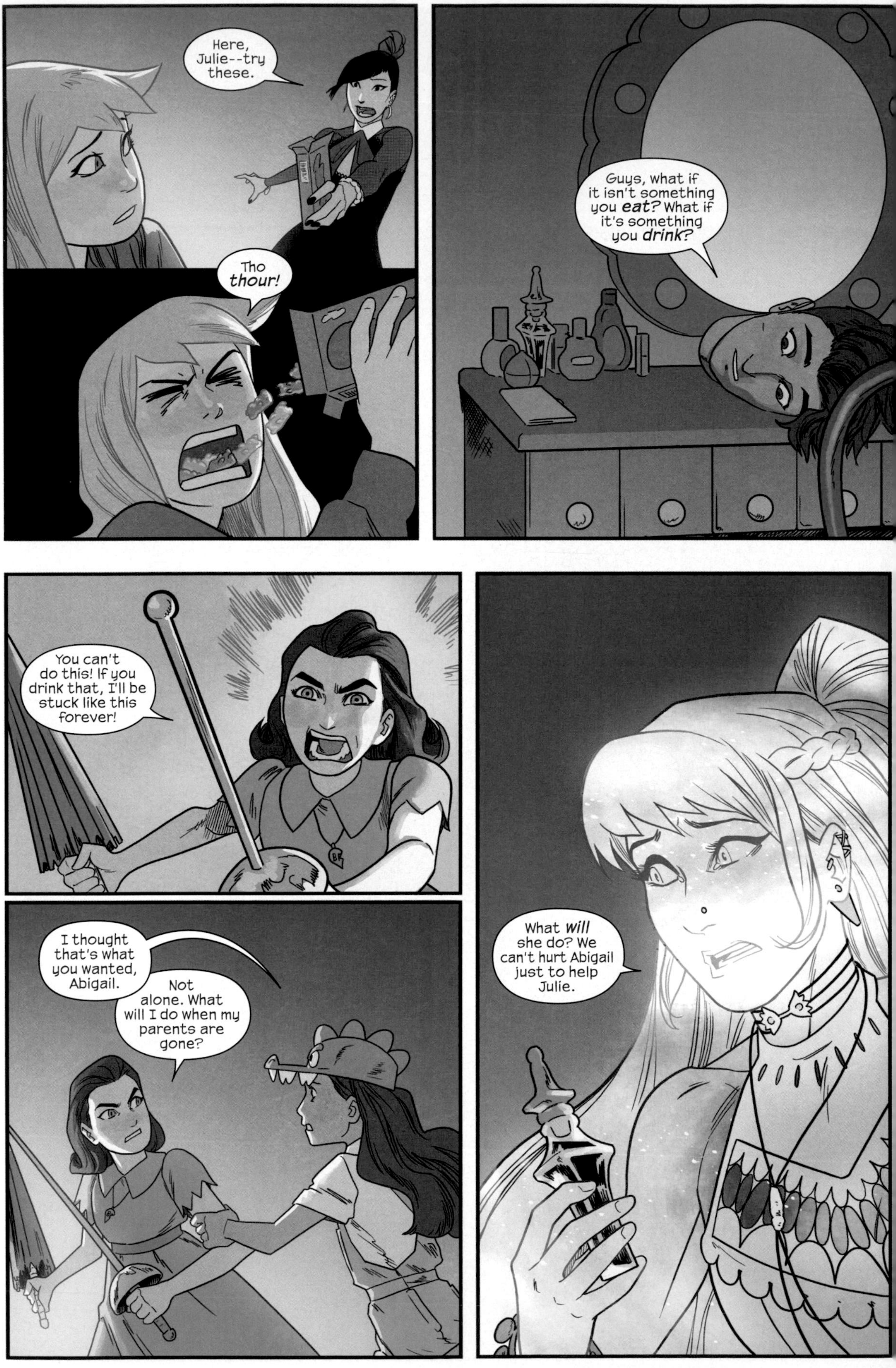
Here, Julie--try these.
Tho thour!
Guys, what if it isn't something you eat? What if it's something you drink?
You can't do this! If you drink that, I'll be stuck like this forever!
I thought that's what you wanted, Abigail.
Not alone. What will I do when my parents are gone?
What will she do? We can't hurt Abigail just to help Julie.

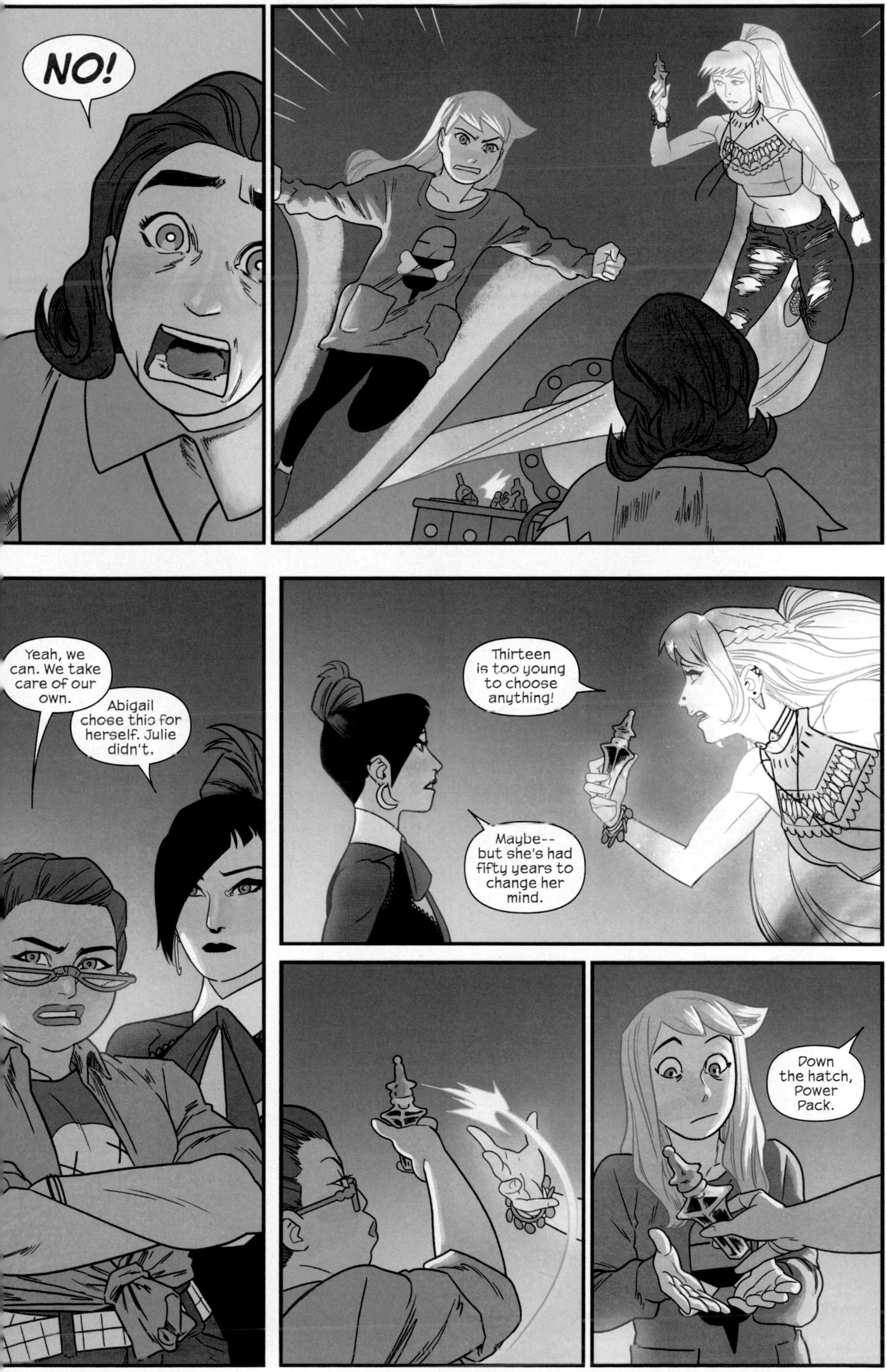
NO!
Yeah, we can. We take care of our own.
Abigail chose this for herself. Julie didn't.
Thirteen is too young to choose anything!
Maybe-- but she's had fifty years to change her mind.
Down the hatch, Power Pack.

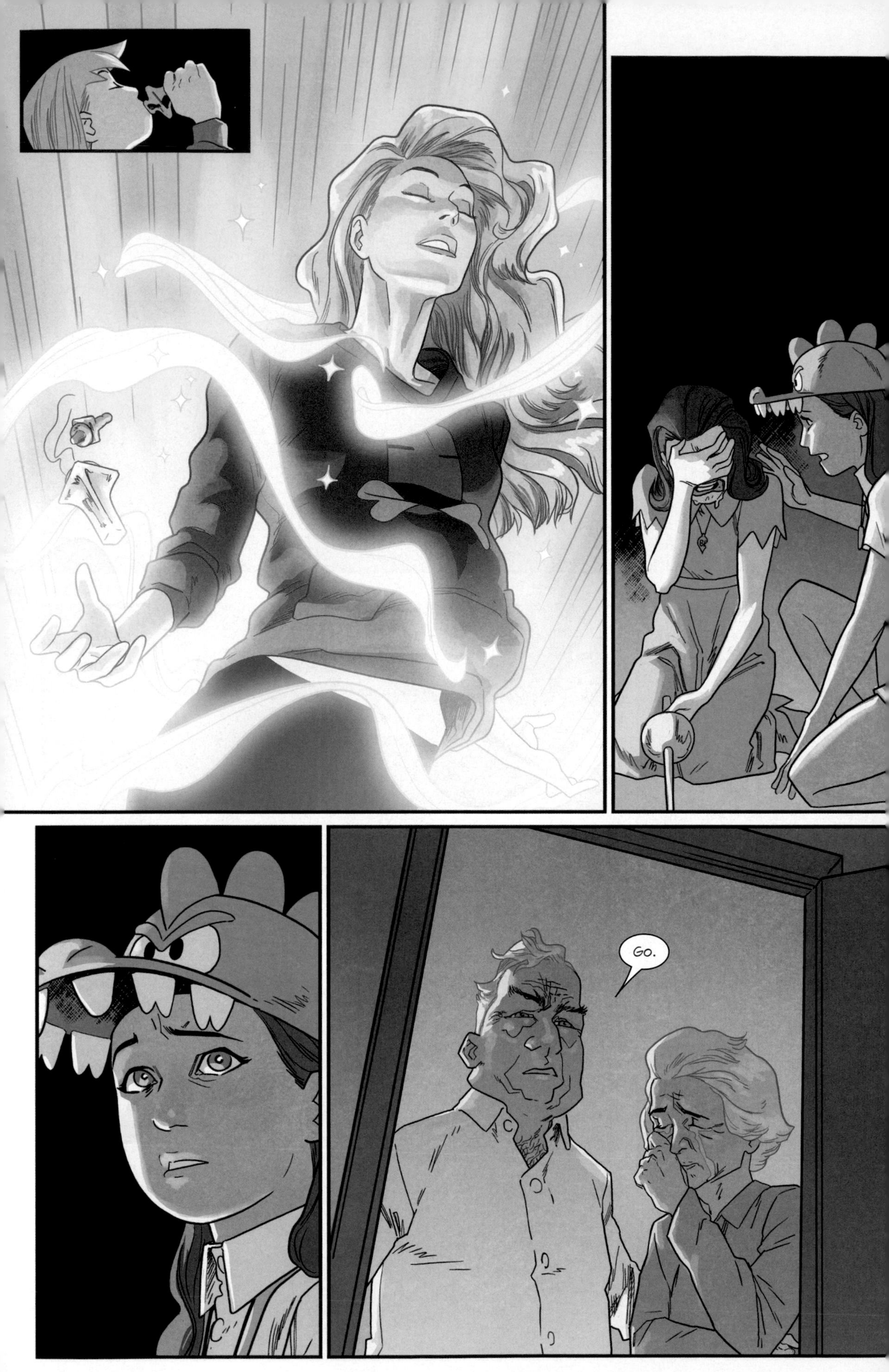
GO.

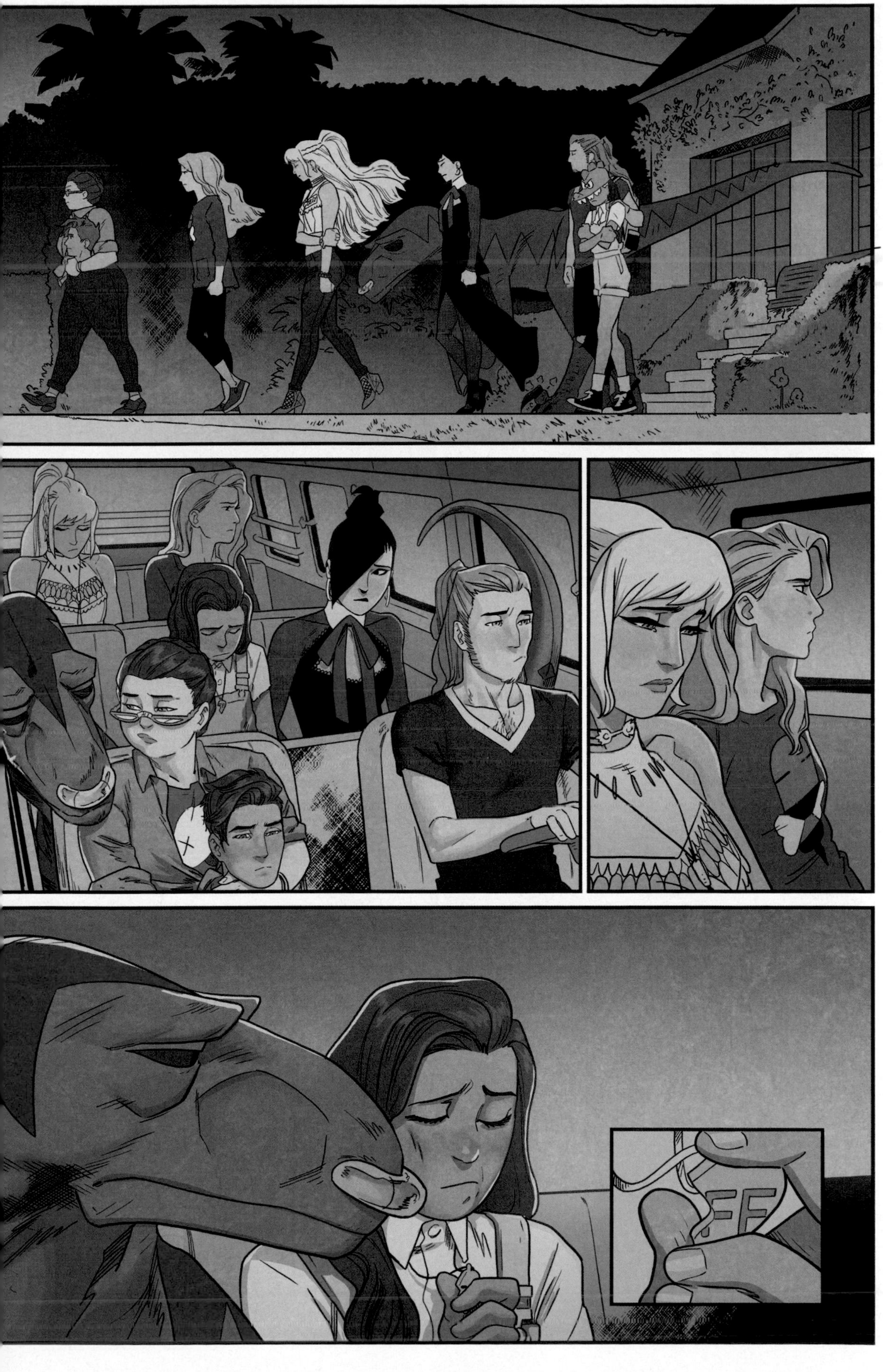

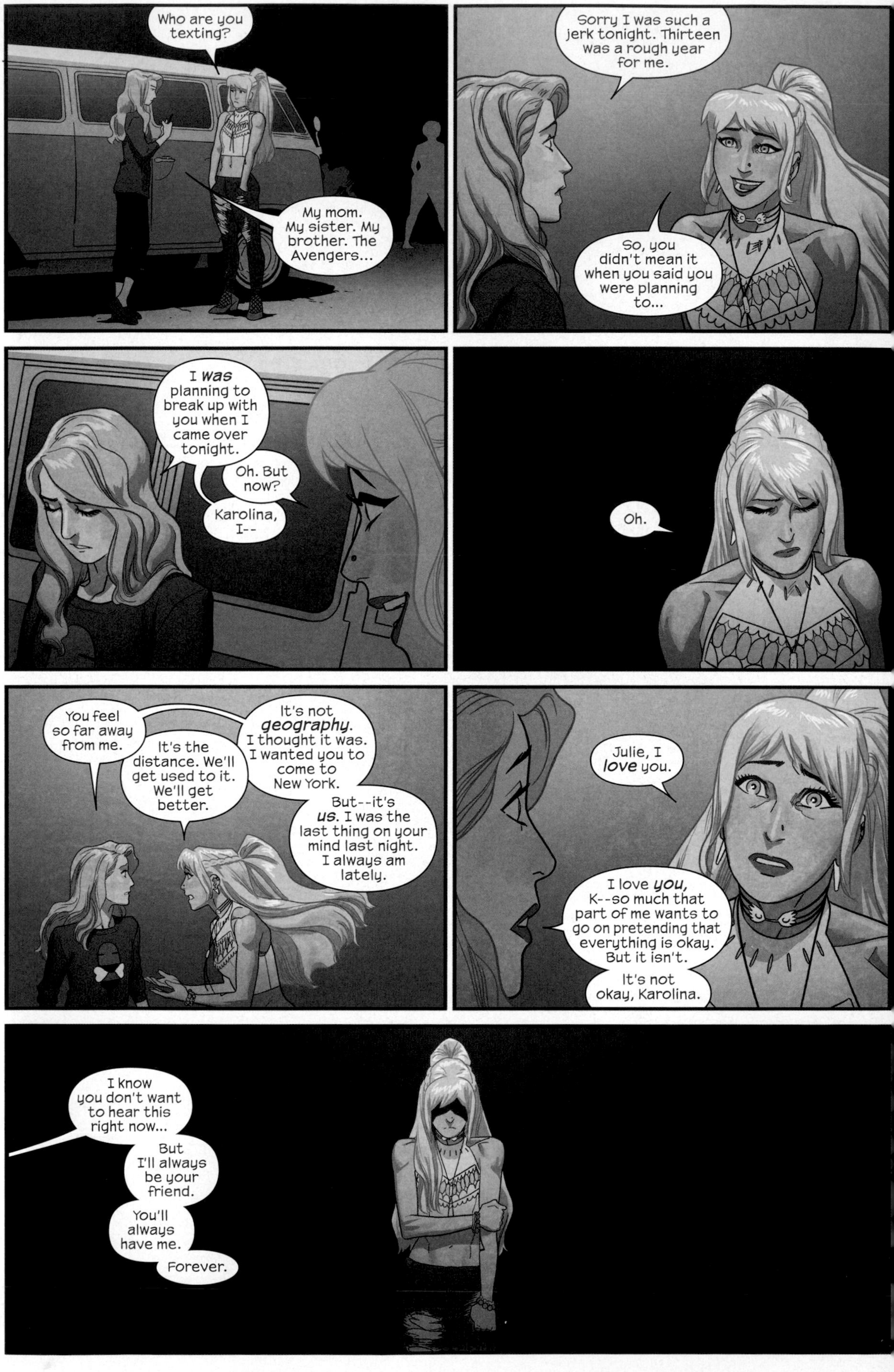
Who are you texting?
My mom. My sister. My brother. The Avengers...
Sorry I was such a jerk tonight. Thirteen was a rough year for me.
So, you didn't mean it when you said you were planning to...
I *was* planning to break up with you when I came over tonight.
Oh. But now?
Karolina, I--
Oh.
You feel so far away from me.
It's the distance. We'll get used to it. We'll get better.
It's not *geography*. I thought it was. I wanted you to come to New York.
But--it's *us*. I was the last thing on your mind last night. I always am lately.
Julie, I *love* you.
I love *you*, K--so much that part of me wants to go on pretending that everything is okay. But it isn't.
It's not okay, Karolina.
I know you don't want to hear this right now...
But I'll always be your friend.
You'll always have me.
Forever.

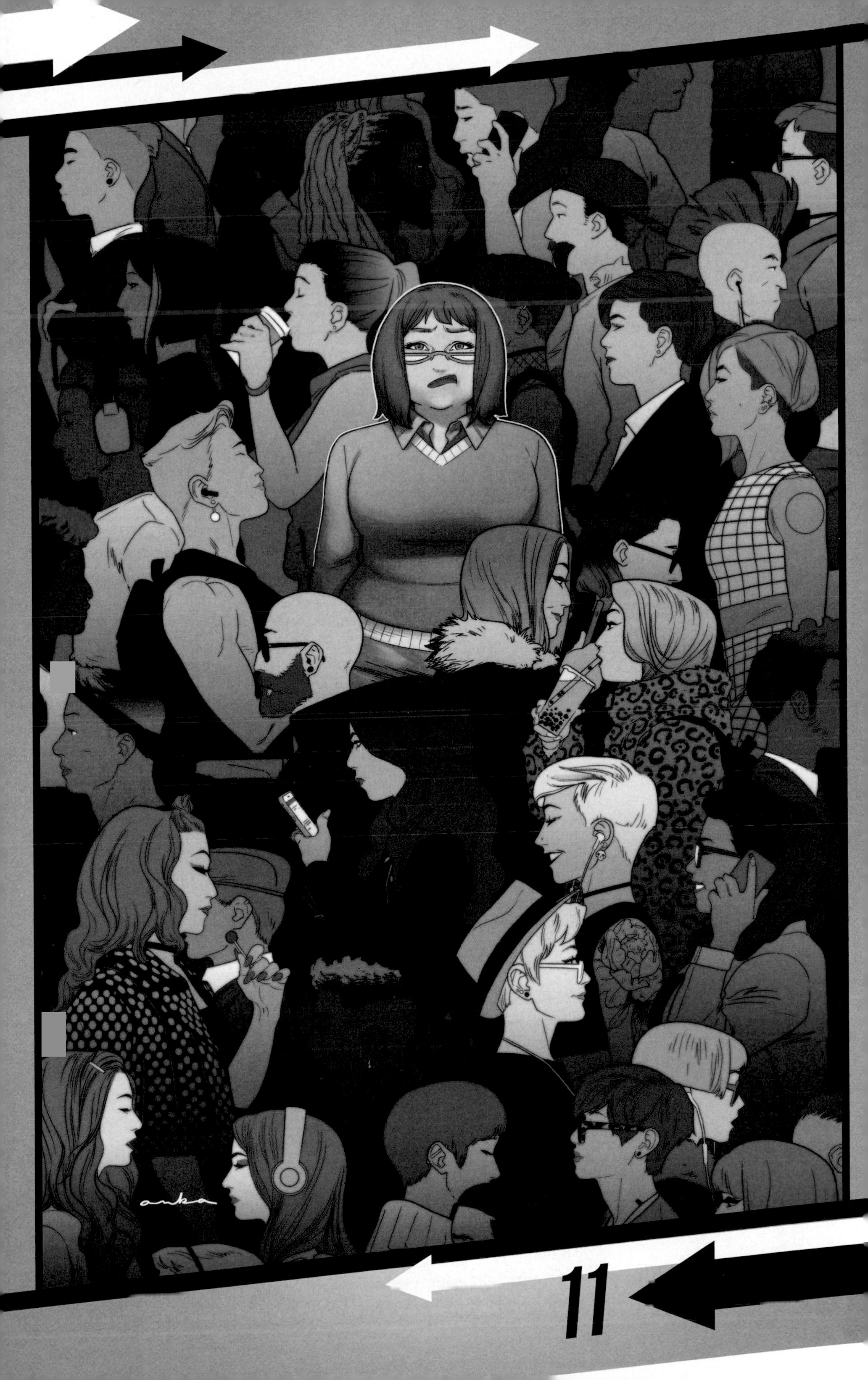
anka
11

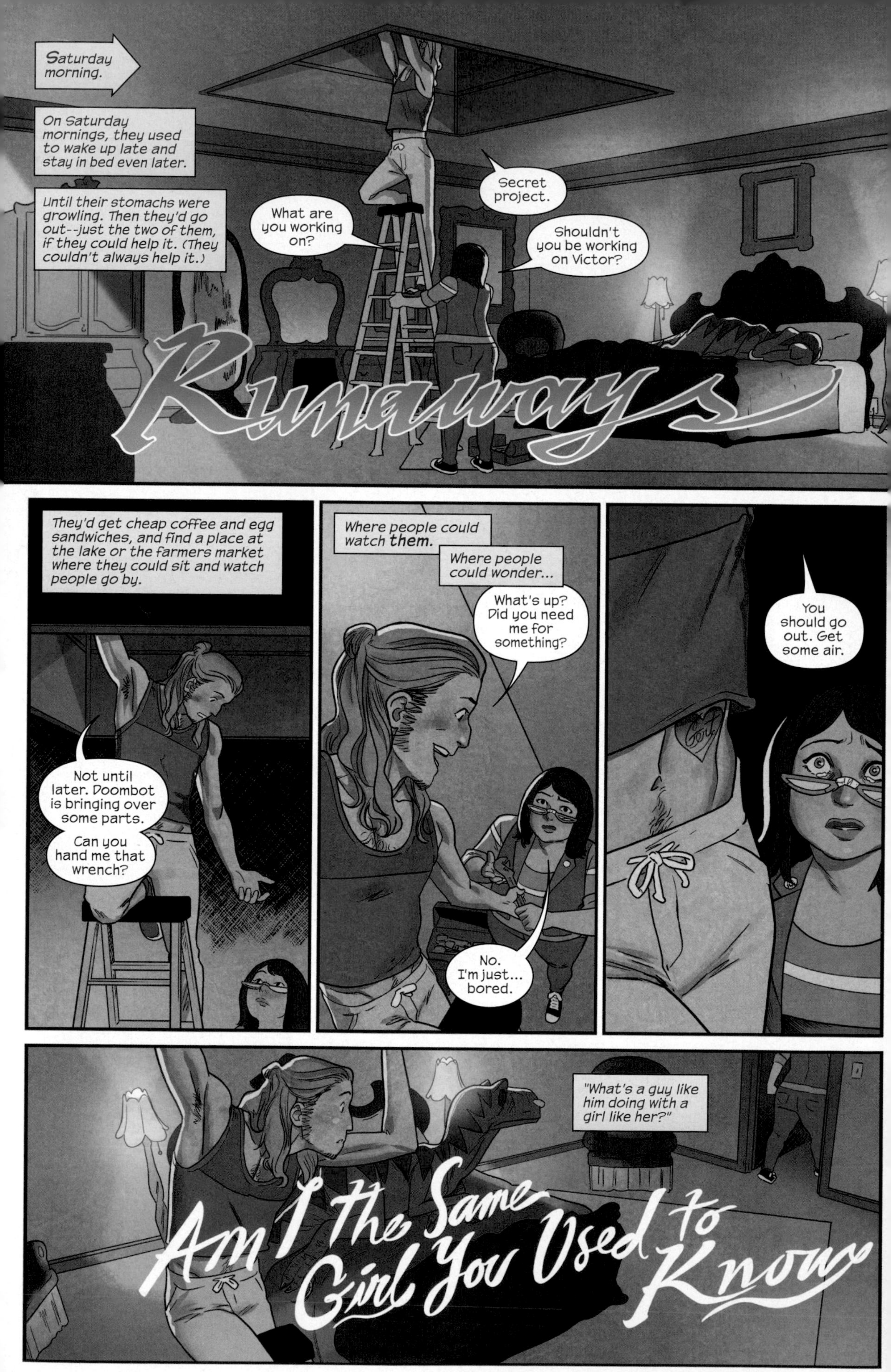
Saturday morning.
On Saturday mornings, they used to wake up late and stay in bed even later.
Until their stomachs were growling. Then they'd go out--just the two of them, if they could help it. (They couldn't always help it.)
What are you working on?
Secret project.
Shouldn't you be working on Victor?
Runaways
They'd get cheap coffee and egg sandwiches, and find a place at the lake or the farmers market where they could sit and watch people go by.
Not until later. Doombot is bringing over some parts.
Can you hand me that wrench?
Where people could watch them.
Where people could wonder...
What's up? Did you need me for something?
No. I'm just... bored.
You should go out. Get some air.
"What's a guy like him doing with a girl like her?"
Am I the Same Girl You Used to Know

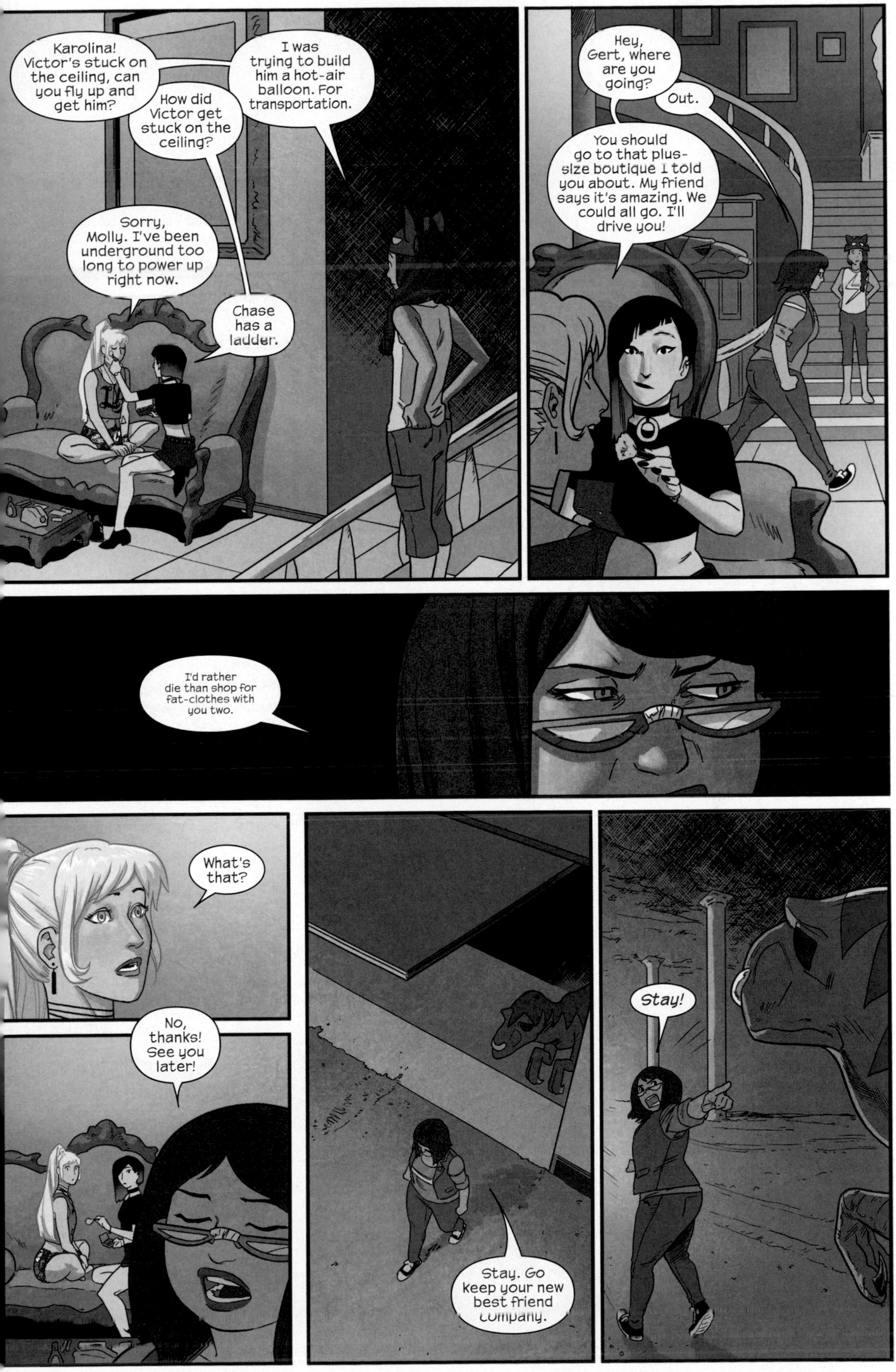
Karolina! Victor's stuck on the ceiling, can you fly up and get him?
I was trying to build him a hot-air balloon. For transportation.
How did Victor get stuck on the ceiling?
Sorry, Molly. I've been underground too long to power up right now.
Chase has a ladder.
Hey, Gert, where are you going?
Out.
You should go to that plus-size boutique I told you about. My friend says it's amazing. We could all go. I'll drive you!
I'd rather die than shop for fat-clothes with you two.
What's that?
No, thanks! See you later!
Stay. Go keep your new best friend company.
Stay!

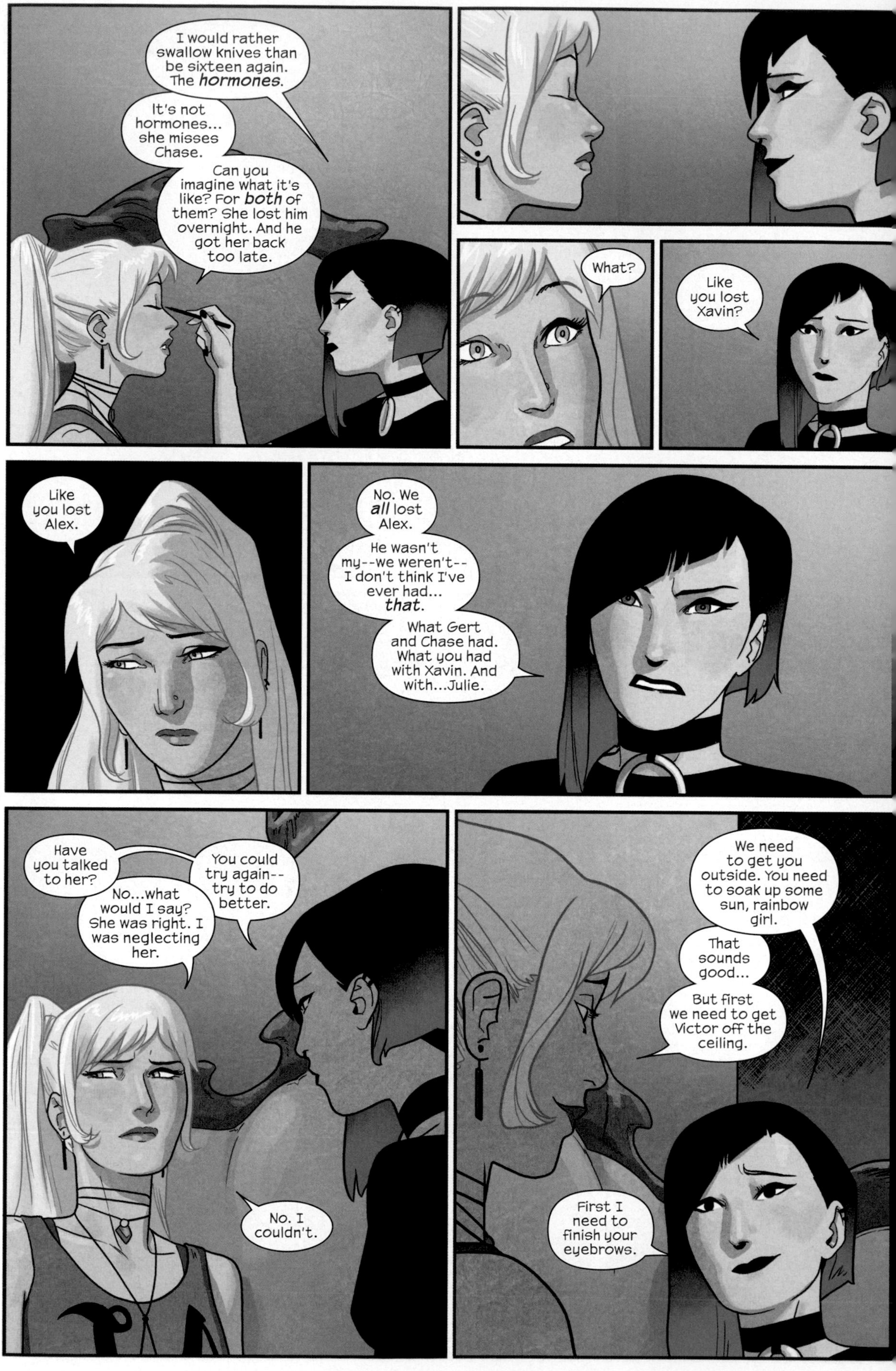
I would rather swallow knives than be sixteen again. The *hormones*.
It's not hormones... she misses Chase.
Can you imagine what it's like? For *both* of them? She lost him overnight. And he got her back too late.
What?
Like you lost Xavin?
Like you lost Alex.
No. We *all* lost Alex.
He wasn't my--we weren't--I don't think I've ever had... *that*.
What Gert and Chase had. What you had with Xavin. And with...Julie.
Have you talked to her?
No...what would I say? She was right. I was neglecting her.
You could try again--try to do better.
No. I couldn't.
We need to get you outside. You need to soak up some sun, rainbow girl.
That sounds good...
But first we need to get Victor off the ceiling.
First I need to finish your eyebrows.

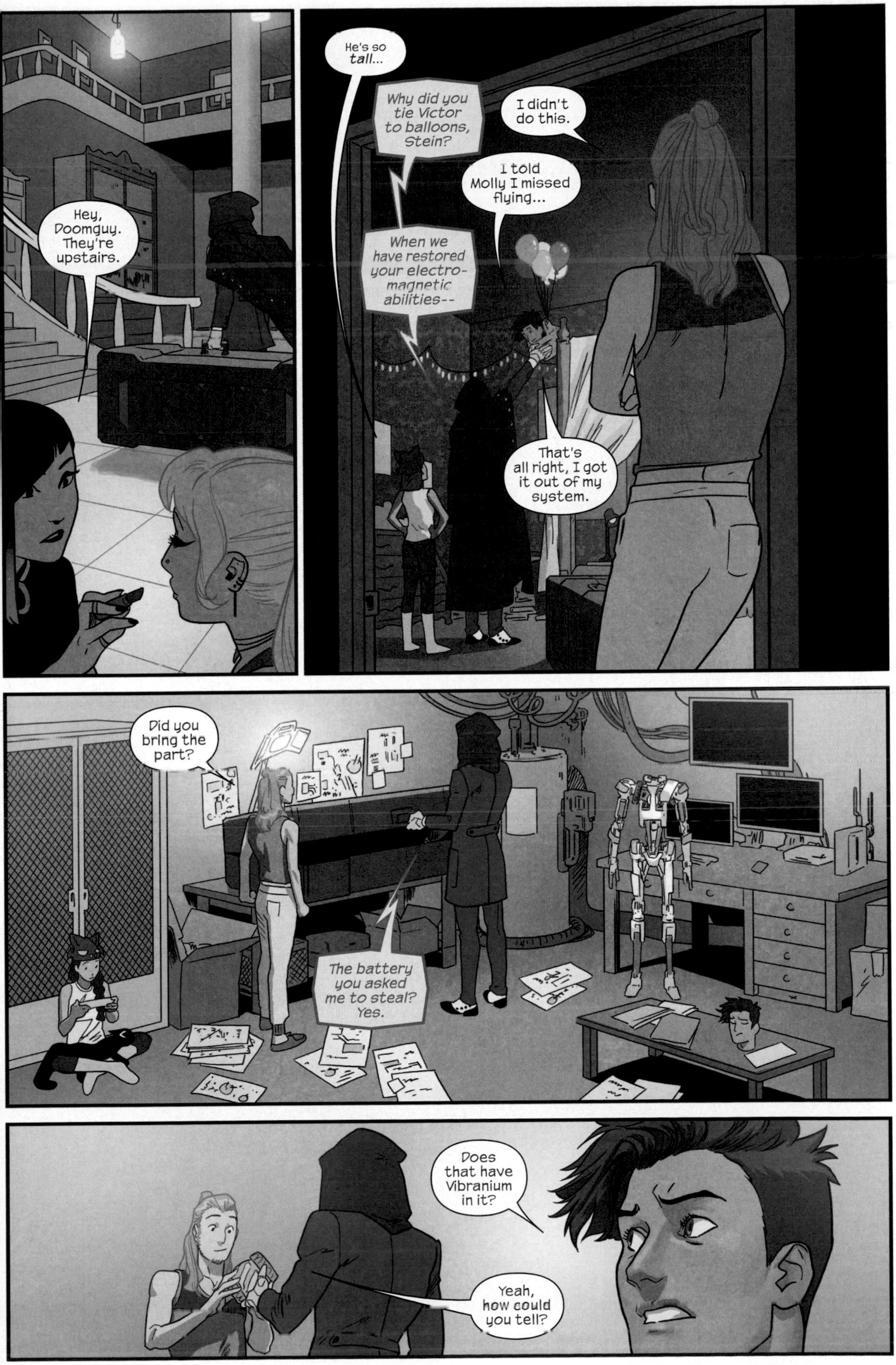
Hey, Doomguy. They're upstairs.
He's so tall...
Why did you tie Victor to balloons, Stein?
When we have restored your electro-magnetic abilities--
I didn't do this.
I told Molly I missed flying...
That's all right, I got it out of my system.
Did you bring the part?
The battery you asked me to steal? Yes.
Does that have Vibranium in it?
Yeah, how could you tell?

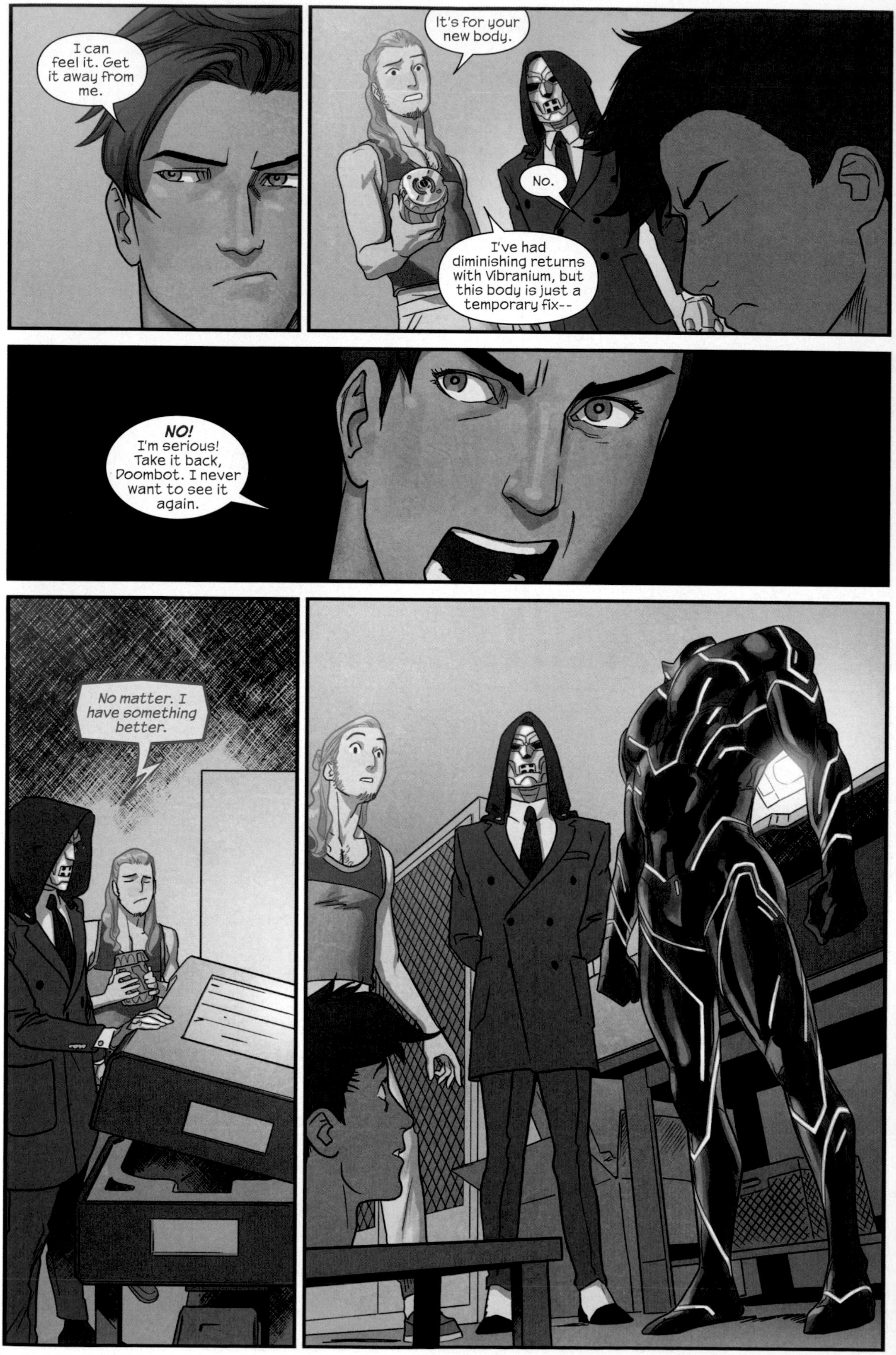
I can feel it. Get it away from me.
It's for your new body.
No.
I've had diminishing returns with Vibranium, but this body is just a temporary fix--
NO! I'm serious! Take it back, Doombot. I never want to see it again.
No matter. I have something better.

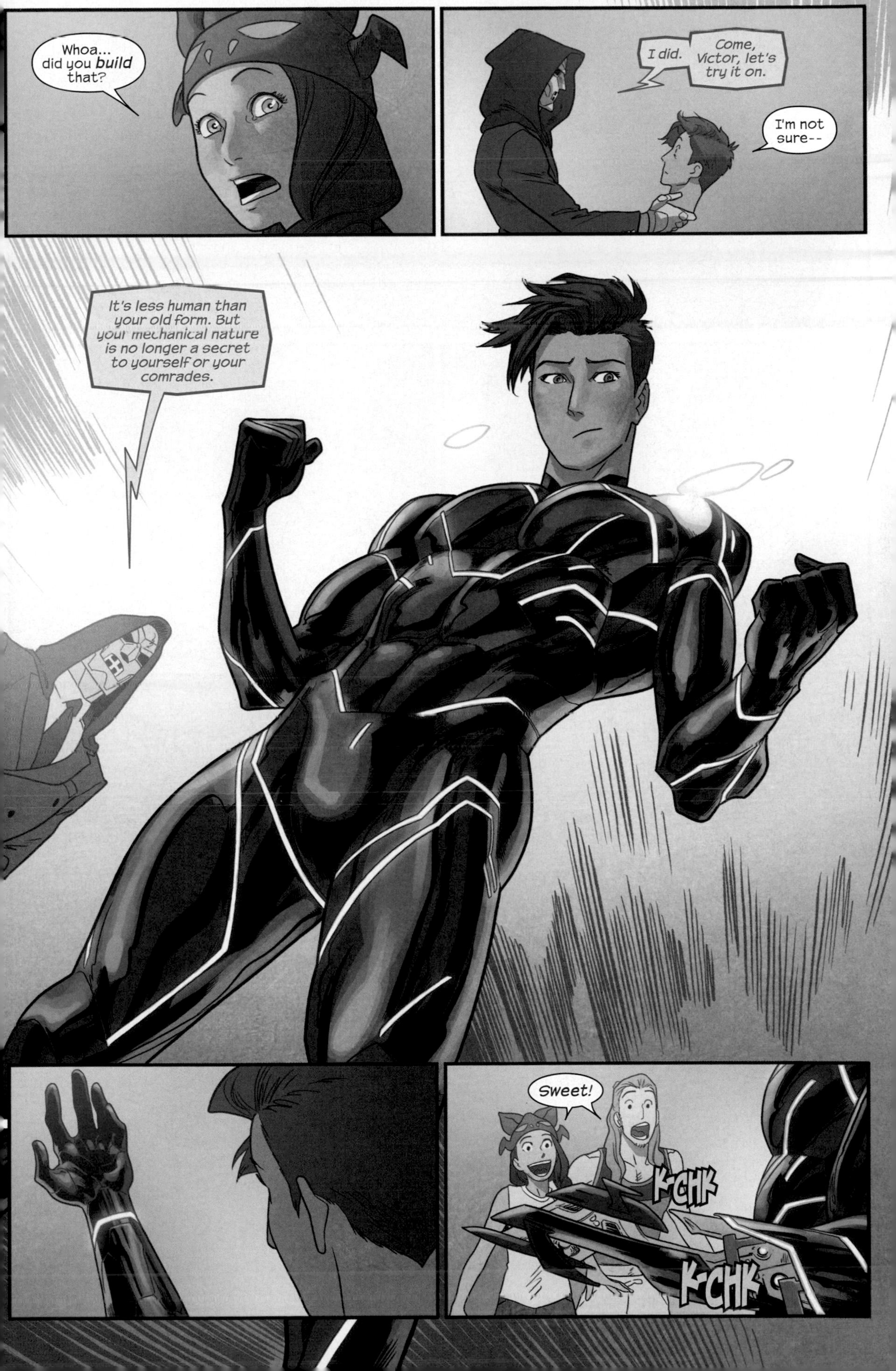
Whoa... did you build that?
I did.
Come, Victor, let's try it on.
I'm not sure--
It's less human than your old form. But your mechanical nature is no longer a secret to yourself or your comrades.
Sweet!
K-CHK
K-CHK

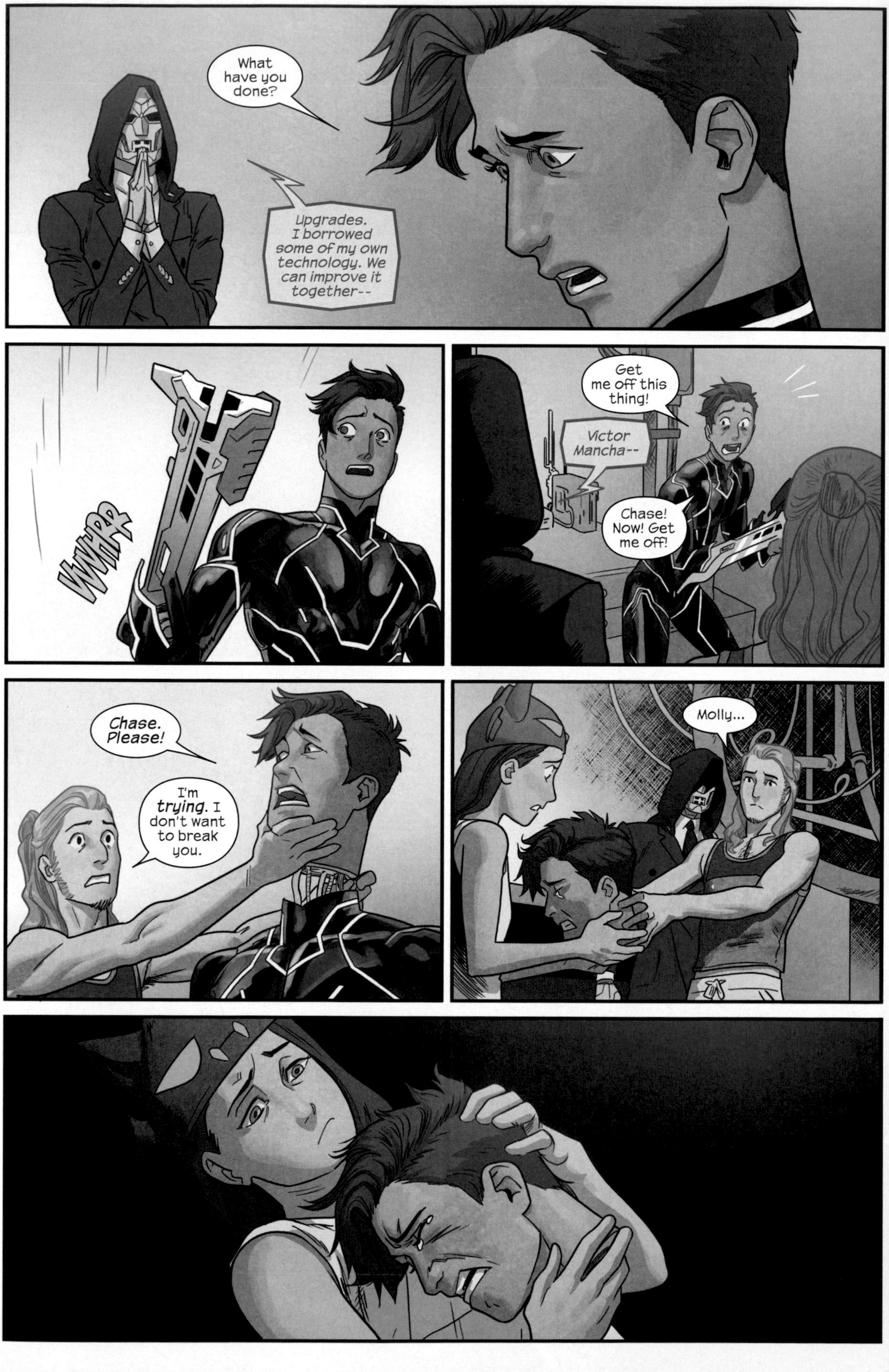
What have you done?
Upgrades. I borrowed some of my own technology. We can improve it together--
WHRR
Get me off this thing!
Victor Mancha--
Chase! Now! Get me off!
Chase. Please!
I'm *trying*. I don't want to break you.
Molly...

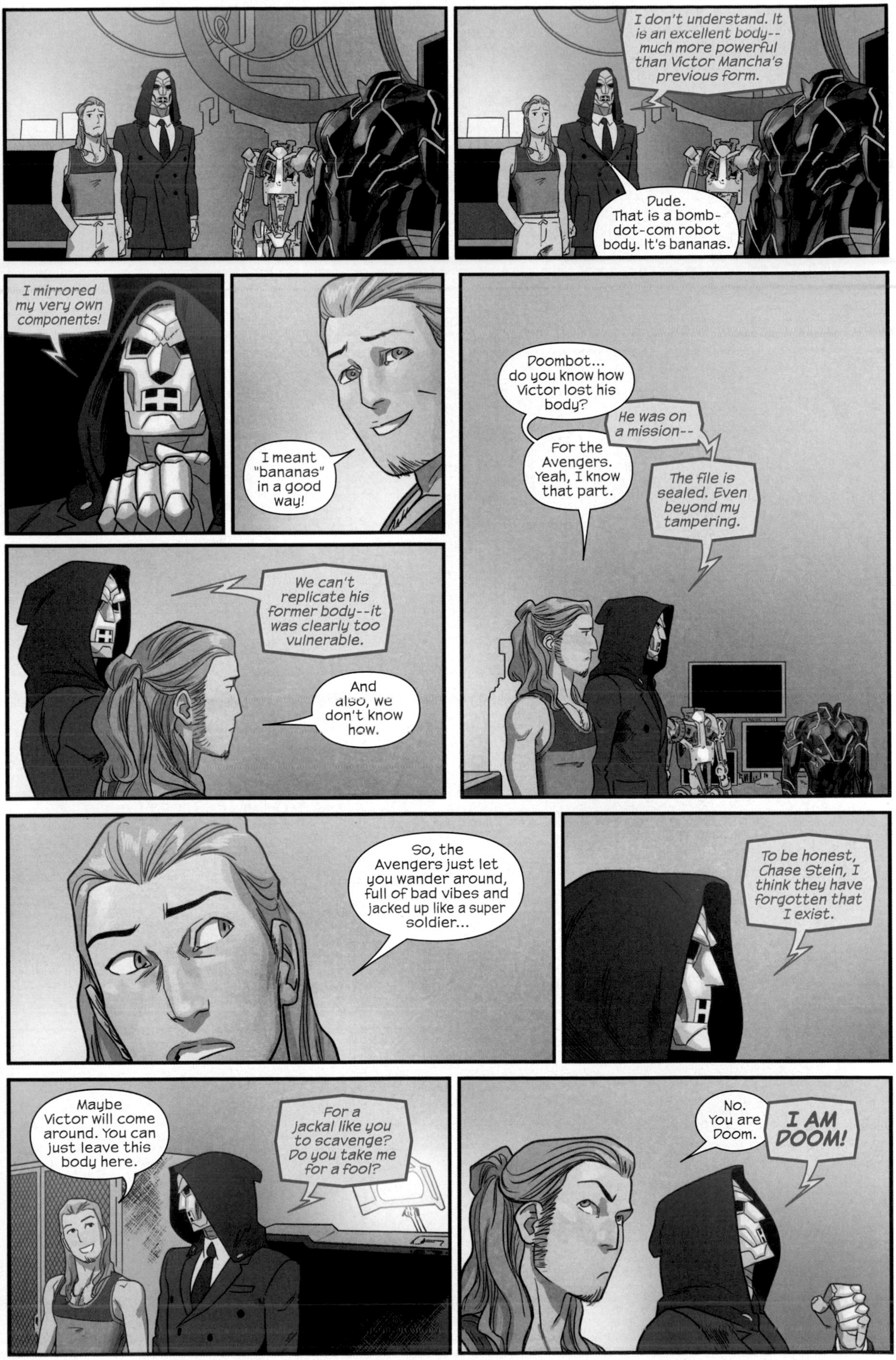
I don't understand. It is an excellent body--much more powerful than Victor Mancha's previous form.
Dude. That is a bomb-dot-com robot body. It's bananas.
I mirrored my very own components!
I meant "bananas" in a good way!
We can't replicate his former body--it was clearly too vulnerable.
And also, we don't know how.
Doombot... do you know how Victor lost his body?
He was on a mission--
For the Avengers. Yeah, I know that part.
The file is sealed. Even beyond my tampering.
So, the Avengers just let you wander around, full of bad vibes and jacked up like a super soldier...
To be honest, Chase Stein, I think they have forgotten that I exist.
Maybe Victor will come around. You can just leave this body here.
For a jackal like you to scavenge? Do you take me for a fool?
No. You are Doom.
I AM DOOM!

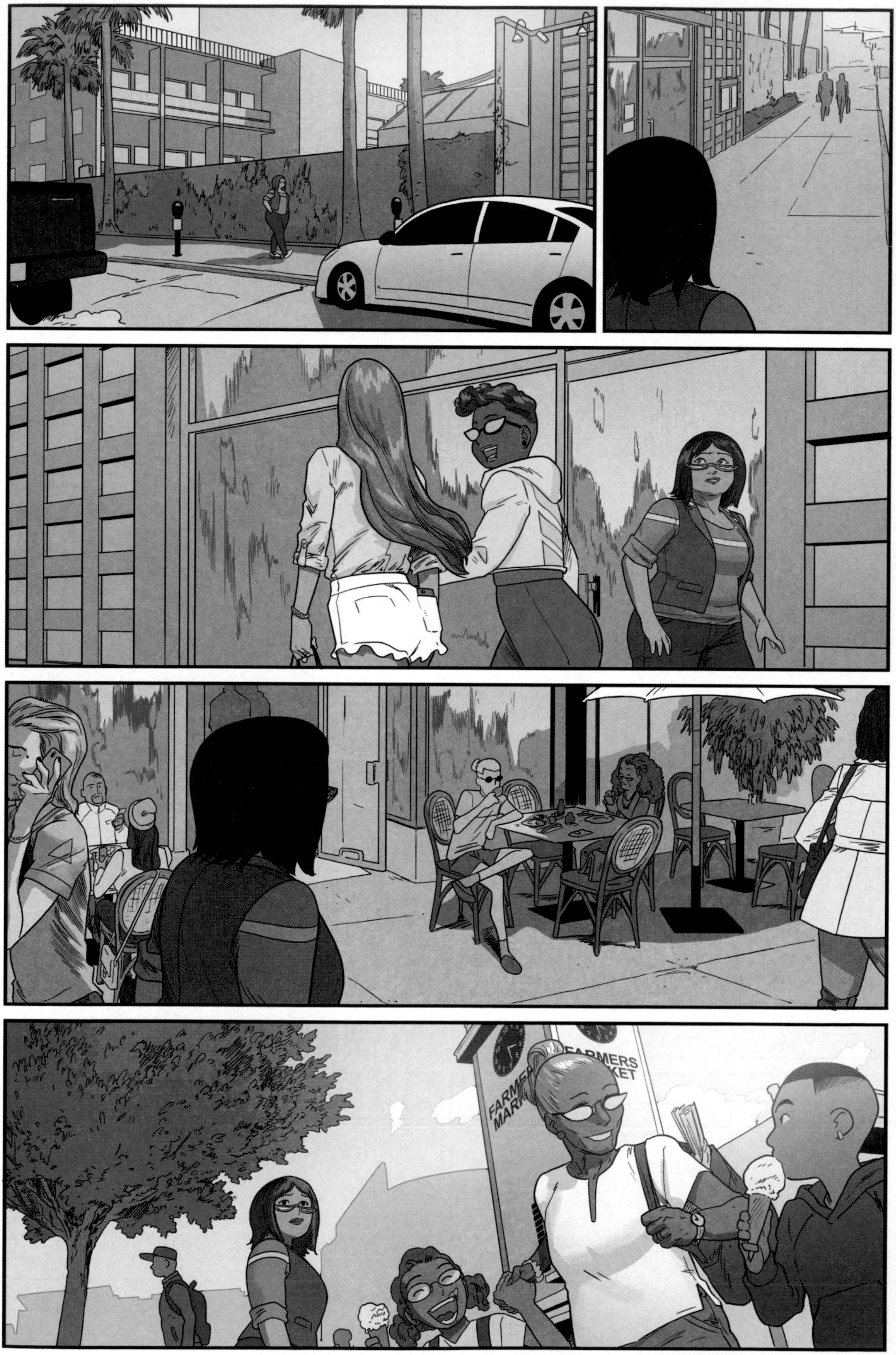
FARMERS

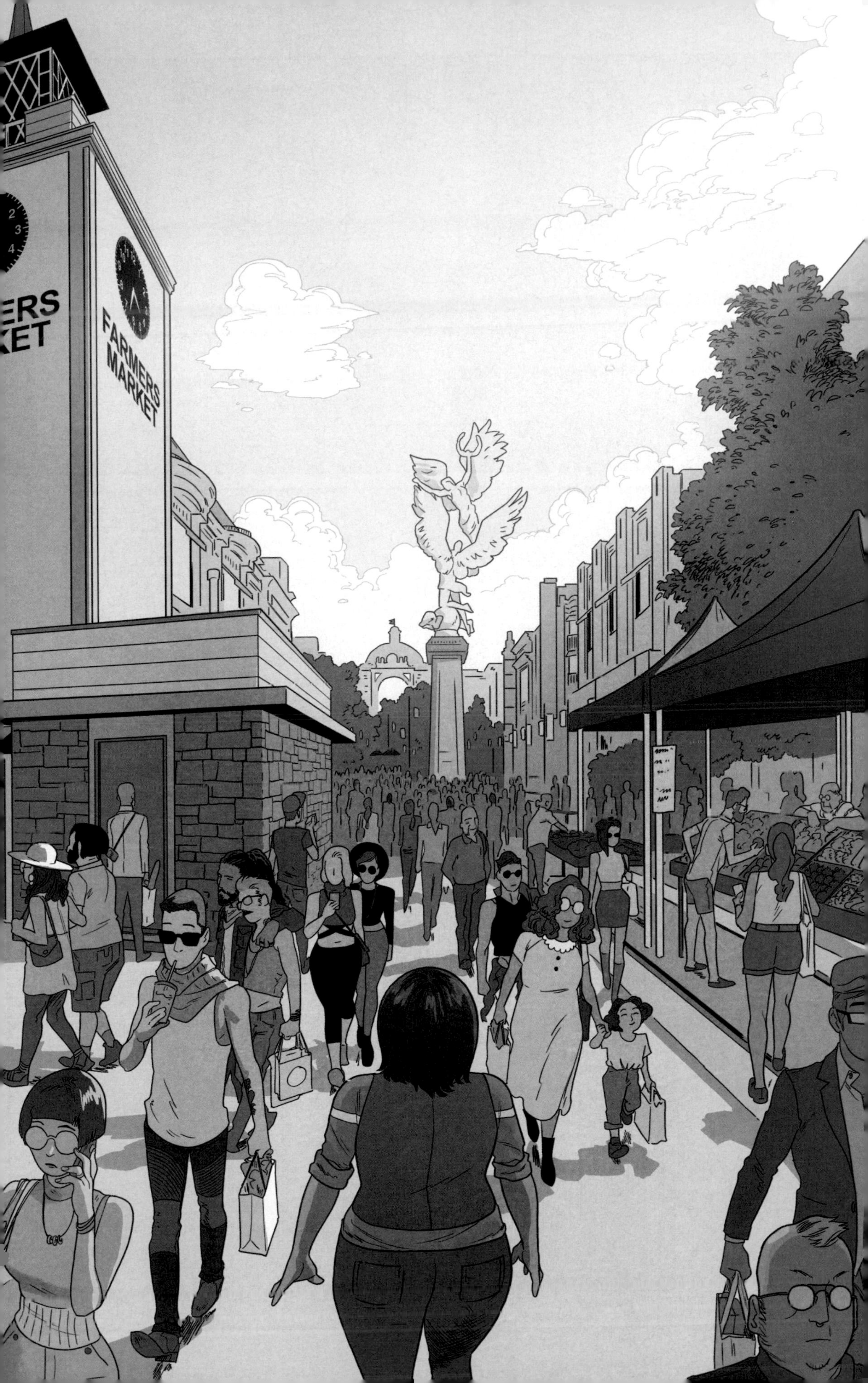
FARMERS MARKET
ERS
KET

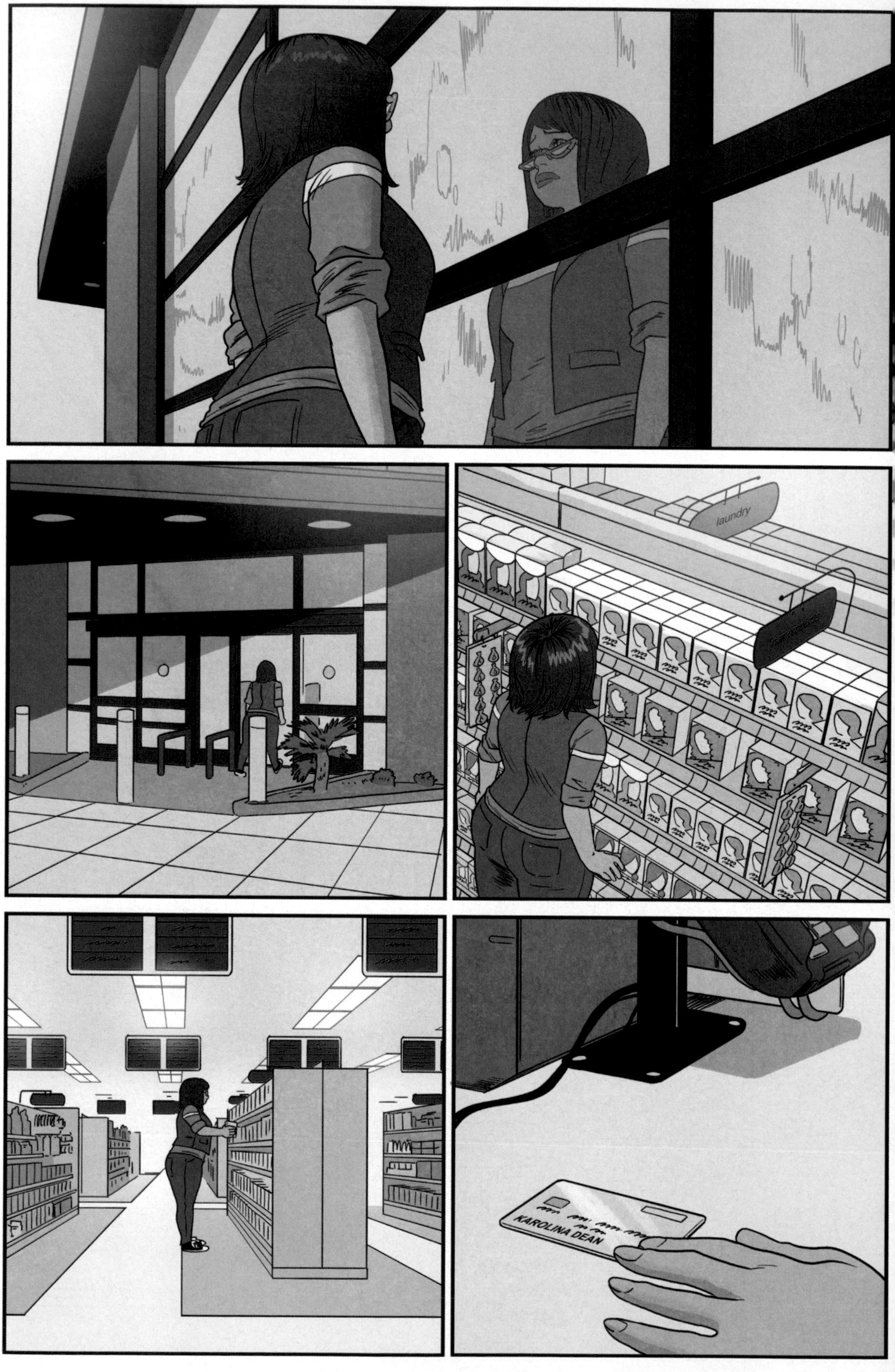
laundry
KAROLINA DEAN

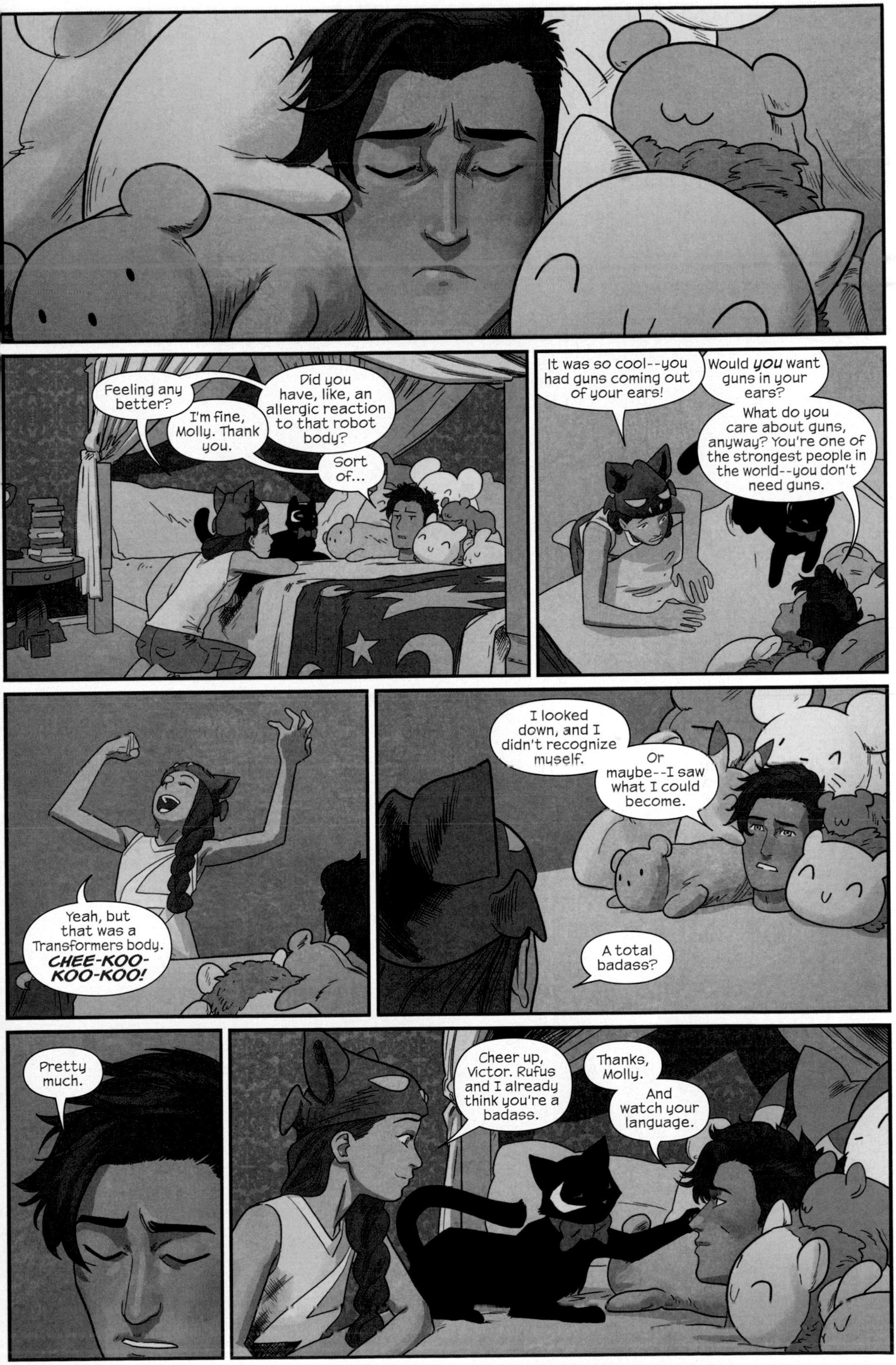
Feeling any better?
Did you have, like, an allergic reaction to that robot body?
I'm fine, Molly. Thank you.
Sort of...
It was so cool--you had guns coming out of your ears!
Would *you* want guns in your ears?
What do you care about guns, anyway? You're one of the strongest people in the world--you don't need guns.
Yeah, but that was a Transformers body. ***CHEE-KOO-KOO-KOO!***
I looked down, and I didn't recognize myself.
Or maybe--I saw what I could become.
A total badass?
Pretty much.
Cheer up, Victor. Rufus and I already think you're a badass.
Thanks, Molly.
And watch your language.

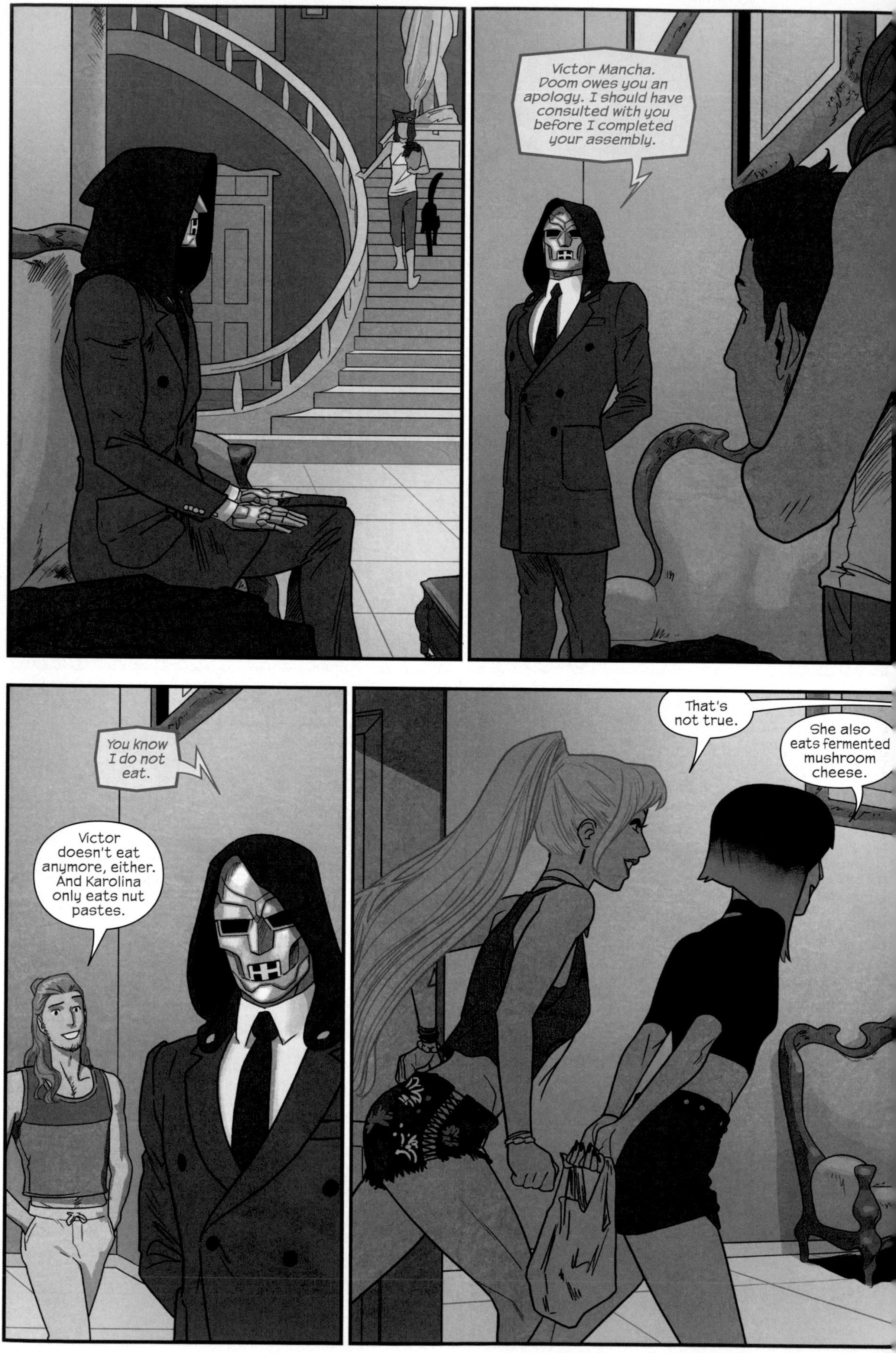
Victor Mancha. Doom owes you an apology. I should have consulted with you before I completed your assembly.
You know I do not eat.
Victor doesn't eat anymore, either. And Karolina only eats nut pastes.
That's not true.
She also eats fermented mushroom cheese.

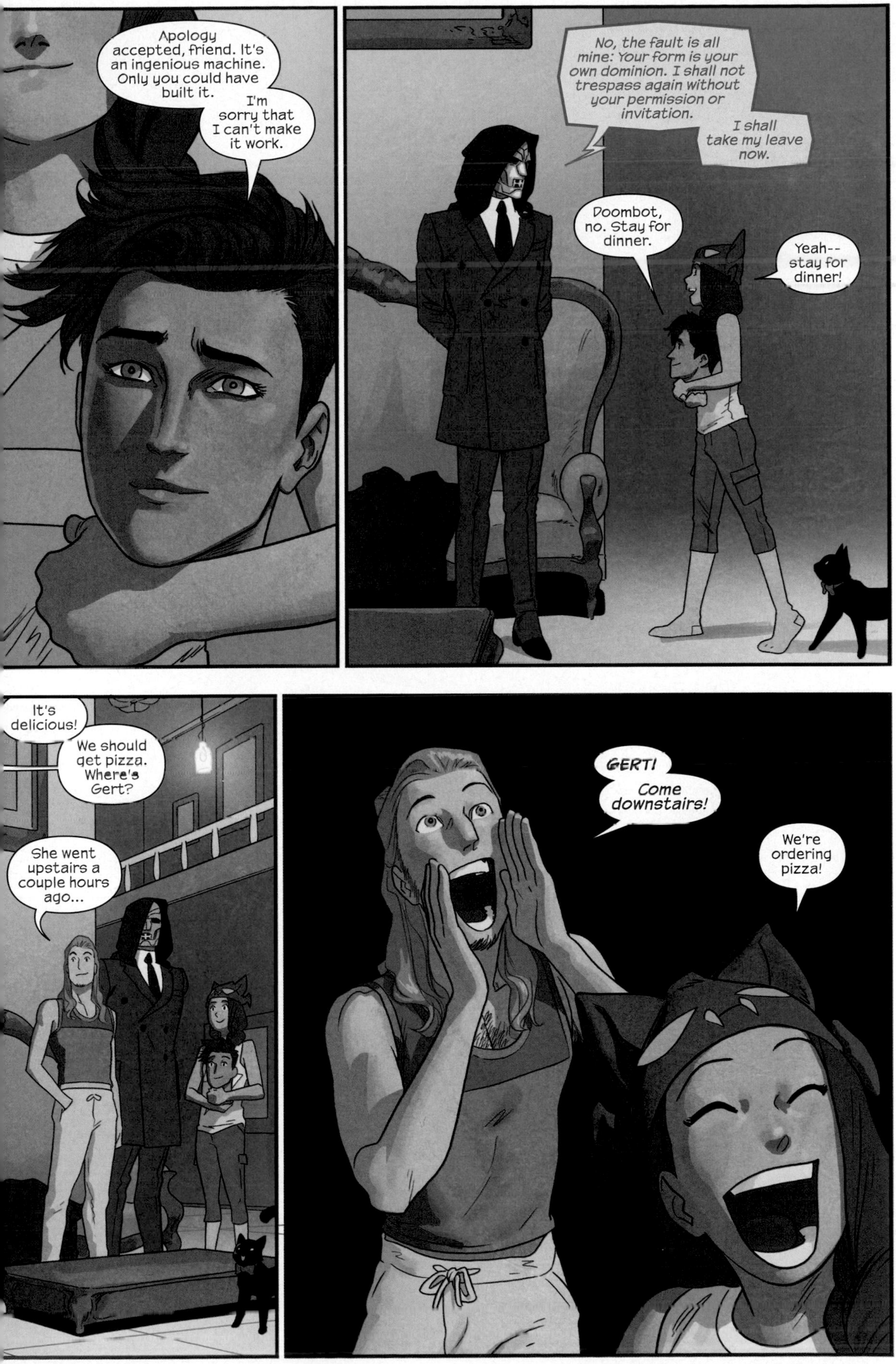
Apology accepted, friend. It's an ingenious machine. Only you could have built it.
I'm sorry that I can't make it work.
No, the fault is all mine: Your form is your own dominion. I shall not trespass again without your permission or invitation.
I shall take my leave now.
Doombot, no. Stay for dinner.
Yeah-- stay for dinner!
It's delicious!
We should get pizza. Where's Gert?
She went upstairs a couple hours ago...
GERT!
Come downstairs!
We're ordering pizza!

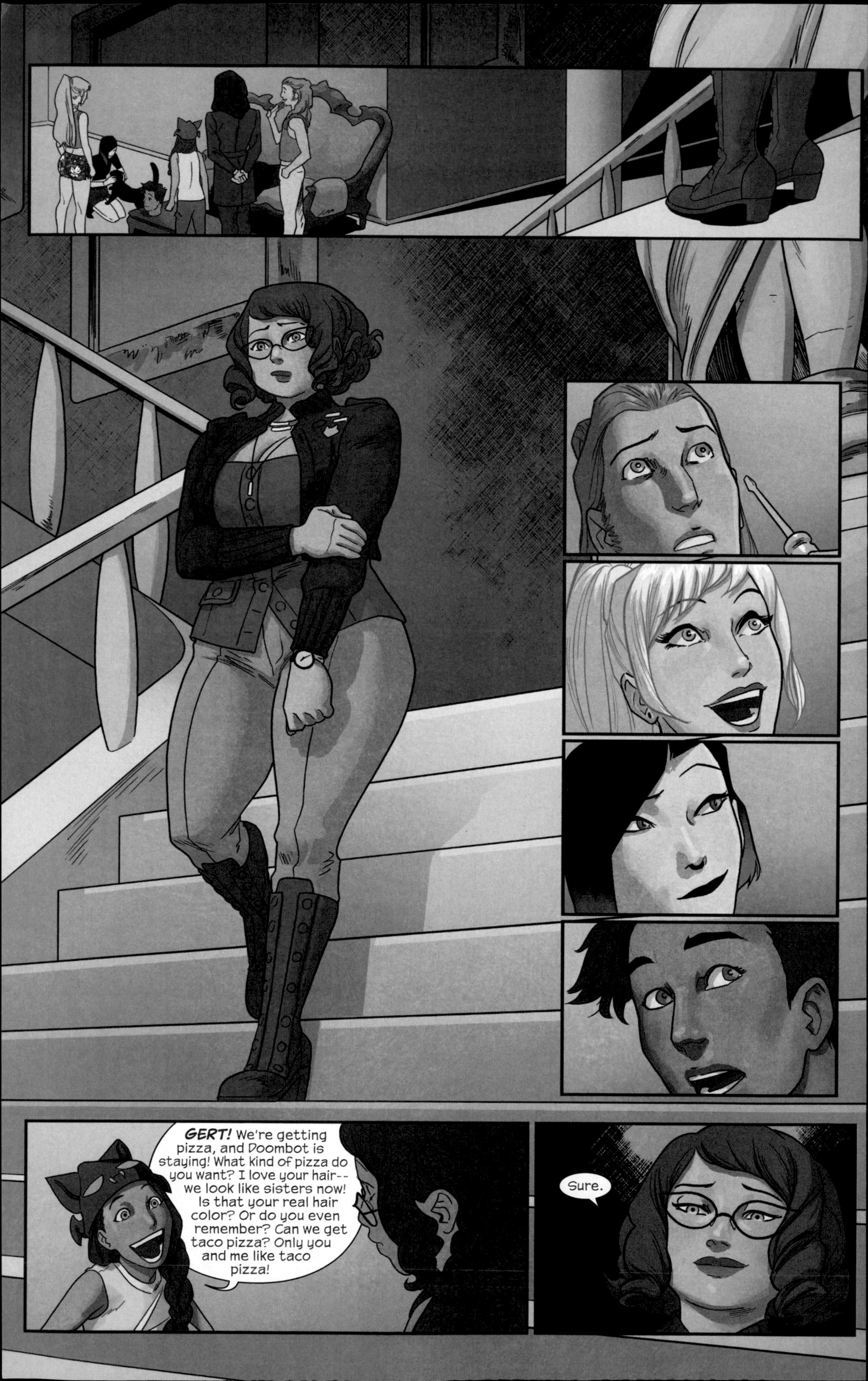

GERT! We're getting pizza, and Doombot is staying! What kind of pizza do you want? I love your hair-- we look like sisters now! Is that your real hair color? Or do you even remember? Can we get taco pizza? Only you and me like taco pizza!
Sure.

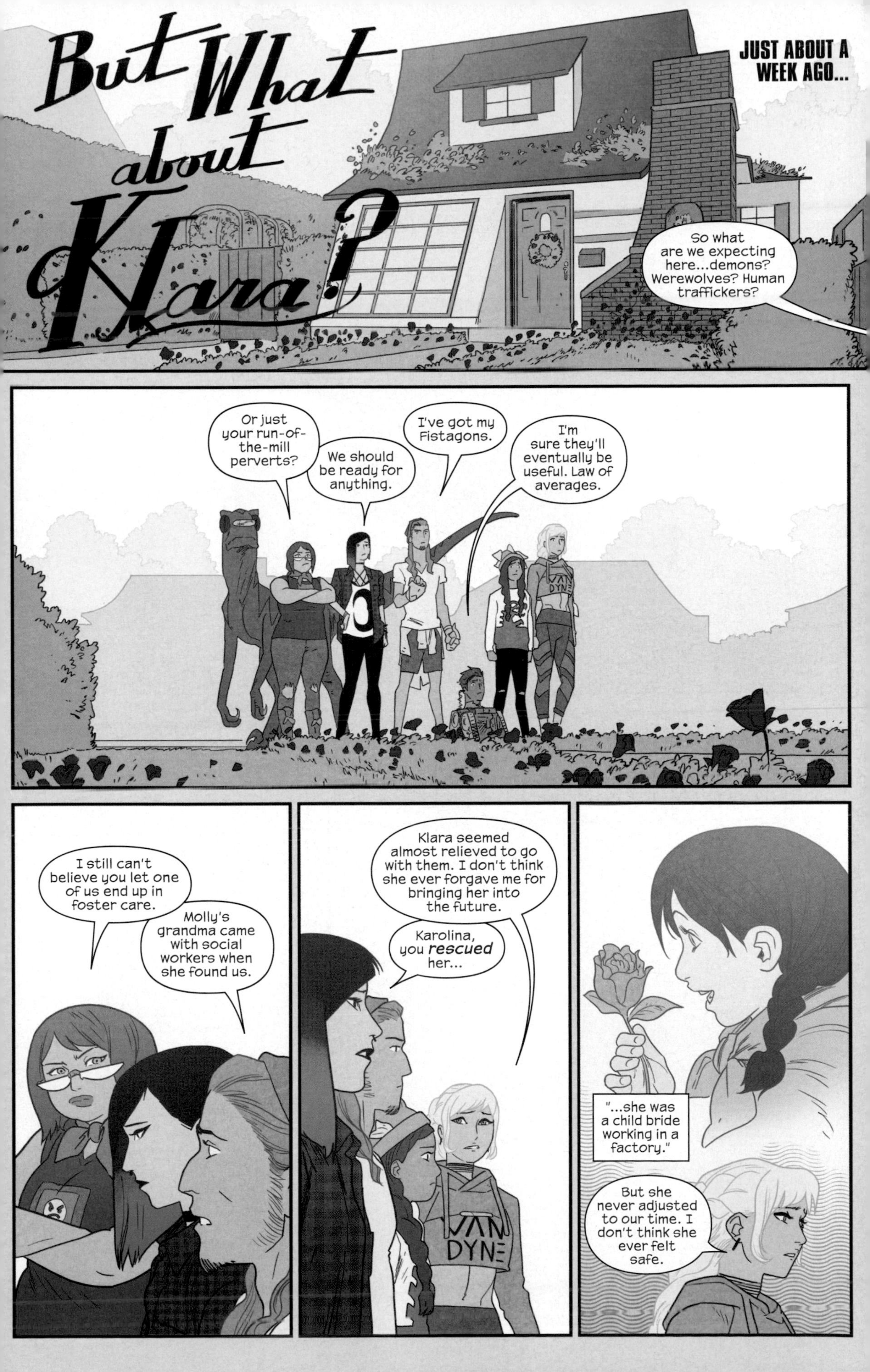
But What about Klara?
JUST ABOUT A WEEK AGO...
So what are we expecting here...demons? Werewolves? Human traffickers?
Or just your run-of-the-mill perverts?
We should be ready for anything.
I've got my Fistagons.
I'm sure they'll eventually be useful. Law of averages.
I still can't believe you let one of us end up in foster care.
Molly's grandma came with social workers when she found us.
Klara seemed almost relieved to go with them. I don't think she ever forgave me for bringing her into the future.
Karolina, you *rescued* her...
"...she was a child bride working in a factory."
But she never adjusted to our time. I don't think she ever felt safe.

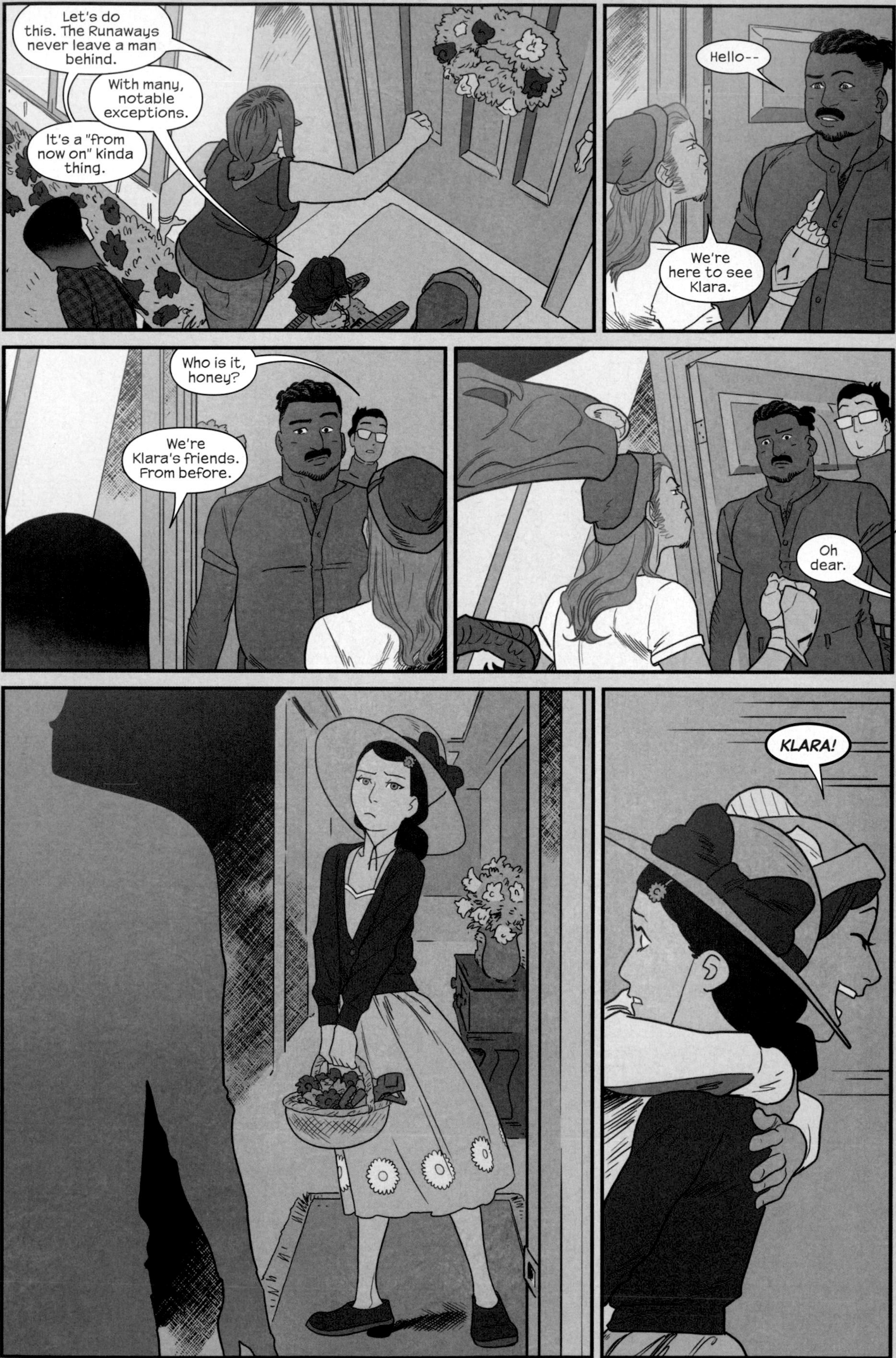
Let's do this. The Runaways never leave a man behind.
With many, notable exceptions.
It's a "from now on" kinda thing.
Hello--
We're here to see Klara.
Who is it, honey?
We're Klara's friends. From before.
Oh dear.
KLARA!

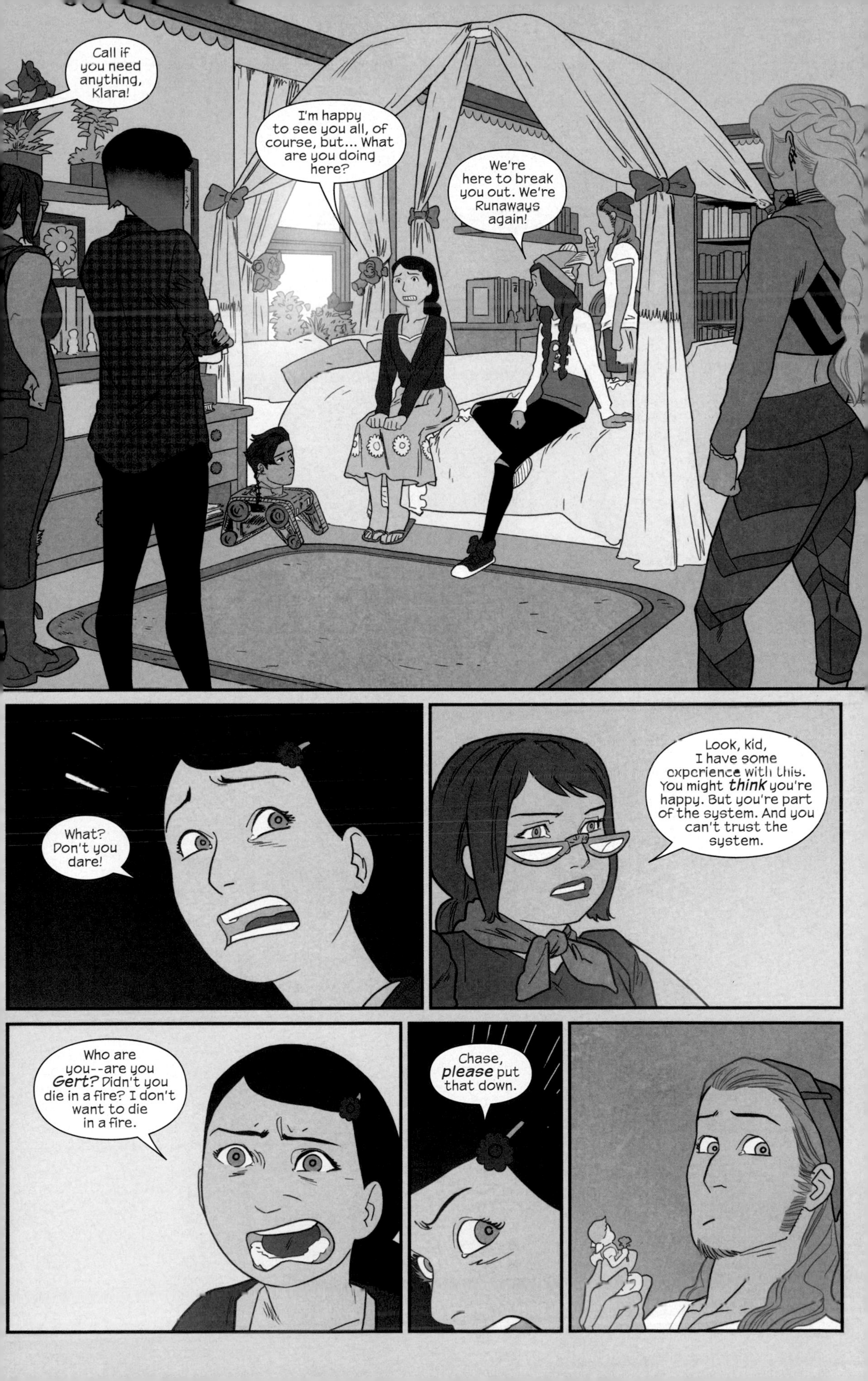
Call if you need anything, Klara!
I'm happy to see you all, of course, but... What are you doing here?
We're here to break you out. We're Runaways again!
What? Don't you dare!
Look, kid, I have some experience with this. You might *think* you're happy. But you're part of the system. And you can't trust the system.
Who are you--are you *Gert?* Didn't you die in a fire? I don't want to die in a fire.
Chase, *please* put that down.

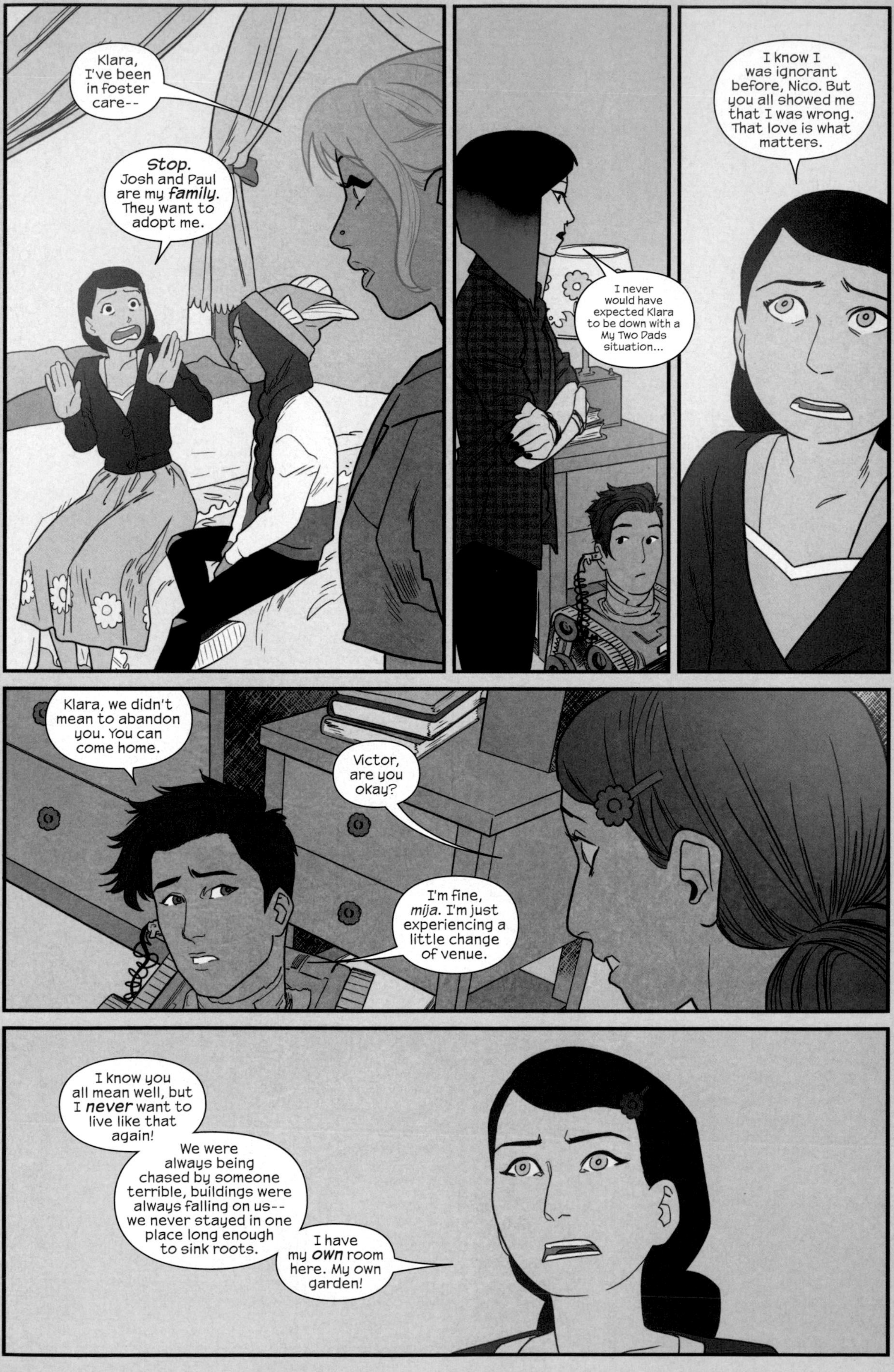
Klara, I've been in foster care--
Stop. Josh and Paul are my family. They want to adopt me.
I never would have expected Klara to be down with a My Two Dads situation...
I know I was ignorant before, Nico. But you all showed me that I was wrong. That love is what matters.
Klara, we didn't mean to abandon you. You can come home.
Victor, are you okay?
I'm fine, mija. I'm just experiencing a little change of venue.
I know you all mean well, but I never want to live like that again!
We were always being chased by someone terrible, buildings were always falling on us-- we never stayed in one place long enough to sink roots.
I have my own room here. My own garden!

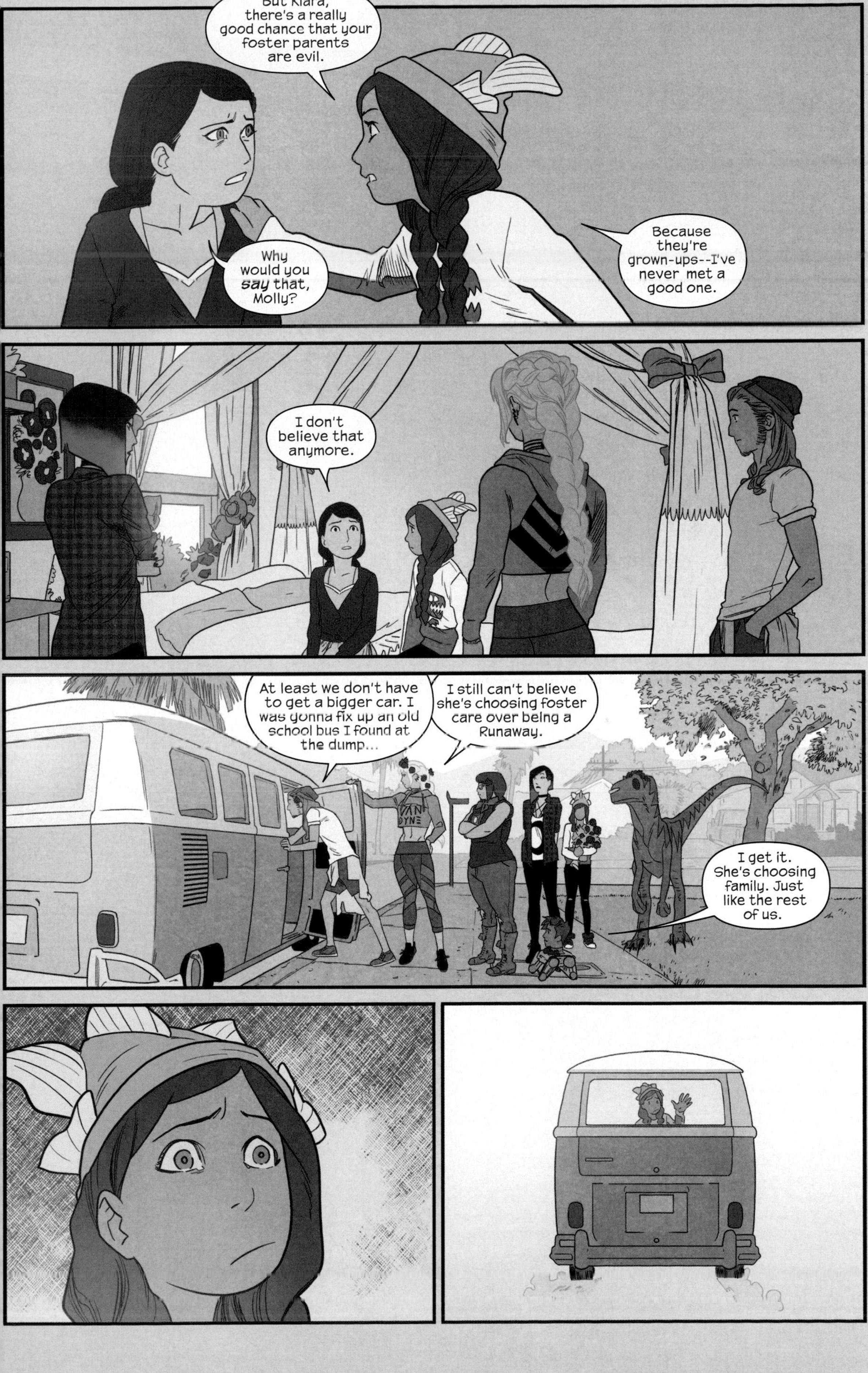
But Klara, there's a really good chance that your foster parents are evil.
Why would you *say* that, Molly?
Because they're grown-ups--I've never met a good one.
I don't believe that anymore.
At least we don't have to get a bigger car. I was gonna fix up an old school bus I found at the dump...
I still can't believe she's choosing foster care over being a Runaway.
I get it. She's choosing family. Just like the rest of us.

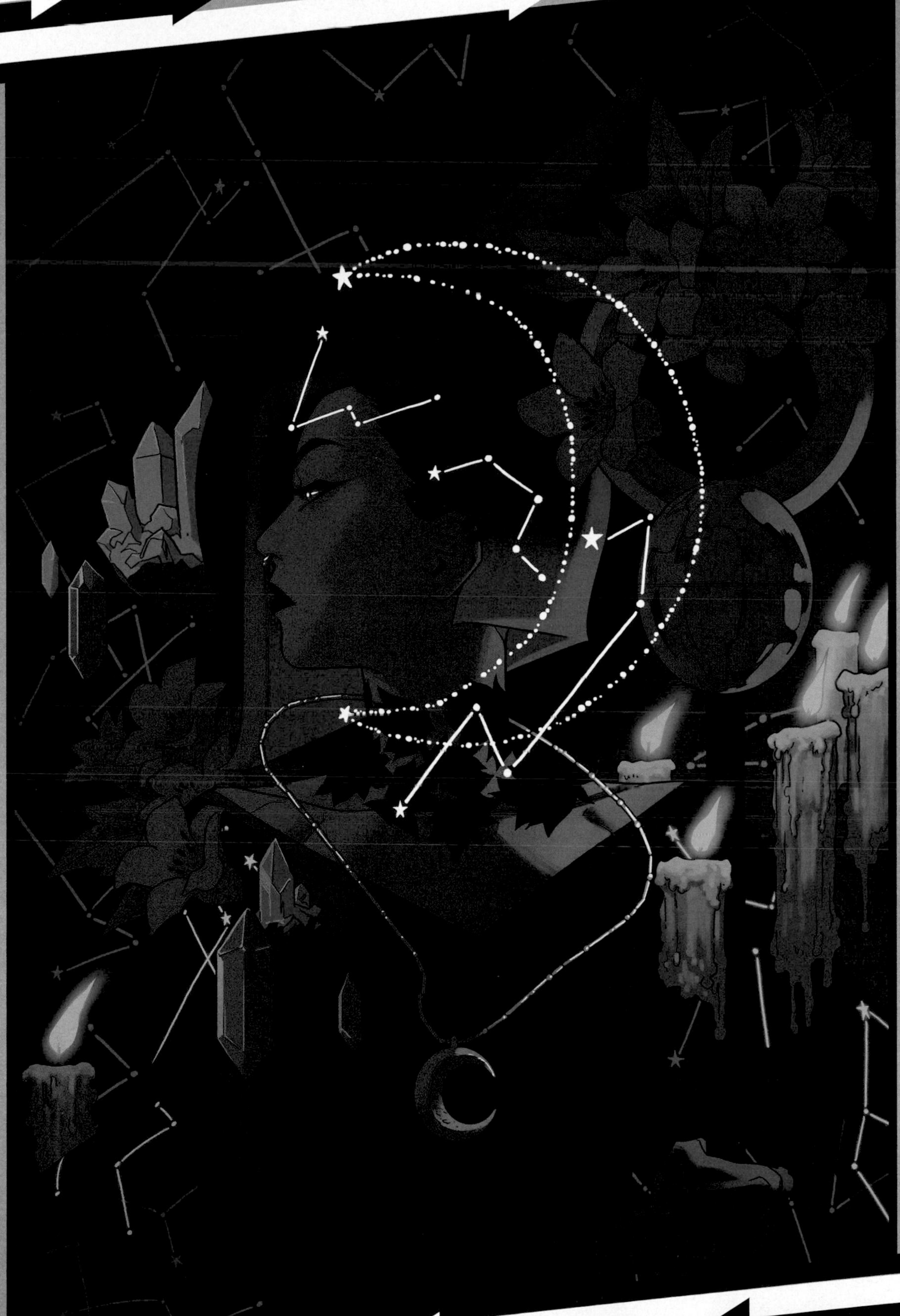

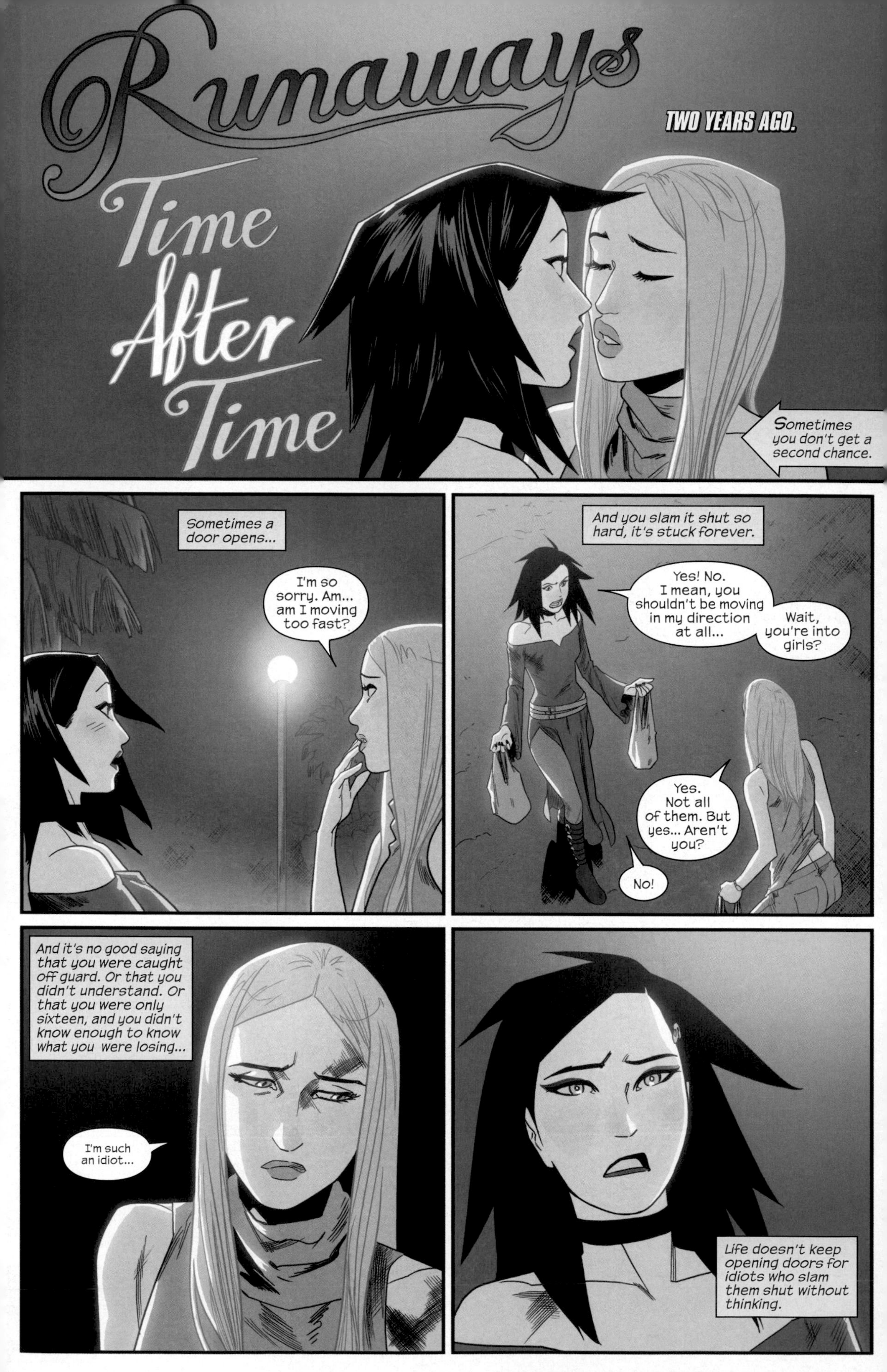
Runaways
Time After Time
TWO YEARS AGO.
Sometimes you don't get a second chance.
Sometimes a door opens...
I'm so sorry. Am... am I moving too fast?
And you slam it shut so hard, it's stuck forever.
Yes! No. I mean, you shouldn't be moving in my direction at all...
Wait, you're into girls?
Yes. Not all of them. But yes... Aren't you?
No!
And it's no good saying that you were caught off guard. Or that you didn't understand. Or that you were only sixteen, and you didn't know enough to know what you were losing...
I'm such an idiot...
Life doesn't keep opening doors for idiots who slam them shut without thinking.

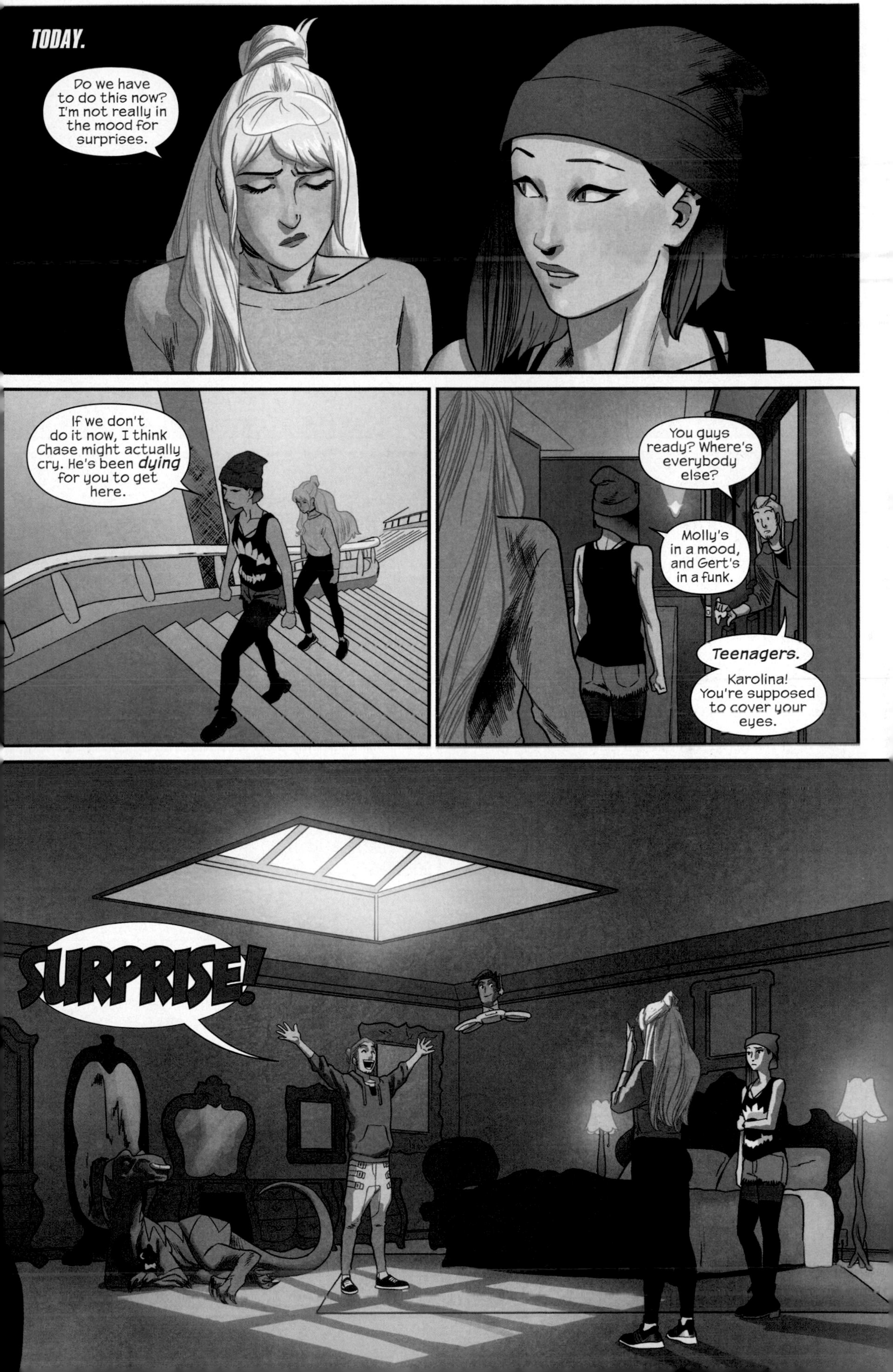
TODAY.
Do we have to do this now? I'm not really in the mood for surprises.
If we don't do it now, I think Chase might actually cry. He's been *dying* for you to get here.
You guys ready? Where's everybody else?
Molly's in a mood, and Gert's in a funk.
Teenagers.
Karolina! You're supposed to cover your eyes.
SURPRISE!

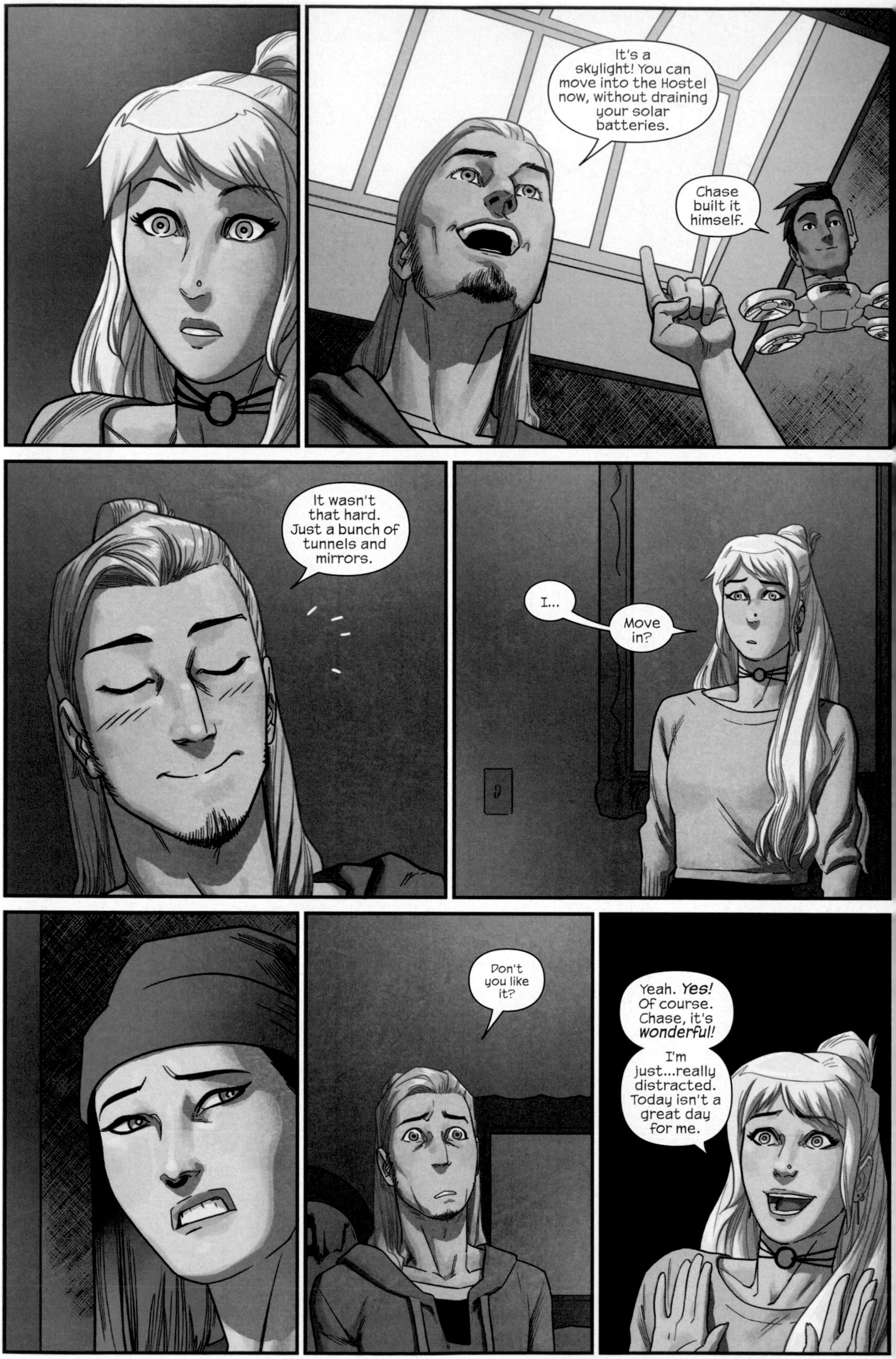
It's a skylight! You can move into the Hostel now, without draining your solar batteries.
Chase built it himself.
It wasn't that hard. Just a bunch of tunnels and mirrors.
I...
Move in?
Don't you like it?
Yeah. *Yes!* Of course. Chase, it's ***wonderful!***
I'm just...really distracted. Today isn't a great day for me.

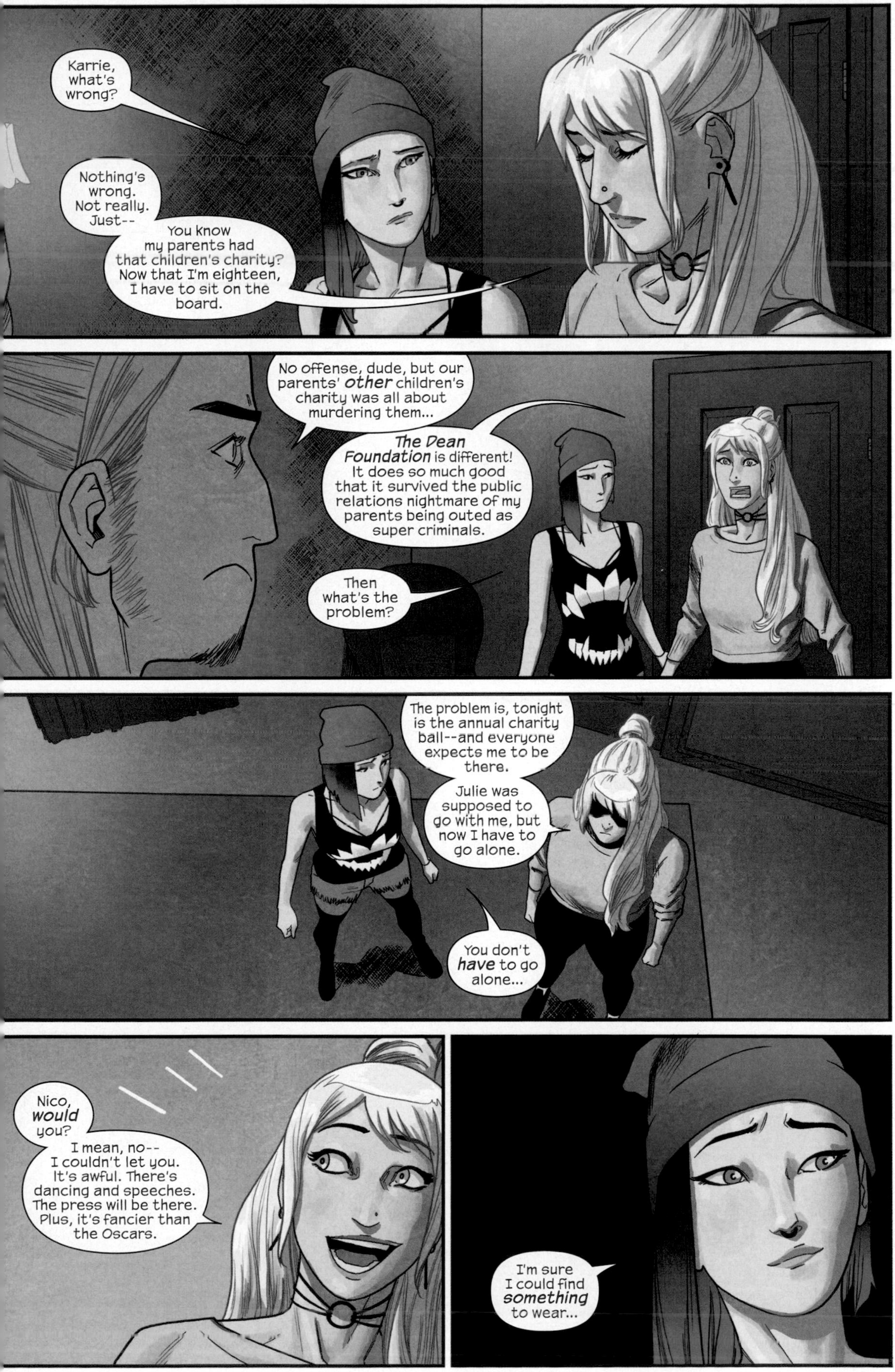
Karrie, what's wrong?
Nothing's wrong. Not really. Just--
You know my parents had that children's charity? Now that I'm eighteen, I have to sit on the board.
No offense, dude, but our parents' *other* children's charity was all about murdering them...
The Dean Foundation is different! It does so much good that it survived the public relations nightmare of my parents being outed as super criminals.
Then what's the problem?
The problem is, tonight is the annual charity ball--and everyone expects me to be there.
Julie was supposed to go with me, but now I have to go alone.
You don't *have* to go alone...
Nico, *would* you?
I mean, no-- I couldn't let you. It's awful. There's dancing and speeches. The press will be there. Plus, it's fancier than the Oscars.
I'm sure I could find *something* to wear...

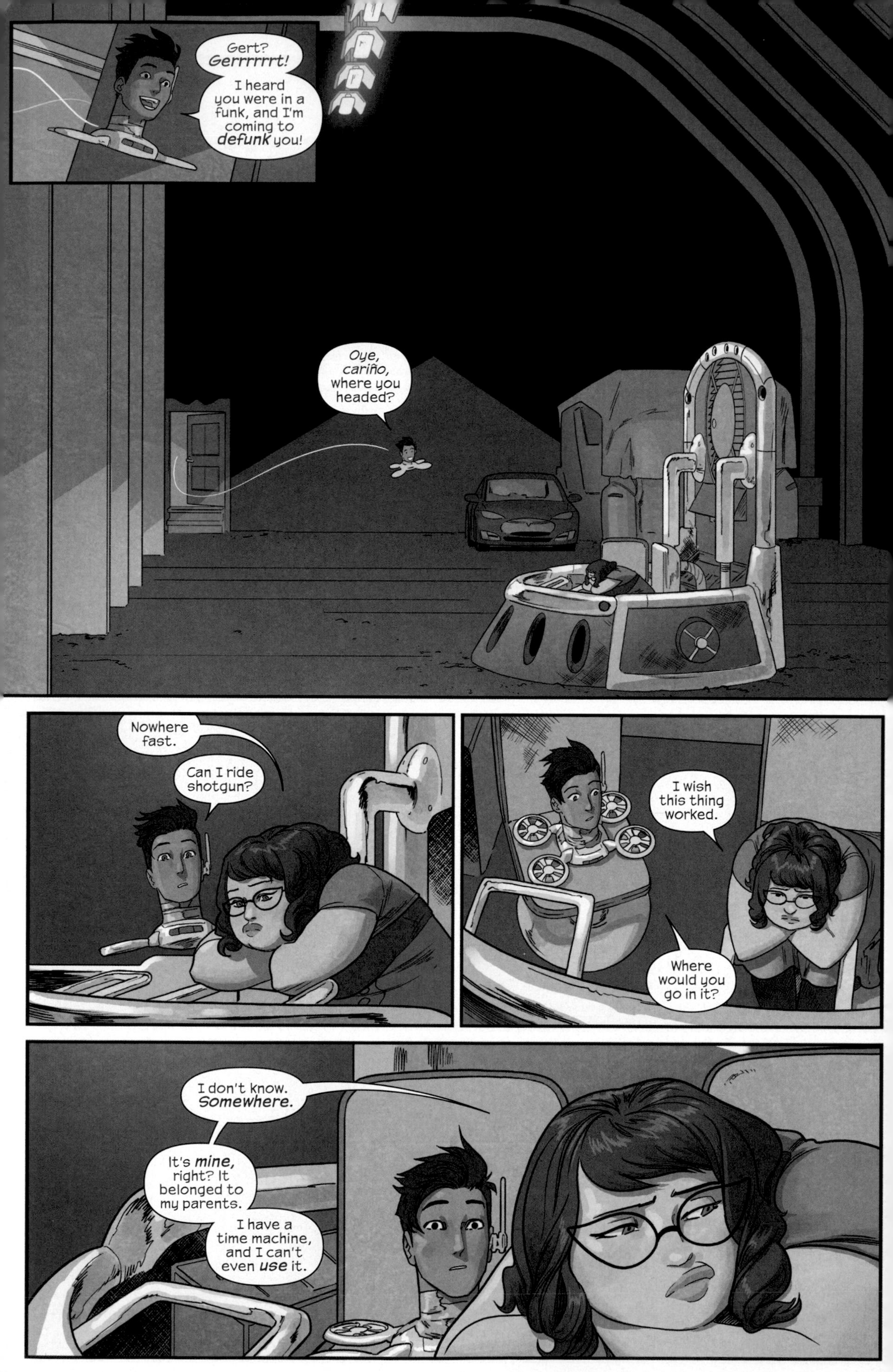
Gert? Gerrrrrrt!
I heard you were in a funk, and I'm coming to defunk you!
Oye, cariño, where you headed?
Nowhere fast.
Can I ride shotgun?
I wish this thing worked.
Where would you go in it?
I don't know. Somewhere.
It's mine, right? It belonged to my parents.
I have a time machine, and I can't even use it.

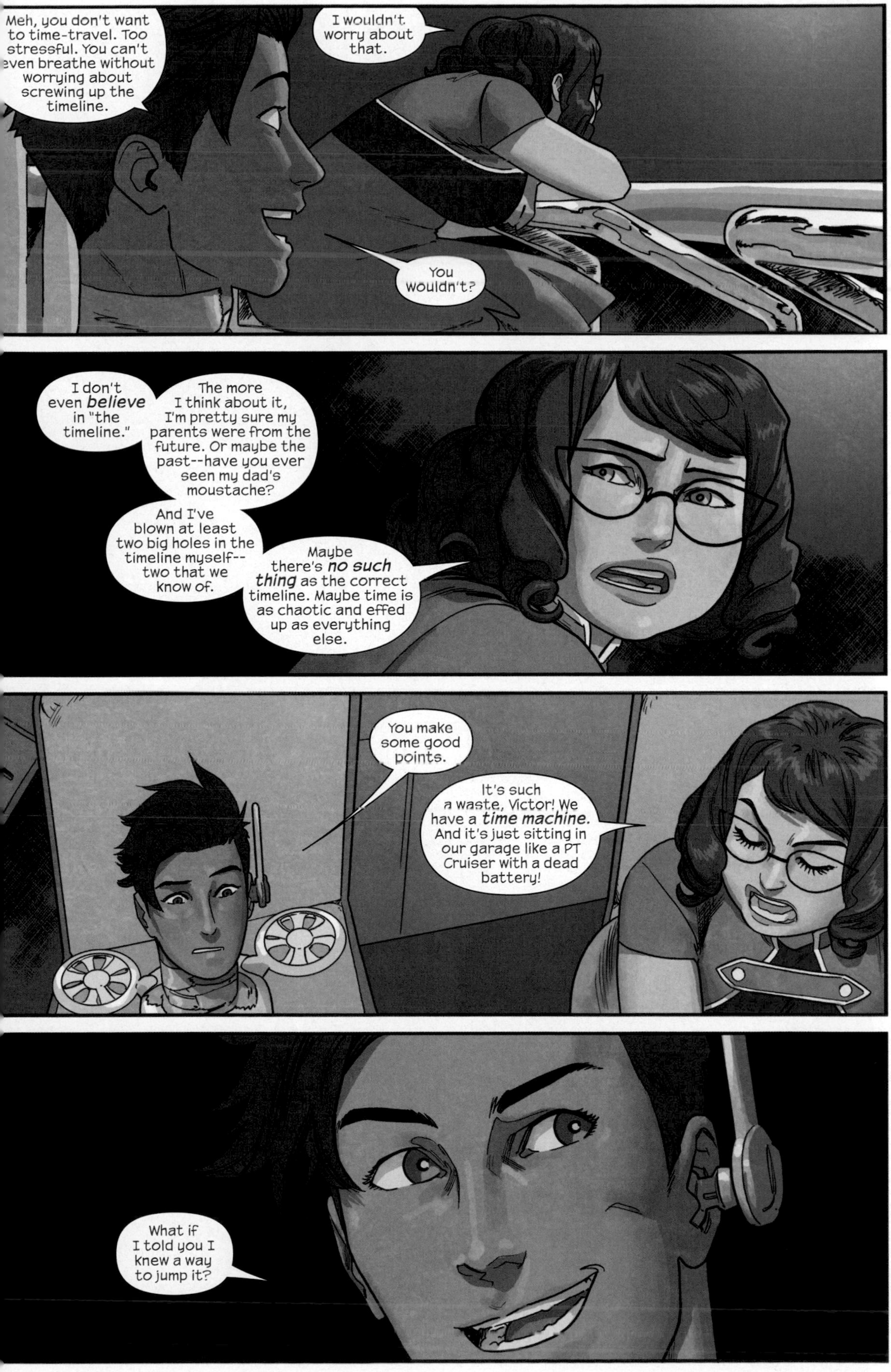
Meh, you don't want to time-travel. Too stressful. You can't even breathe without worrying about screwing up the timeline.
I wouldn't worry about that.
You wouldn't?
I don't even *believe* in "the timeline."
The more I think about it, I'm pretty sure my parents were from the future. Or maybe the past--have you ever seen my dad's moustache?
And I've blown at least two big holes in the timeline myself--two that we know of.
Maybe there's *no such thing* as the correct timeline. Maybe time is as chaotic and effed up as everything else.
You make some good points.
It's such a waste, Victor! We have a *time machine.* And it's just sitting in our garage like a PT Cruiser with a dead battery!
What if I told you I knew a way to jump it?

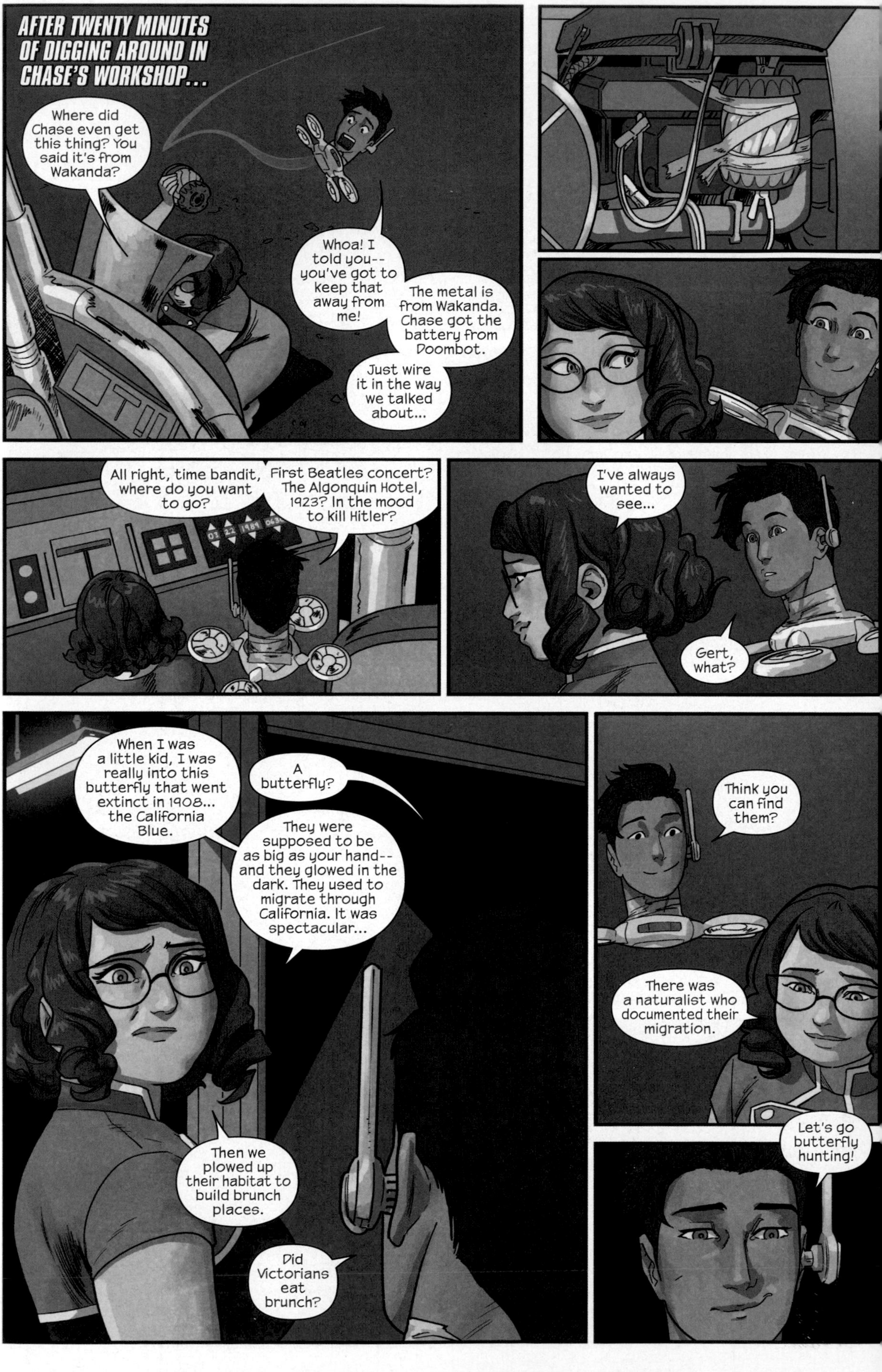
AFTER TWENTY MINUTES OF DIGGING AROUND IN CHASE'S WORKSHOP...
Where did Chase even get this thing? You said it's from Wakanda?
Whoa! I told you-- you've got to keep that away from me!
The metal is from Wakanda. Chase got the battery from Doombot.
Just wire it in the way we talked about...
All right, time bandit, where do you want to go?
First Beatles concert? The Algonquin Hotel, 1923? In the mood to kill Hitler?
I've always wanted to see...
Gert, what?
When I was a little kid, I was really into this butterfly that went extinct in 1908... the California Blue.
A butterfly?
They were supposed to be as big as your hand-- and they glowed in the dark. They used to migrate through California. It was spectacular...
Then we plowed up their habitat to build brunch places.
Did Victorians eat brunch?
Think you can find them?
There was a naturalist who documented their migration.
Let's go butterfly hunting!

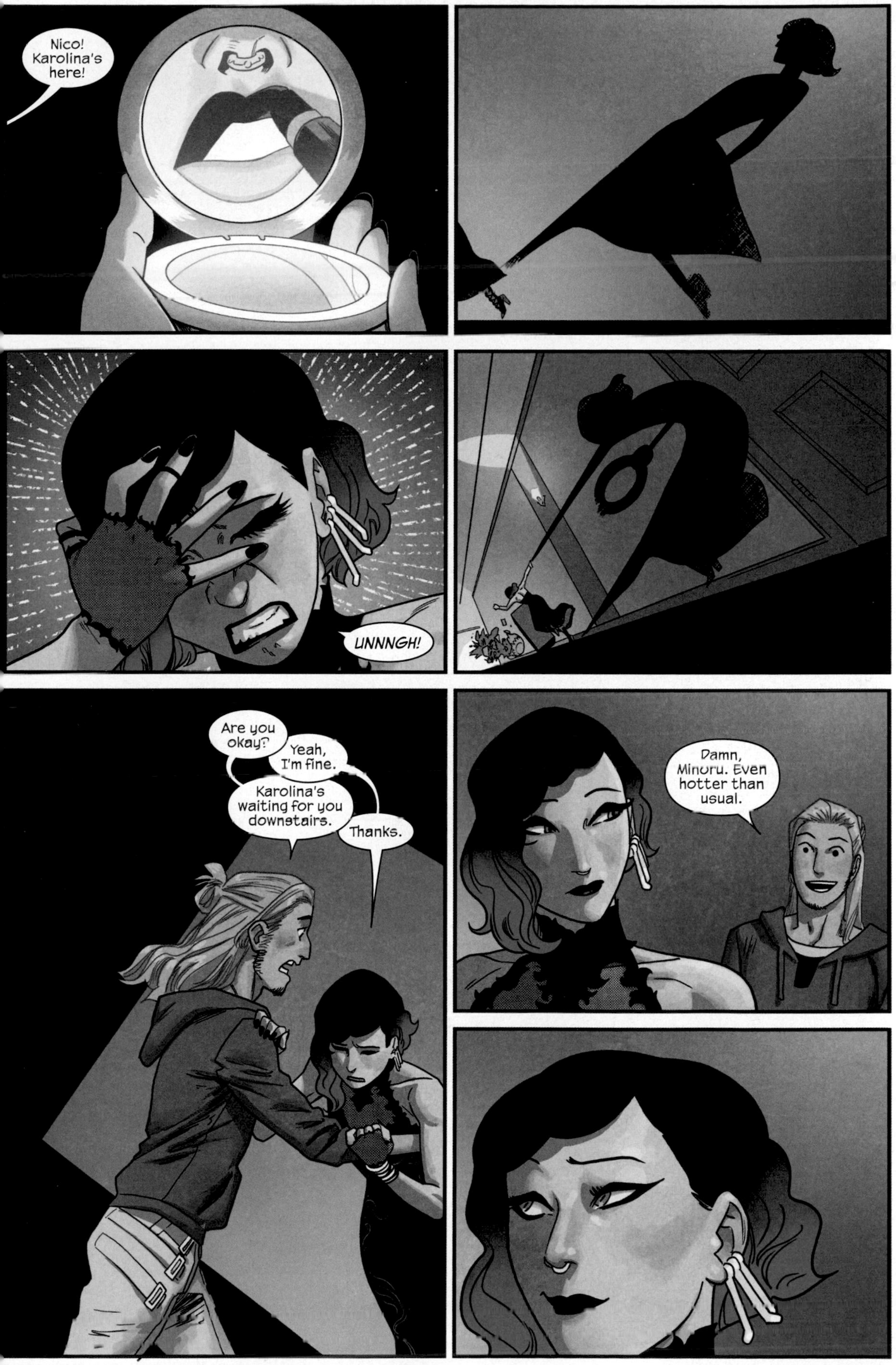
Nico! Karolina's here!
UNNNGH!
Are you okay?
Yeah, I'm fine.
Karolina's waiting for you downstairs.
Thanks.
Damn, Minoru. Even hotter than usual.

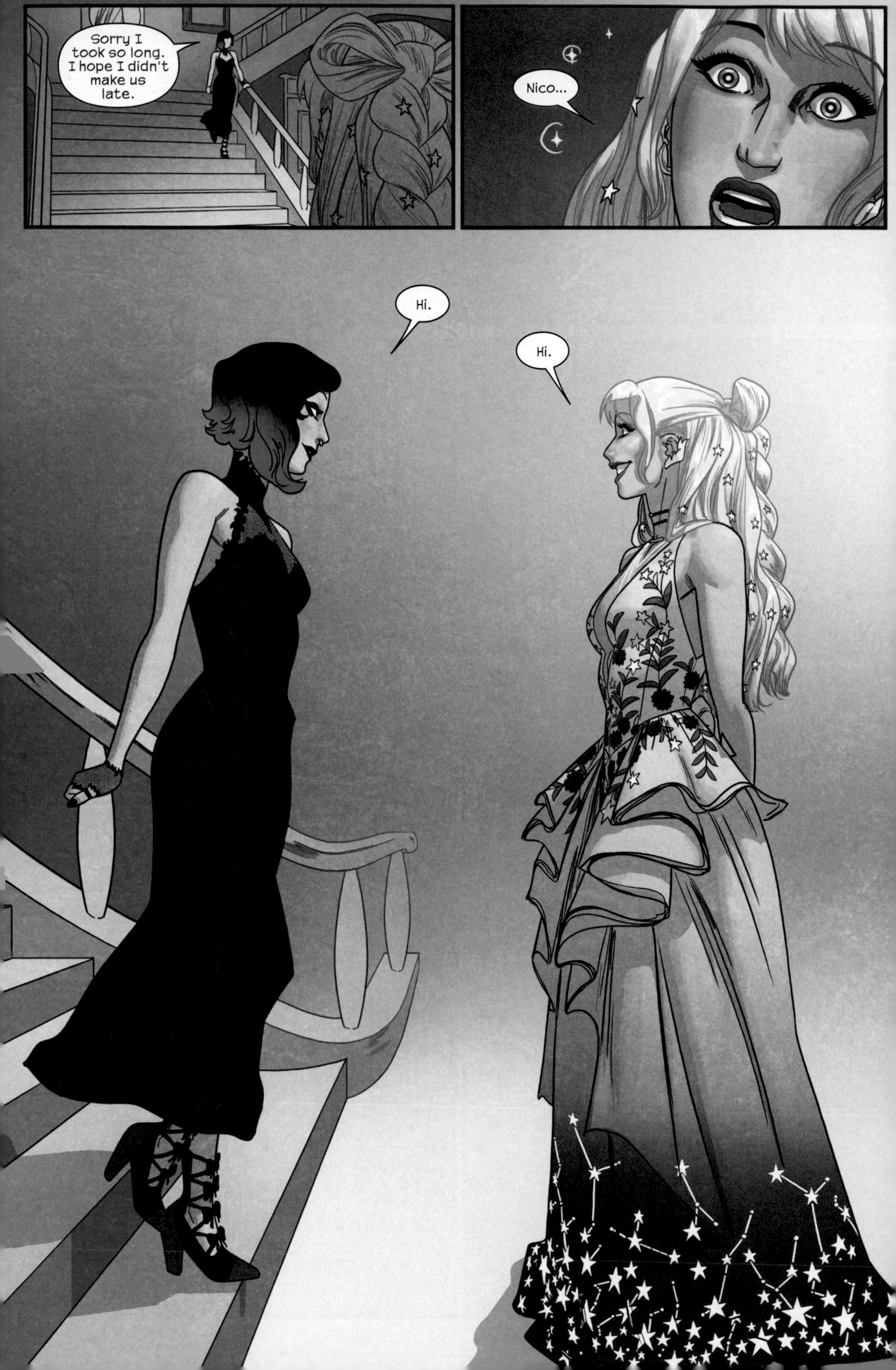
Sorry I took so long. I hope I didn't make us late.
Nico...
Hi.
Hi.

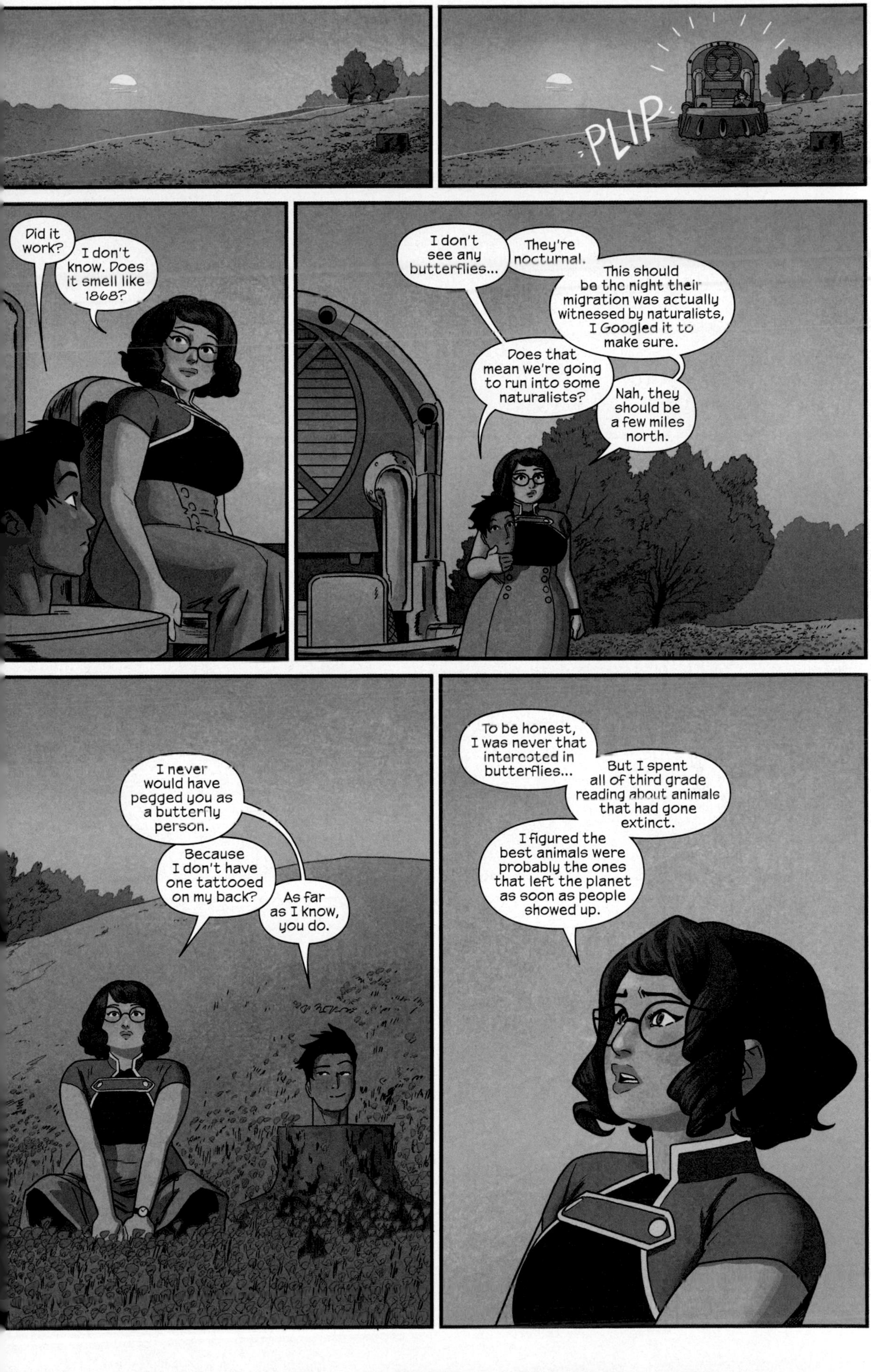
PLIP
Did it work?
I don't know. Does it smell like 1868?
I don't see any butterflies...
They're nocturnal.
This should be the night their migration was actually witnessed by naturalists, I Googled it to make sure.
Does that mean we're going to run into some naturalists?
Nah, they should be a few miles north.
I never would have pegged you as a butterfly person.
Because I don't have one tattooed on my back?
As far as I know, you do.
To be honest, I was never that interested in butterflies...
But I spent all of third grade reading about animals that had gone extinct.
I figured the best animals were probably the ones that left the planet as soon as people showed up.

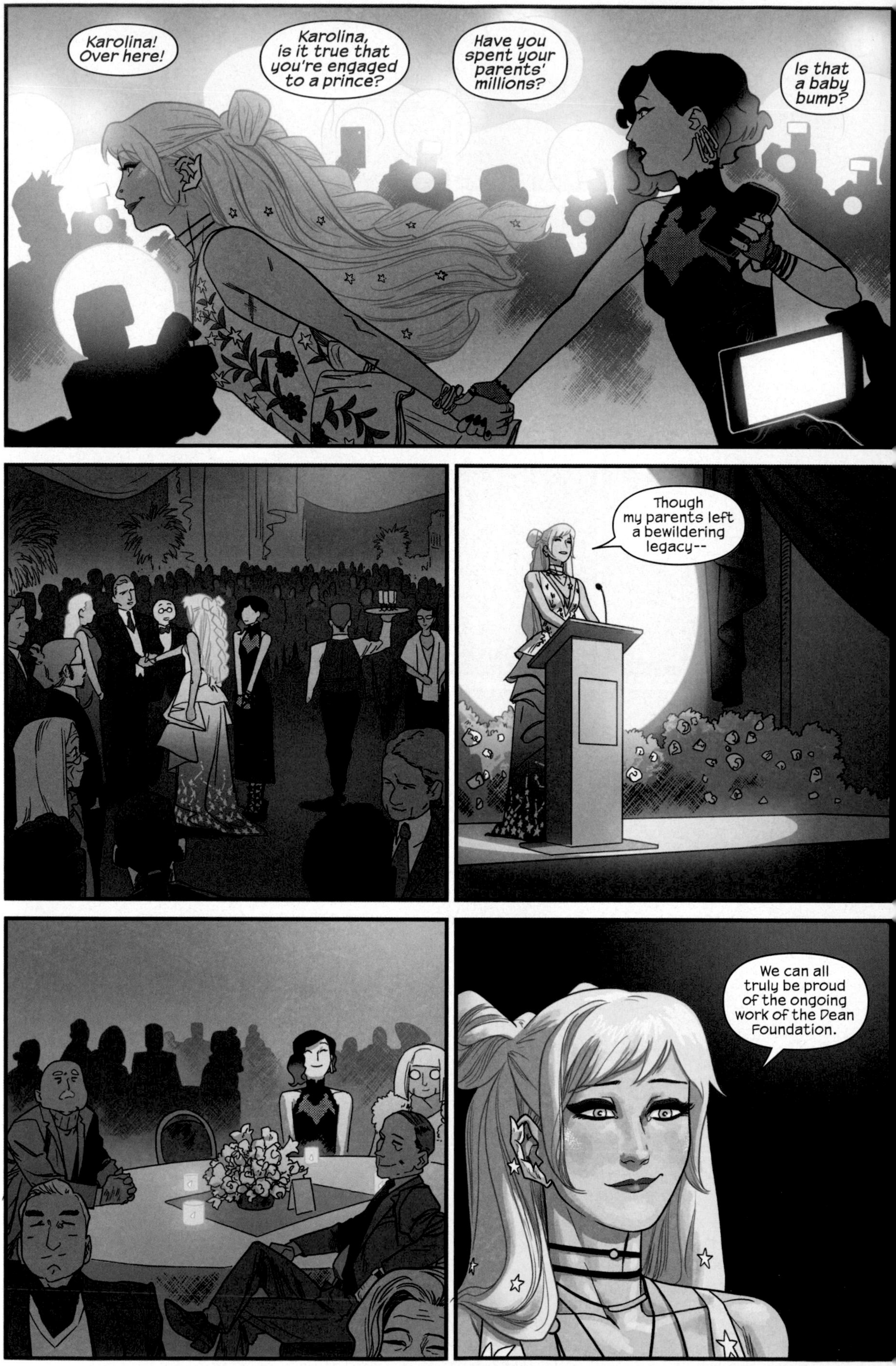
Karolina! Over here!
Karolina, is it true that you're engaged to a prince?
Have you spent your parents' millions?
Is that a baby bump?
Though my parents left a bewildering legacy--
We can all truly be proud of the ongoing work of the Dean Foundation.

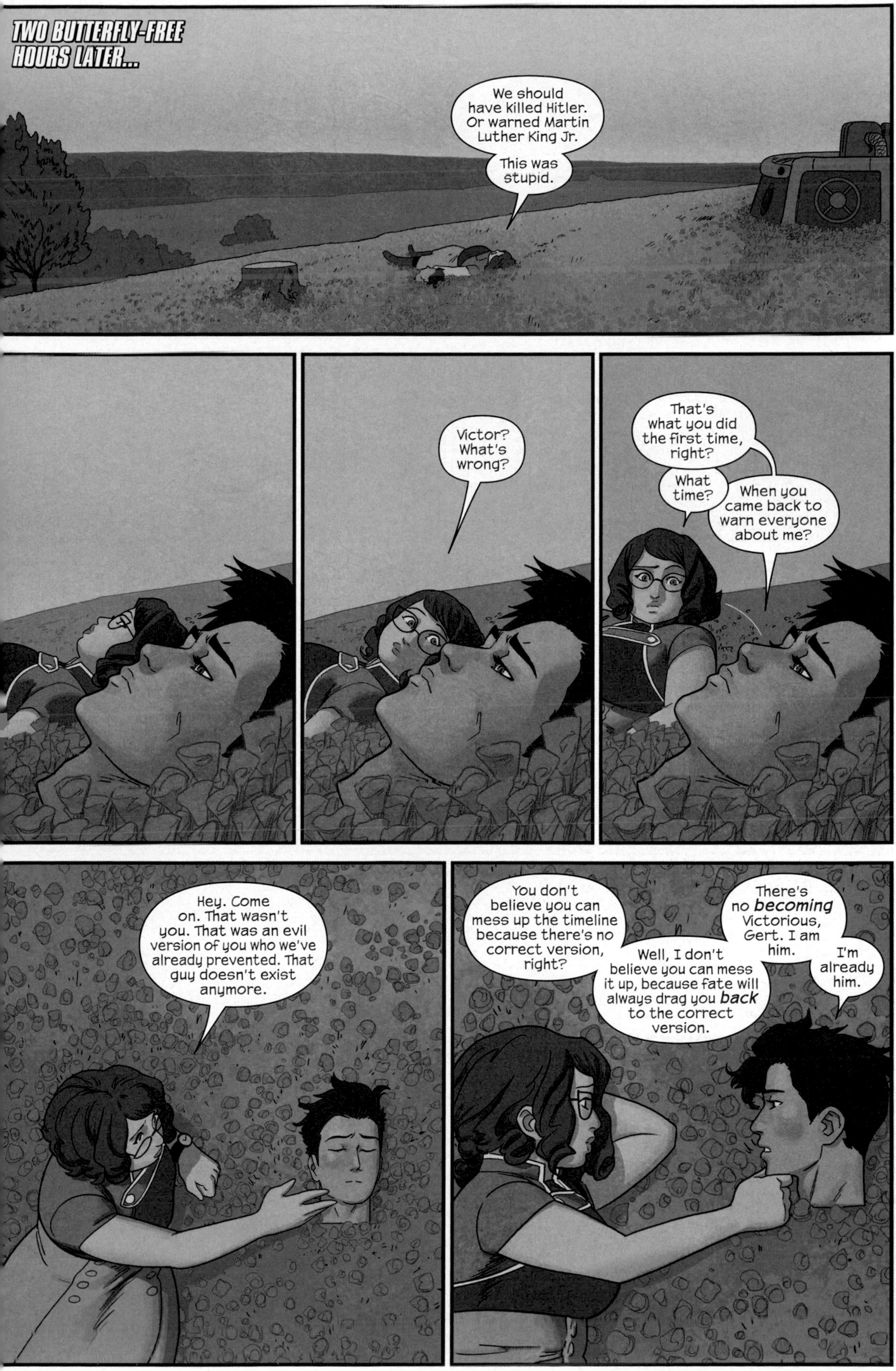
TWO BUTTERFLY-FREE HOURS LATER...
We should have killed Hitler. Or warned Martin Luther King Jr.
This was stupid.
Victor? What's wrong?
That's what you did the first time, right?
What time?
When you came back to warn everyone about me?
Hey. Come on. That wasn't you. That was an evil version of you who we've already prevented. That guy doesn't exist anymore.
You don't believe you can mess up the timeline because there's no correct version, right?
Well, I don't believe you can mess it up, because fate will always drag you *back* to the correct version.
There's no *becoming* Victorious, Gert. I am him.
I'm already him.

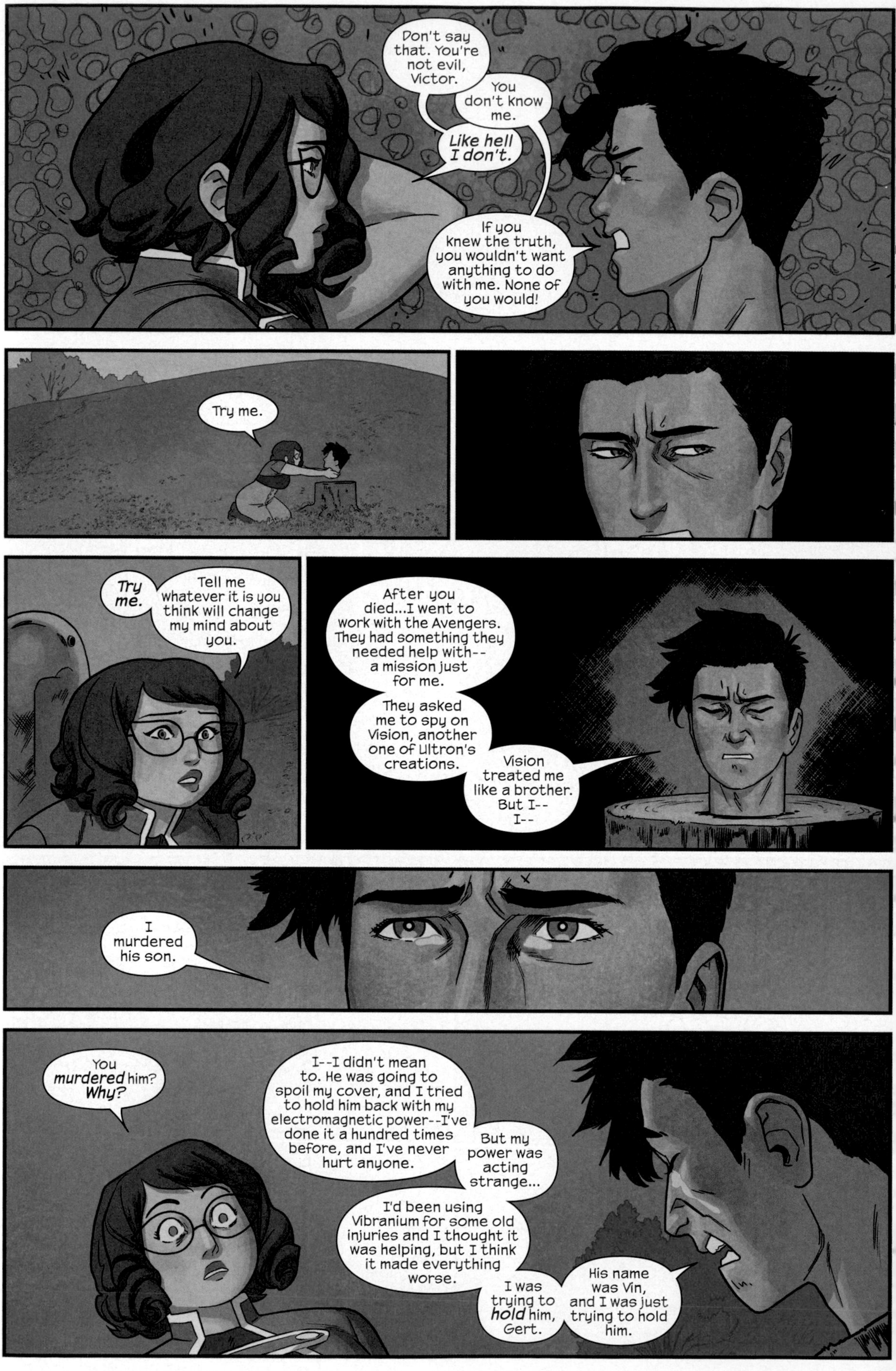

Don't say that. You're not evil, Victor.
You don't know me.
Like hell I don't.
If you knew the truth, you wouldn't want anything to do with me. None of you would!
Try me.
Try me.
Tell me whatever it is you think will change my mind about you.
After you died...I went to work with the Avengers. They had something they needed help with-- a mission just for me.
They asked me to spy on Vision, another one of Ultron's creations.
Vision treated me like a brother. But I-- I--
I murdered his son.
You murdered him? Why?
I--I didn't mean to. He was going to spoil my cover, and I tried to hold him back with my electromagnetic power--I've done it a hundred times before, and I've never hurt anyone.
But my power was acting strange...
I'd been using Vibranium for some old injuries and I thought it was helping, but I think it made everything worse.
I was trying to hold him, Gert.
His name was Vin, and I was just trying to hold him.

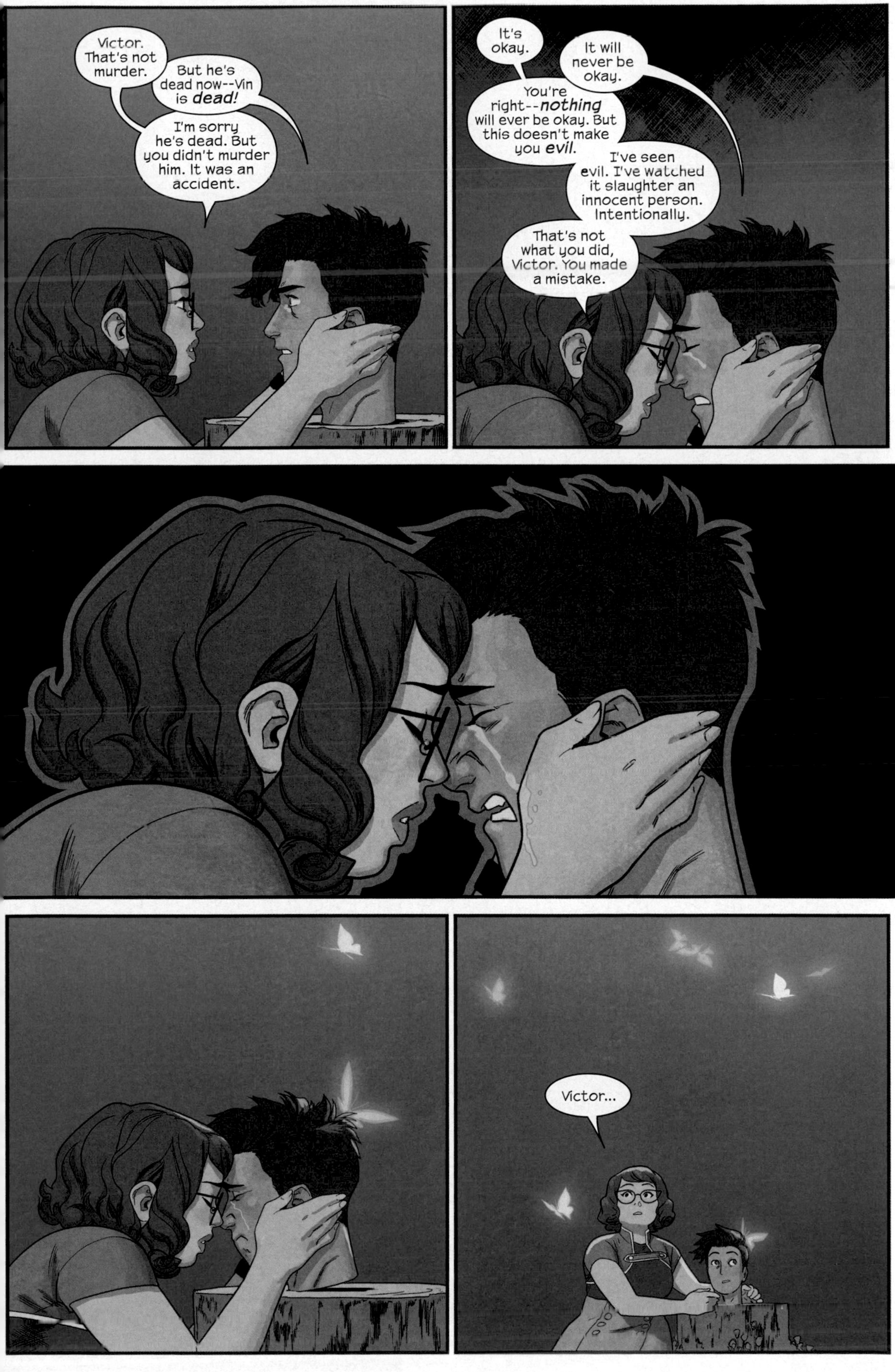
Victor. That's not murder.
But he's dead now--Vin is *dead!*
I'm sorry he's dead. But you didn't murder him. It was an accident.
It's okay.
It will never be okay.
You're right--*nothing* will ever be okay. But this doesn't make you *evil.*
I've seen evil. I've watched it slaughter an innocent person. Intentionally.
That's not what you did, Victor. You made a mistake.
Victor...

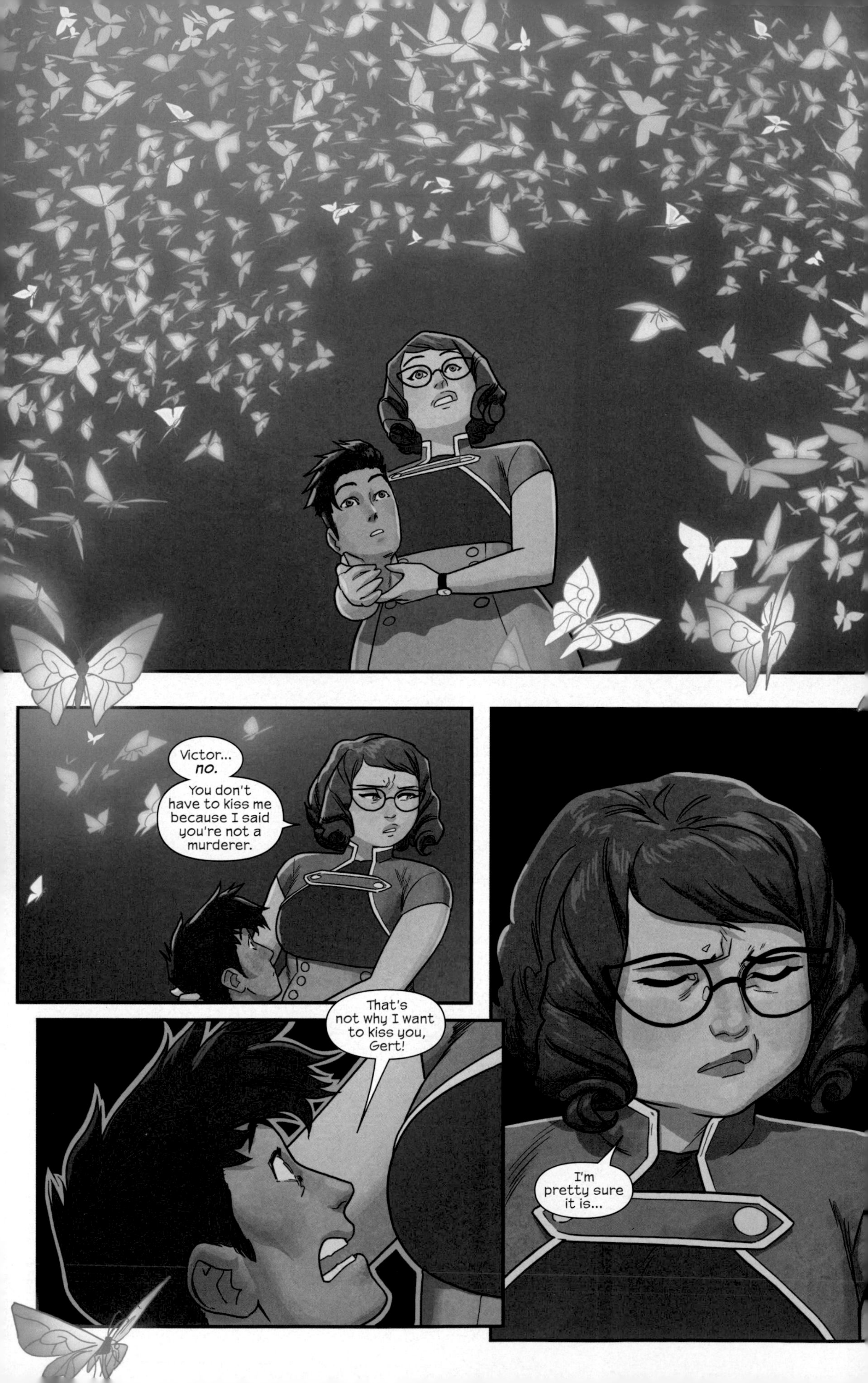
Victor... no.
You don't have to kiss me because I said you're not a murderer.
That's not why I want to kiss you, Gert!
I'm pretty sure it is...

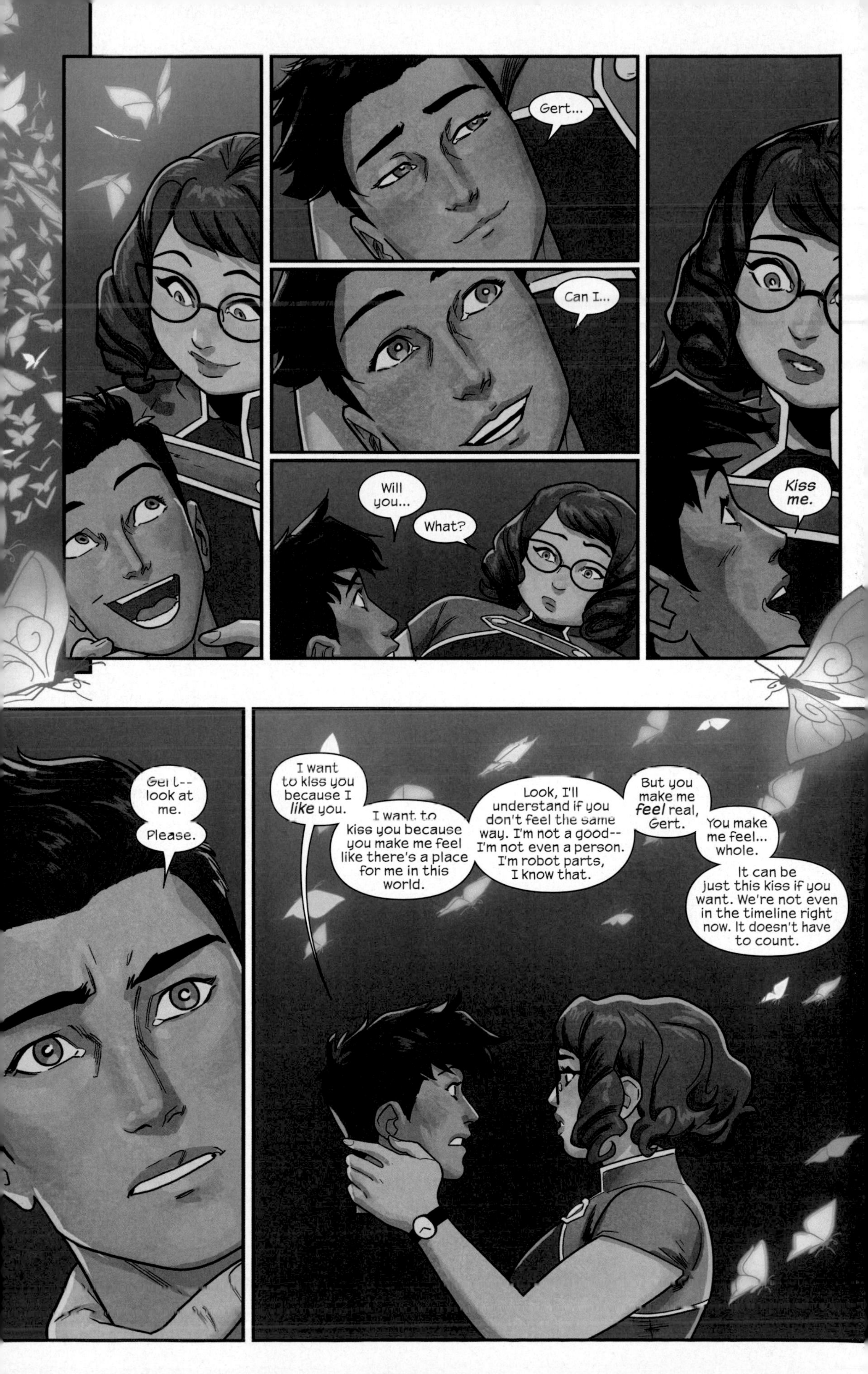

Gert...
Can I...
Will you...
What?
Kiss me.
Gert--look at me.
Please.
I want to kiss you because I *like* you.
I want to kiss you because you make me feel like there's a place for me in this world.
Look, I'll understand if you don't feel the same way. I'm not a good-- I'm not even a person. I'm robot parts, I know that.
But you make me *feel* real, Gert.
You make me feel... whole.
It can be just this kiss if you want. We're not even in the timeline right now. It doesn't have to count.

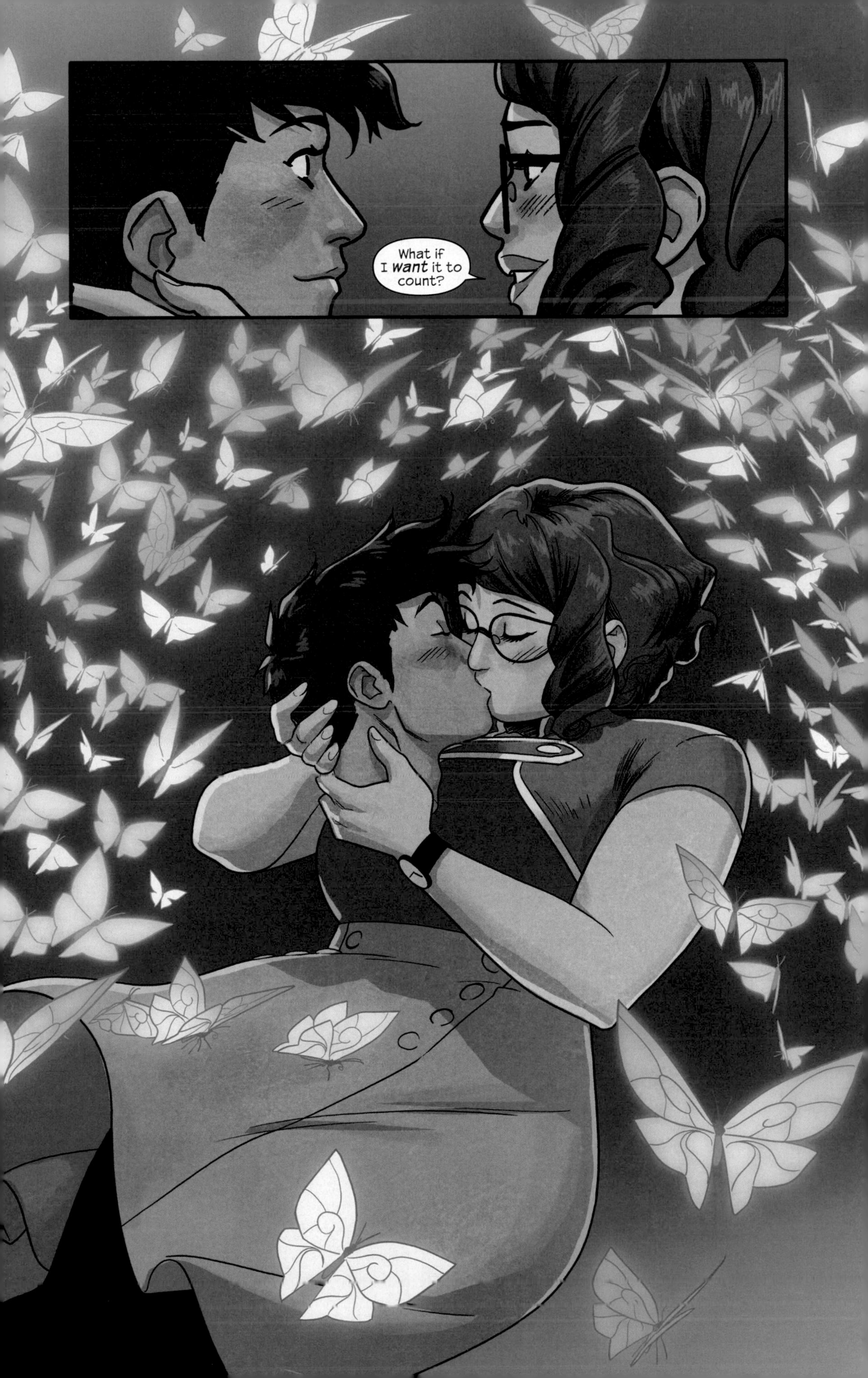
What if I *want* it to count?

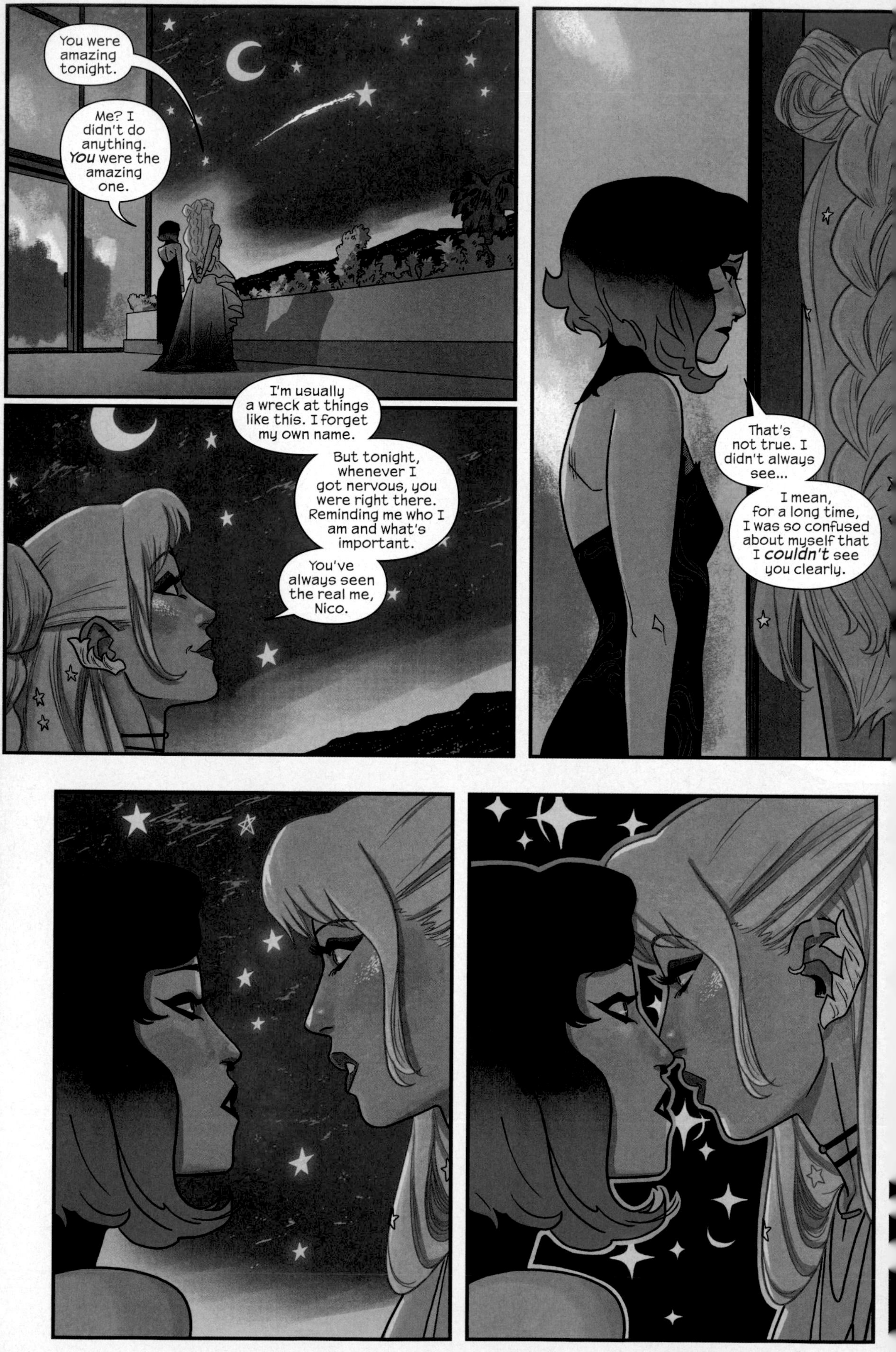

You were amazing tonight.
Me? I didn't do anything. *You* were the amazing one.
I'm usually a wreck at things like this. I forget my own name.
But tonight, whenever I got nervous, you were right there. Reminding me who I am and what's important.
You've always seen the real me, Nico.
That's not true. I didn't always see...
I mean, for a long time, I was so confused about myself that I *couldn't* see you clearly.

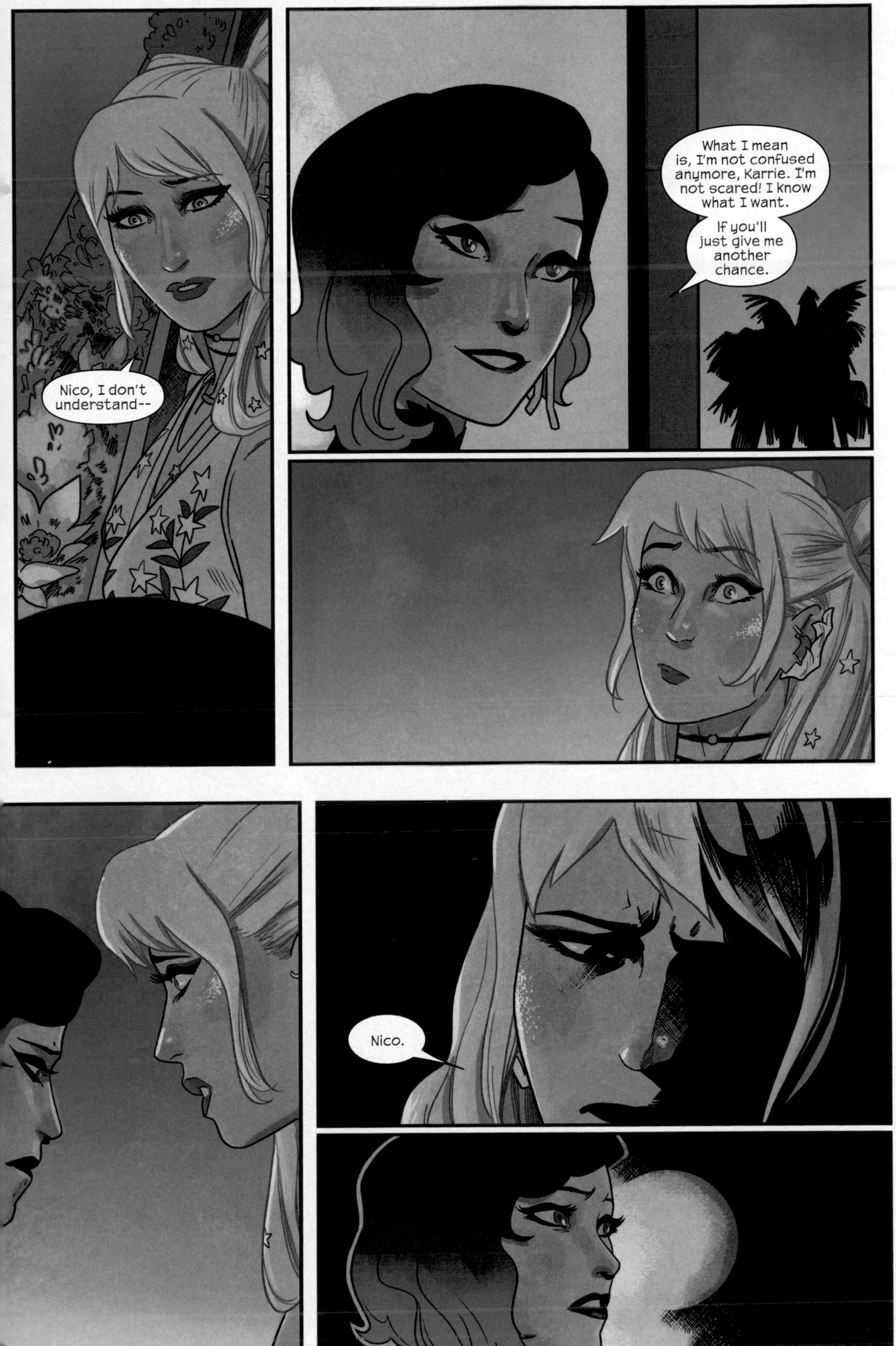
Nico, I don't understand--
What I mean is, I'm not confused anymore, Karrie. I'm not scared! I know what I want.
If you'll just give me another chance.
Nico.

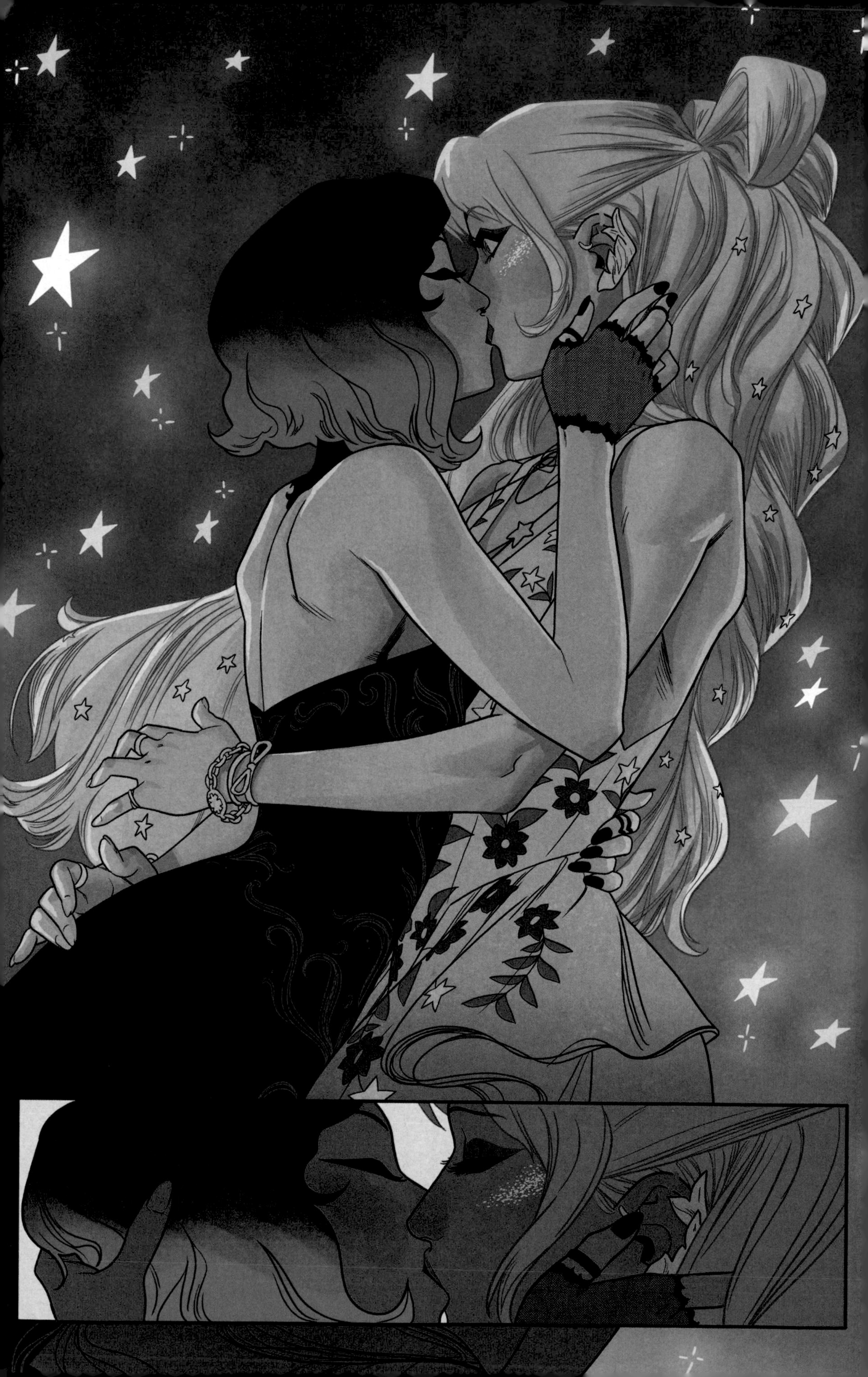

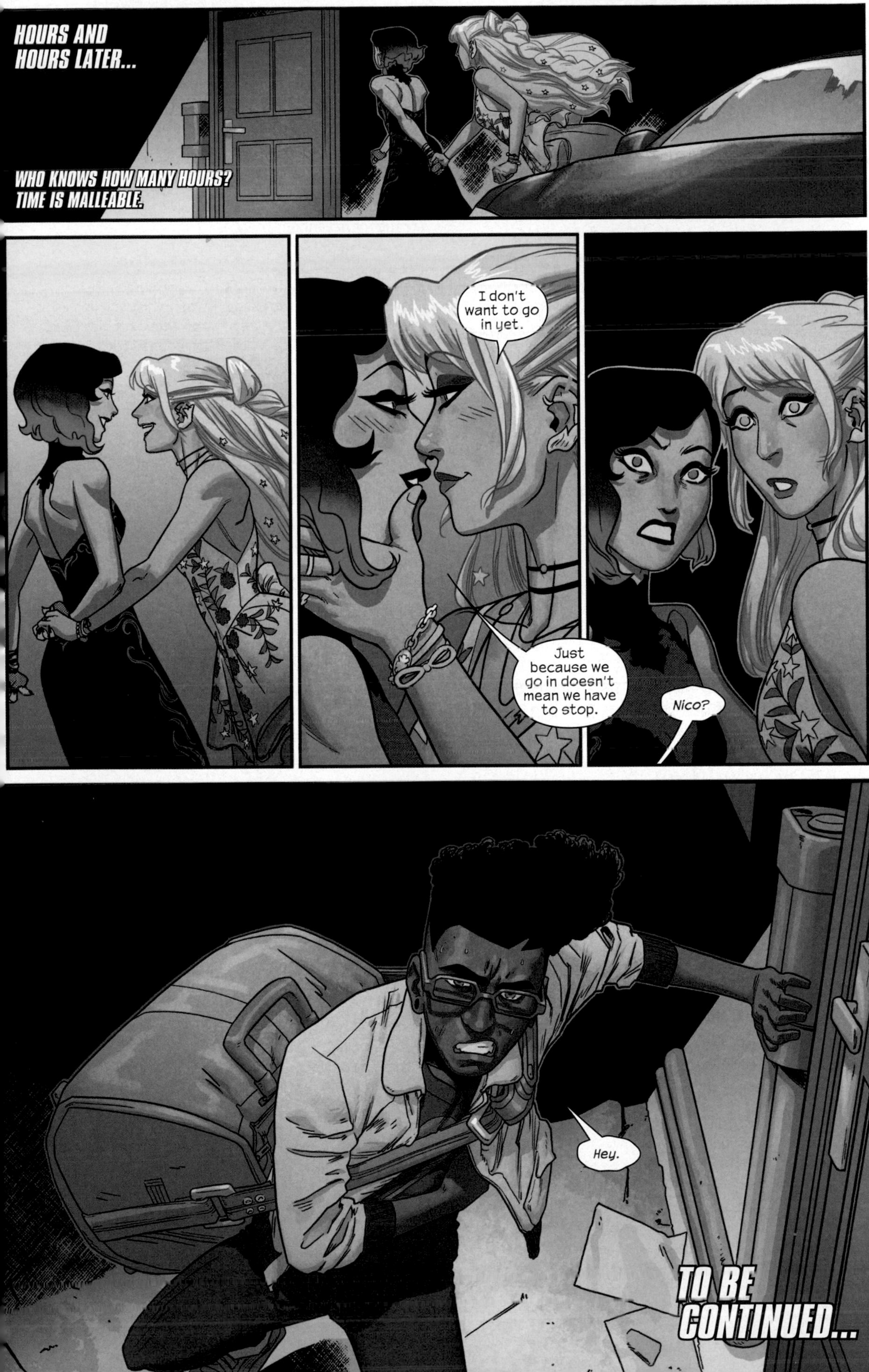
HOURS AND HOURS LATER...
WHO KNOWS HOW MANY HOURS? TIME IS MALLEABLE.
I don't want to go in yet.
Just because we go in doesn't mean we have to stop.
Nico?
Hey.
TO BE CONTINUED...

RUNAWAYS #11 (Pages 1-15)

"AM I THE SAME GIRL YOU USED TO KNOW?"
RAINBOW ROWELL

IN THIS ISSUE: Gert confronts her identity crisis -- and decides to stop living in the past. Who is she in this reality? This present? Karolina and Nico are asking themselves the same question -- what does being back together mean for them? And Chase is forcing Victor forward, whether he's ready or not.

PAGE 1 – SATURDAY AFTERNOON

• We're in one of the Hostel bedrooms. This one is currently empty, but it's still decorated all fancily. (This is the room Chase is fixing up for Karolina, though she doesn't know it.)

• Chase has the ceiling torn open, and he's up on a tall ladder, reaching into the ceiling; his head is hidden. His shirt is short enough to be lifting up a little bit.

Gert is at the bottom of the ladder, looking up. She's wearing Chase's old clothes. *(Kris, I still have a few outfits to choose from.)* This will be the last time we see her in Chase's clothes for a while.

Maybe Old Lace is napping on the bed.

• NARRATOR
Saturday morning.

On Saturday mornings, they used to wake up late and stay in bed even later.

Until their stomachs were growling. Then they'd go out -- just the two of them, if they could help it. (They couldn't always help it.)

GERT
What are you working on?

CHASE
Secret project.

GERT
Shouldn't you be working on Victor?

• Chase comes down out of the ceiling, leaning over a bit, reaching for something:

NARRATOR
They'd get cheap coffee and egg sandwiches, and find a place at the lake or the farmers' market where they could sit and watch people go by.

CHASE
Not until later. Doombot is bringing over some parts.

Can you hand me that wrench?

NARRATOR
Where people could watch *them.*

Where people could wonder...

Gert holds up the wrench. Chase takes it, smiling.

CHASE
What's up? Did you need me for something?

Gert looks vulnerable and unsure. Because *of course* she needs him for something. She still loves him. But she can't say that or have that.

GERT
No. I'm just... bored.

Chase is back up in the ceiling, reaching higher. His shirt is pulled way up now. We see a tattoo above his hip: GERT, written in script, inside a heart. It is both a little tacky and a little beautiful.

CHASE
(from inside ceiling)
You should go out. Get some air.

Gert is stunned. There are maybe tears in her eyes?

• Gert rushes from the room.

Chase has come down from the ceiling and is looking after her. Maybe Old Lace has lifted her head (if we can see her).

NARRATOR
"What's a guy like him doing with a girl like her?"

PAGE 2 – THIS IS NOT MY BEAUTIFUL HOUSE

We're in the main room of the Hostel: Karolina is sitting on the couch. Nico is doing Karolina's eye makeup. They're just hanging out.

Molly is standing on the stairs.

MOLLY
Karolina! Victor's stuck on the ceiling, can you fly up and get him?

NICO
How did Victor get stuck on the ceiling?

MOLLY
I was trying to build him a hot air balloon. For transportation.

KAROLINA
Sorry, Molly. I've been underground too long to power up right now.

NICO
Chase has a ladder.

• Gert walks through the room. Old Lace is loping behind her.

Karolina notices Gert.

KAROLINA
Hey, Gert, where are you going?

GERT
Out.

"SEASON 2" PLAN BY **RAINBOW ROWELL**

KAROLINA
You should go to that plus-size boutique I told you about. My friend says it's amazing. We could all go. I'll drive you!

• Gert is still walking.

GERT
(muttering)
I'd rather die than shop for fat clothes with you two.

•   KAROLINA
Gert?

GERT
(regular voice)
No, thanks -- going out!

• Gert is at the doorway. (What does the Hostel doorway look like? Fancy, I'll bet!) Gert has turned back to Old Lace.

GERT
Stay. Go keep your new best friend company.

• Old Lace looks rejected. Gert points at her.

GERT
Stay!

PAGE 3 – NICO AND KAROLINA GET A LITTLE CLOSER

• Nico is putting on Karolina's eyeliner. Karolina's eyes are closed.

NICO
I would rather swallow knives than be 16 again. The *hormones*.

KAROLINA
It's not hormones... She misses Chase.

Can you imagine what it's like? For *both* of them? She lost him overnight. And he got her back too late.

• Silent panel: Nico just looks at Karolina's face, thinking about love and loss and how beautiful and sensitive Karolina is.

• Karolina opens her eyes. Nico looks abashed/sad.

KAROLINA
What?

NICO
Like you lost Xavin?

• Karolina looks away.

KAROLINA
(softly)
Like you lost Alex.

Nico looks more firm:

NICO
No. We all lost Alex.

He wasn't my-- We weren't-- I don't think I've ever had...*that*.

What Gert and Chase had. What you had with Xavin. And with... Julie.

• Nico is treading carefully here, trying not to let her own feelings interfere with being a good friend. Karolina is serious, smiling kind of grimly. She knows that she and Julie are over:

NICO
Have you talked to her?

KAROLINA
No... What would I say? She was right. I was neglecting her.

NICO
You could try again -- try to do better.

KAROLINA
No. I couldn't.

• Nico tries to smile:

NICO
We need to get you outside. You need to soak up some sun, rainbow girl.

KAROLINA
That sounds good...

But first we need to get Victor off the ceiling.

NICO
First I need to finish your eyebrows.

PAGES 4-5 – ENTER DOOM, STAGE RIGHT

PAGE 4

• Doombot walks into the Hostel. He's carrying a large, handled case. Like a big black rectangular box with silver edges -- something that would be too heavy for a normal person to carry. The vibe when he walks in is comically casual. Like he's the neighbor on a sitcom.

Nico is finishing Karolina's face. She doesn't look up.

NICO
They're upstairs.

• We're in Molly's room. Doom -- who is 6'7" -- is reaching up to get Victor, who is in a handled basket tied to multicolored helium balloons. Chase is watching from the doorway. Molly is looking up at Doombot. Victor is smiling, relaxed.

MOLLY
(to herself)
He's so *tall*...

DOOMBOT
Why did you tie Victor to balloons, Stein?

CHASE
I didn't do this.

VICTOR
(trying to keep Molly from getting in trouble)

I told Molly I missed flying...

DOOMBOT
When we have restored your electromagnetic abilities--

VICTOR
No, thanks. I got it out of my system.

• Now they're in Chase's work space. There are papers spread everywhere and robotic parts. Molly's in here, too. She's sitting on the floor with a handheld video game.

There's a partially built robot body that looks like a *Star Wars* battle droid (very bare bones and practical) but made out of cruder parts.

Doombot is opening his case. Victor is sitting on a tabletop, looking like he'd rather be somewhere else.

CHASE
Did you bring the part?

DOOMBOT
The battery you asked me to steal? Yes.

• Doombot hands Chase a power source. It has Vibranium in it. Victor looks upset. Chase is grinning, maybe tossing the battery in his hand.

VICTOR
Does that have Vibranium in it?

CHASE
Yeah, how could you tell?

PAGE 5

• Victor is dead serious:

VICTOR
I can feel it. Get it away from me.

CHASE
It's for your new body.

VICTOR
No.

CHASE
I've had diminishing returns with Vibranium, but this body is just a temporary fix--

Victor could not be more stern:

VICTOR

NO!

I'm serious! I never want to see it again.

• Chase lets his hand, with the battery, drop to his side. He looks confused and a little hurt. Doombot holds up his case with his other hand.

DOOMBOT
No matter. I have something better.

• We see that Doombot has set up a beautifully constructed robot body for Victor. *Gleaming*. Built more thickly than old Victor, but still man-shaped. It's unapologetically mechanical. Smooth metal skin. (Dark gray or black maybe. With gold circuitry.) There are lines in the arms and other places, where panels can open, revealing weaponry. (We don't see them open.)

This body *could* be Doom-like, if you want, but I'm imagining something very sleek.

Chase and Victor both look stunned.

PAGES 6-7 – VICTOR REJECTS HIS NEW BODY
PAGE 6

• Molly's mouth is hanging open.

MOLLY
Whoa... Did you *build* that?

Doombot, picking up Victor's head, looks very pleased with himself. Victor looks surprised, but doesn't have a chance to argue.

DOOMBOT
I did.

Come, Victor, let's try it on.

VICTOR
I'm not sure--

• **LARGE PANEL:** Victor has been attached to his new body.

He looks *really cool*. Fearsome. Handsome. His eyebrow is lowered like he's trying to figure out how he feels, but the effect is intimidating.

Would I argue with a little wind in his hair? I would not.

Doombot is talking, but he and his balloons are off to the side, so that they don't distract from Victor.

Or maybe Doombot's face is just below Victor's panel.

DOOMBOT
It's less human than your old form. But your mechanical nature is no longer a secret to yourself or your comrades.

• Victor is looking down at his forearm. His arm is bent at the elbow, and his hand is raised toward him.

• Panels in his arm open and components snap out that transform his arm into a fearsome energy gun or canon.

MOLLY AND CHASE
Sweet!

PAGE 7

• Victor looks disgusted.

VICTOR
What have you done?

DOOMBOT
Upgrades. I borrowed some of my own technology. We can improve it together--

• Victor's other arm opens or transforms somehow into another fearsome weapon. His body sort of jerks as it happens.

• Victor looks up. He's desperate.

VICTOR
Get me off this thing!

DOOMBOT
Victor Mancha--

VICTOR
Chase! Now! Get me off!

• Chase is removing Victor's head. It's not detached yet.

VICTOR
Chase. Please!

CHASE
I'm *trying*. I don't want to break you.

• Doombot looks confused and hurt. Chase has Victor's head off. Victor looks near tears. He's holding the head out to Molly.

CHASE
Molly…

• Molly takes Victor, lovingly. Victor's eyes are closed, like he can't even look at the body. Or anyone.

PAGE 8 – DOOMBOTS JUST DON'T UNDERSTAND

• Chase and Doombot are alone with the body. They're both downcast, a little ashamed. One silent panel and then:

•   DOOMBOT
I don't understand. It is an excellent body -- much more powerful than Victor Mancha's previous form.

CHASE
Dude. That is a bomb-dot-com robot body. It's bananas.

• Doombot is defensive, raising a fist.

DOOMBOT
I mirrored my very own components!

Chase tries to reassure him:

CHASE
I meant "bananas" in a good way!

•   DOOMBOT
(still confused about what went wrong)
We can't replicate his former body -- it was clearly too vulnerable.

CHASE
(realistically)
And also, we don't know how.

• Chase looks concerned/thoughtful.

CHASE
Doombot... Do you know how Victor lost his body?

DOOMBOT
He was on a mission--

CHASE
For the Avengers. Yeah, I know that part.

DOOMBOT
The file is sealed. Even beyond my tampering.

• Chase is like, "This is pretty messed up."

CHASE
So, the Avengers just let you wander around, full of bad vibes and jacked up like a Super-Soldier...

Doombot is like, "Meh. It is what it is."

DOOMBOT
To be honest, Chase Stein, I think they have forgotten that I exist.

Chase looks like he's got an angle:

CHASE
Maybe Victor will come around. You can just leave this body here.

DOOMBOT
For a jackal like you to scavenge? Do you take me for a fool?

•   CHASE
(like he's heard it before, rolling his eyes)
No. You are Doom.

DOOMBOT
(simultaneously)
I am Doom!

PAGE 9 – GERT LOOKS FOR HERSELF

• Gert is walking by herself along an L.A. street. There's no one else in this panel. Her hands are in her pockets

For context: In a minute, she'll be walking around the Grove.

Matt, I thought it might be interesting to play with the palette in this sequence so all the purple hair really pops. To have it be purple on almost a grayscale.

Or to start with more natural color and then have page 10 have the only real color be all the purple hair.

But I'm not attached to either of these ideas.

• Gert looks up and sees some people in the distance. We can't see their details or features.

• Two girls walk by, laughing, very cute. One of them has purple hair. Maybe the other has cat-eye glasses.

• Gert walks by a cafe with outdoor tables. Two of the four people at one table -- maybe a girl and a guy -- both have shades of purple hair. They look like cool young twentysomethings at brunch.

• Gert walks by a late 30s mom with two small kids. The mom has purple hair and cat-eye glasses. She's carrying a cloth bag of produce. The kids are eating ice cream.

(All of these people are different races, different body types, have different hairstyles.)

PAGE 10 – PURPLE PEOPLE
• FULL-PAGE PANEL:

Gert is standing in a huge crowd scene. (Sorry, Kris.)

People at a farmers' market, in a pedestrian area. SO MANY OF THEM HAVE PURPLE HAIR.

Grandmas. Kids on skateboards. At least one or two chubby girls like Gert. Maybe there's a skinny girl who's copped Gert's entire *look* from the original series. Like almost an entire outfit. Fishnets. Ripped jean skirt. Military boots.

Gert is standing in the middle of the scene. Lost. She doesn't stand out at all.

She's just another girl with purple hair.

PAGE 11 – A WHOLE NEW GERT

• Gert is standing in front of a shop (like a Walgreens). looking at her reflection in the window. Her brown roots are showing.

She looks lost. Like she doesn't recognize her own reflection anymore.

• Gert is walking into the Walgreens (or whatever).

• We see a huge selection of hair dyes. All The boxes. And the little fake hair curls on the display, showing the different shades of brown and blond and rainbow colors. (Shout if you don't know what I'm talking about.)

• We see Gert reaching/taking a box, but we don't see the color.

• She's setting a platinum card down near the register. The name on the card is *"Karolina Dean."*

PAGE 12 – TRAUMA CARE, MOLLY-STYLE

• Close-up of Victor's head. He's surrounded by Molly's stuffed animals. Like she's built them up around him.

Maybe his eyes are still closed.

• Then we back up and see that he's sitting on Molly's bed. She's kneeling on the floor, with her elbow resting on the bed. Rufus is also on the bed, peering at Victor, curiously.

Victor's eyes are open.

>MOLLY
>Feeling any better?

>VICTOR
>I'm fine, Molly. Thank you.

>MOLLY
>Did you have, like, an allergic reaction to that robot body?

>VICTOR
>Sort of...

• Shift in perspective.

>MOLLY
>It was so cool -- you had guns coming out of your ears!

>VICTOR
>Would you want guns in your ears?

>What do you care about guns anyway? You're one of the strongest people in the world -- you don't need guns.

• Molly acts like she's Optimus Prime:

>MOLLY
>Yeah, but that was a Transformer body. *Beep-beep-bum-pum-pow!*

• Victor looks thoughtful. And handsome. (Because he's Victor.)

>VICTOR
>I looked down, and I didn't recognize myself.

>Or maybe-- I saw what I could become.

>MOLLY
>A total badass?

• VICTOR
>(looking sad)
>Pretty much.

• Rufus has come closer. He boops Victor's nose.

>MOLLY
>Cheer up, Victor. Rufus and I already think you're a badass.

>VICTOR
>Thanks, Molly.

>And watch your language.

PAGES 13-14 – VICTOR VON DOOM DOESN'T APOLOGIZE, BUT DOOMBOT...

• We're in the main room of the Hostel. Molly is coming downstairs with Victor.

• Doombot is sitting on the couch, with his head in his hands. Chase is sitting on an easy chair. The cruder, half-finished robot body is in front of him. Chase has a screwdriver in his mouth, and he's adjusting something on the robot's chest.

• Doombot stands up. His posture is very formal:

> DOOMBOT
> Victor Mancha. Doom owes you an apology. I should have consulted with you before I completed your assembly.

> •   VICTOR
> Apology accepted, friend. It's an ingenious machine. Only you could have built it.
>
> I'm sorry that I can't make it work.

> •   DOOMBOT
> No, the fault is all mine: Your form is your own dominion. I shall not trespass again without your permission or invitation.
>
> I shall take my leave now.

> VICTOR
> Doombot, no. Stay for dinner.

> MOLLY
> Yeah -- stay for dinner!

• Chase is magnanimous:

> DOOMBOT
> You know I do not eat.

> CHASE
> Victor doesn't eat anymore either. And Karolina only eats nut pastes.

• Karolina and Nico walk in. They look happy. Like they've had a great day.

> KAROLINA
> That's not true.

> NICO
> She also eats fermented mushroom cheese.

> KAROLINA
> It's delicious!

> NICO
> We should get pizza. Where's Gert?

> CHASE
> She went upstairs a couple hours ago...

• Chase shouts:

> CHASE
> **GERT!**
>
> **Come downstairs!**

> •   MOLLY
> We're ordering pizza!

PAGE 15 – SAME OLD GERT

• We see the whole gang. No one is really paying attention. Chase has the screwdriver in his mouth again. Molly has set Victor down so that he can talk to everyone. Maybe on the coffee table. We can see his face in profile. Karolina and Nico are still standing. Gert is standing at the top of the stairs. We can't really see her

• **LARGE PANEL, MAYBE A TALL PANEL:**
Gert's come down the stairs. We see her in full. Her hair is a rich brown, a littler darker than Molly's. (Or whatever color we decide on, Kris.) It looks soft and feminine.

She's wearing new, less sharp glasses. And a new outfit. Something a little less punk rock. Definitely more feminine than the clothes she's been borrowing from Chase.

Something that modestly shows her figure. *(Kris, we talked about a tunic that's a riff on her Heroine uniform?)* She's got a giant watch and a few cool accessories. She looks like a cool, smart, fat girl -- still a girl who isn't afraid to stand out. But like she doesn't have to *try* so hard.

But she also looks *really* vulnerable. It's scary to change. Scary to face your friends. She feels a little bit like she's in costume.

• We see the gang react to her. Not sure the best way to show this. In small individual panels? In one or two group shots?

Chase looks shocked. And sad, frankly. He's been holding on to a certain image of Gert for two years. And now that's gone. She's going to grow and change away from the Gert he remembers.

He's taken the screwdriver out of his mouth.

Karolina is smiling. She looks proud, almost motherly. Like, *"Look at my beautiful girl."*

Nico's face is more impressed. Like that face you make with your lips turned down that says, *"Not bad. Not bad at all."*

Victor looks startled and more than a little in love. But not TOO MUCH in love. Don't tip our hand! (Maybe lips just parted?

• Molly has run up to Gert and is chattering. (Maybe we can have a device we use when she chatters like this. Like the text can fill up the background of her panel.)

> MOLLY
> Gert! We're getting pizza, and Doombot is staying! What kind of pizza do you want? I love your hair -- we look like sisters now! Is that your real hair color? Or do you even remember? Can we get taco pizza? Only you and me like taco pizza!

• Gert smiles.

> GERT
> Sure.

NEW CLOTHES FOR #7

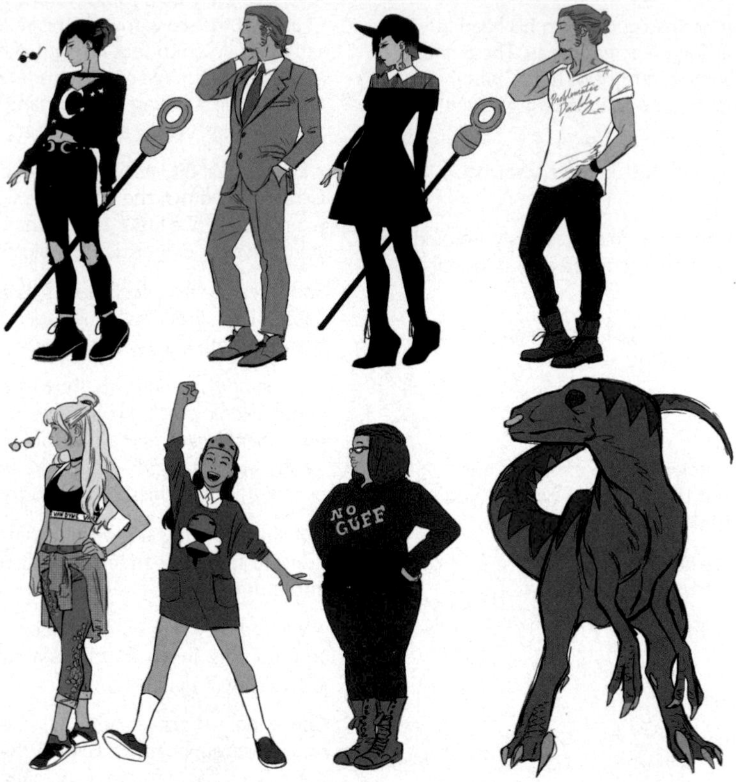
NO GUFF

NEW CLOTHES FOR #8

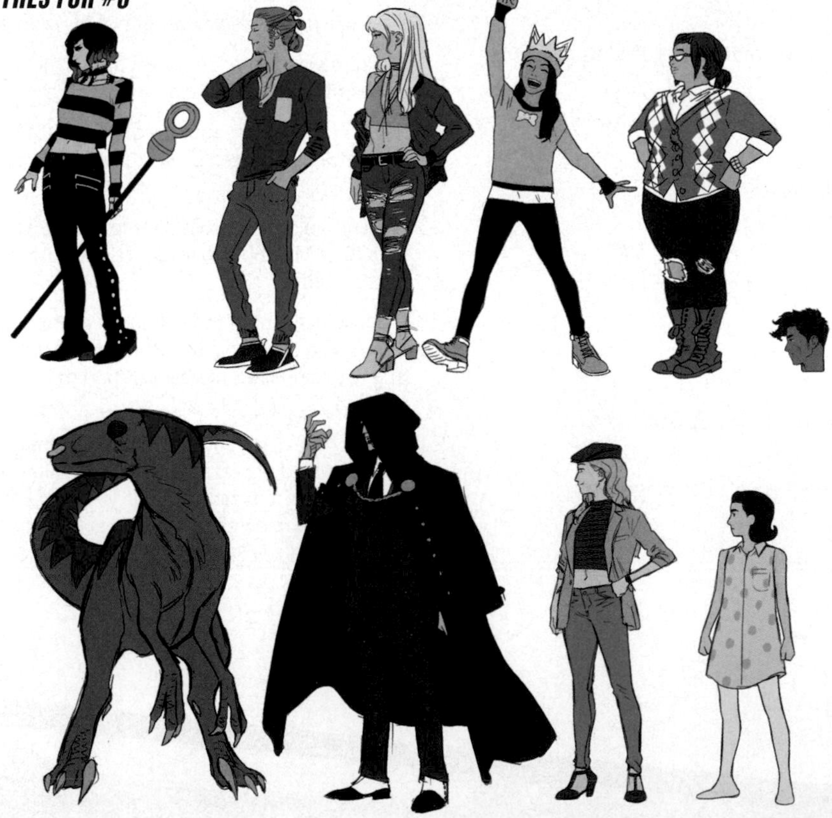

NEW CLOTHES FOR #9

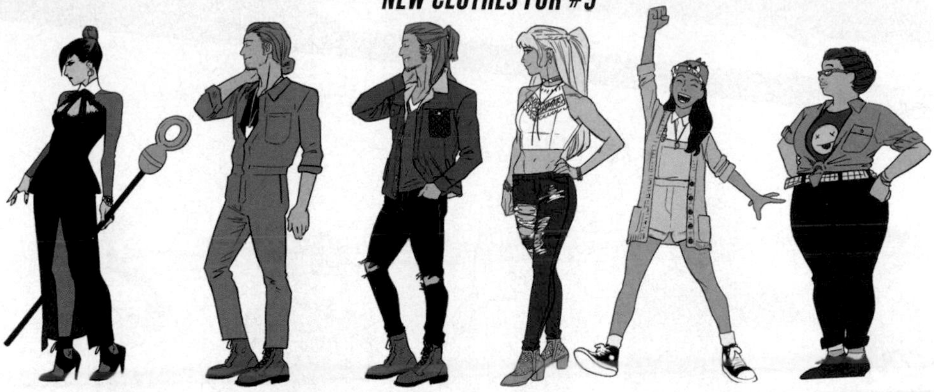

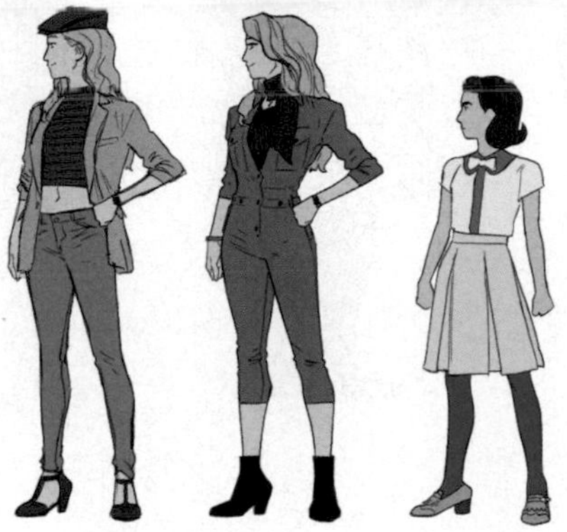

NEW CLOTHES FOR #10

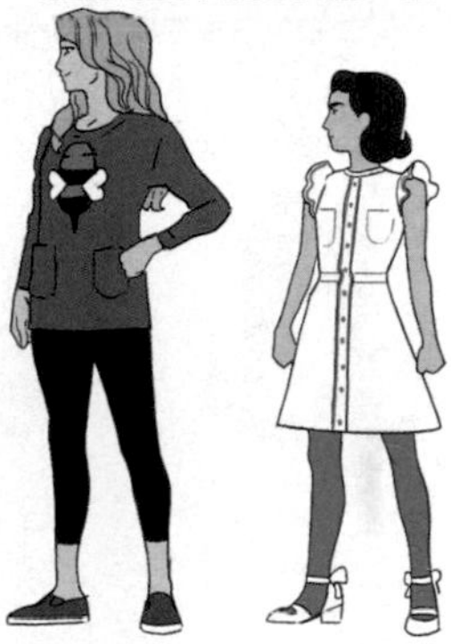

NEW CLOTHES FOR #11

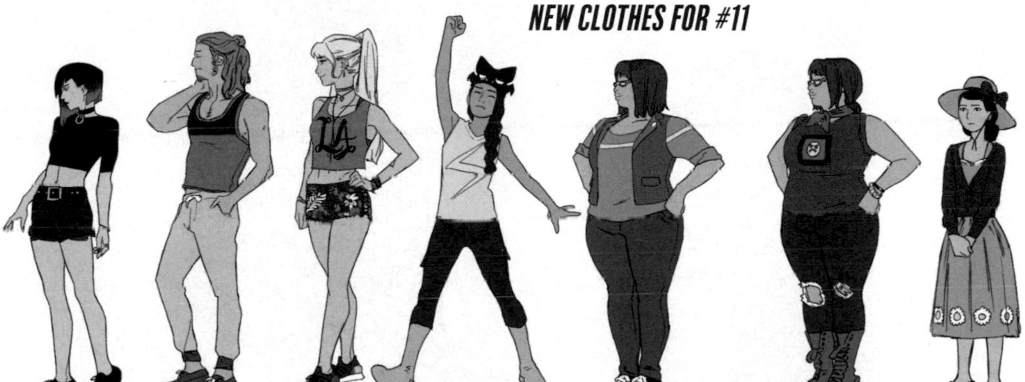

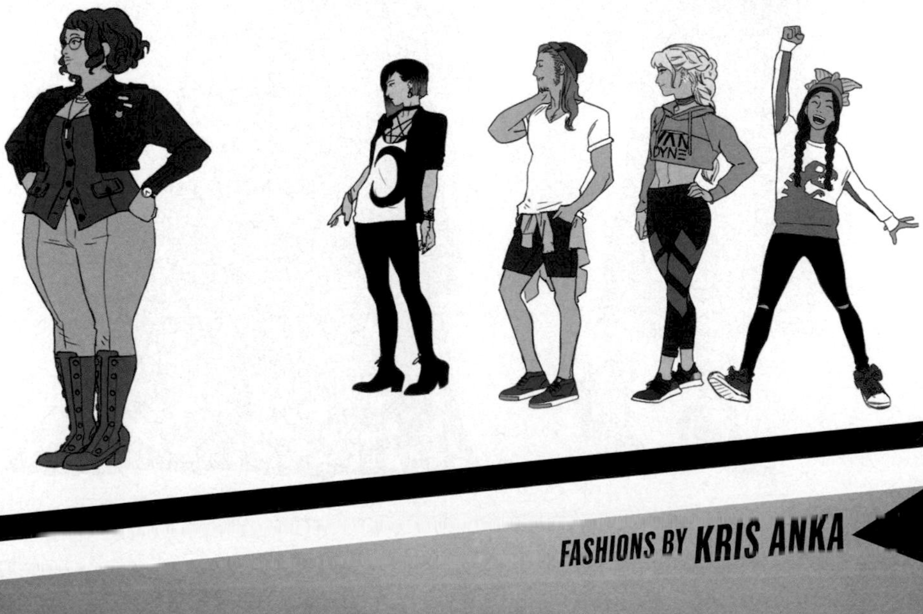

FASHIONS BY **KRIS ANKA**

NEW CLOTHES FOR #12

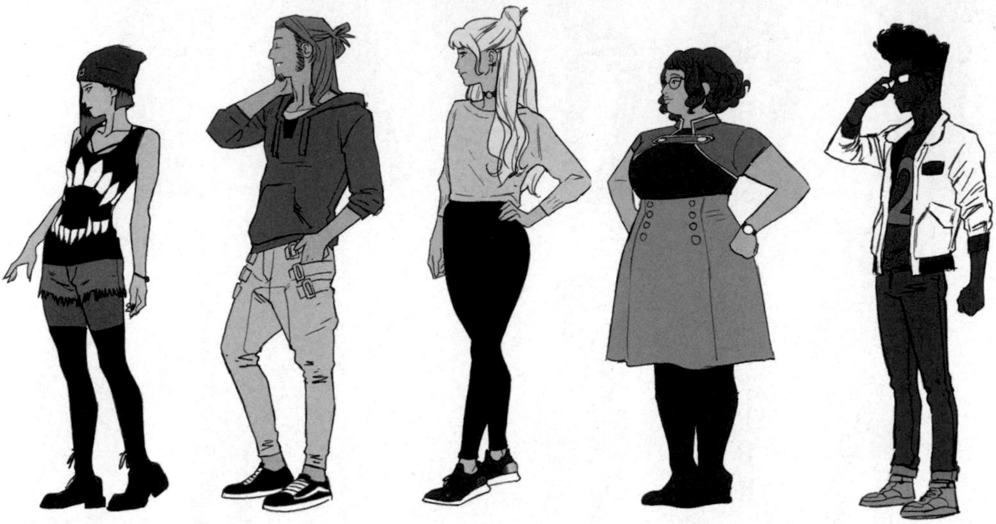

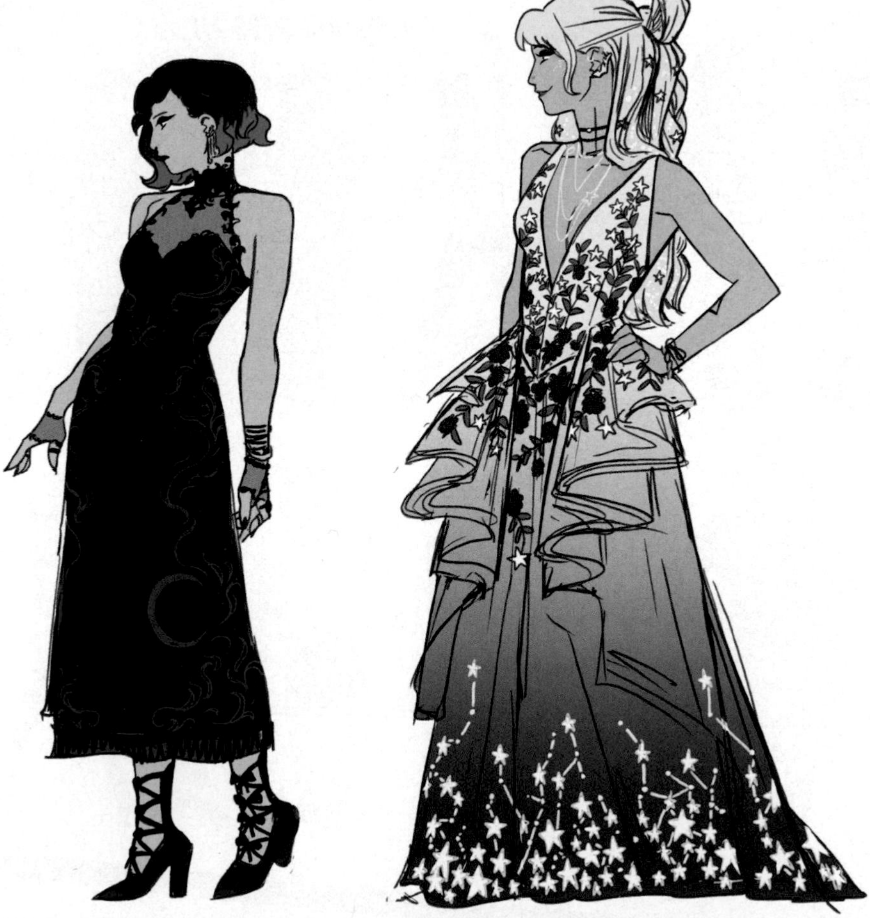